RADIANT

RADIANT

*The Dancer, The Scientist, and
a Friendship Forged in Light*

LIZ HEINECKE

GRAND CENTRAL
PUBLISHING

NEW YORK BOSTON

Grand Central Publishing
Hachette Book Group
1290 Avenue of the Americas, New York, NY 10104
grandcentralpublishing.com
twitter.com/grandcentralpub

First Edition: February 2021

Grand Central Publishing is a division of Hachette Book Group, Inc. The Grand Central Publishing name and logo is a trademark of Hachette Book Group, Inc.

The publisher is not responsible for websites (or their content) that are not owned by the publisher.

The Hachette Speakers Bureau provides a wide range of authors for speaking events. To find out more, go to www.hachettespeakersbureau.com or call (866) 376-6591.

Library of Congress Cataloging-in-Publication Data
Names: Heinecke, Liz Lee, author.
Title: Radiant : the dancer, the scientist, and a friendship forged in light/ Liz Heinecke.
Description: First edition. | New York : Grand Central Publishing, 2020. | Includes
   bibliographical references.
Identifiers: LCCN 2020030161 | ISBN 9781538717363 (hardcover) | ISBN
   9781538717370 (ebook)
Subjects: LCSH: Fuller, Loie, 1862–1928. | Curie, Marie, 1867–1934—Friends and
   associates. | Women dancers—United States—Biography. | Women physicists—France—
   Biography. | Women scientists—France—Biography. | Modern dance—France—History.
   | Stage lighting—History. | Radium—Social aspects.
Classification: LCC GV1785.F8 H45 2020 | DDC 792.802/8092 [B]—dc23
LC record available at https://lccn.loc.gov/2020030161

ISBN: 978-1-5387-1736-3 (hardcover), 978-1-5387-1737-0 (ebook)

Printed in the United States of America

LSC-C

Printing 1, 2020

for Ken

"Come what, come may
Time & the hour runs
Through the roughest day."
(& alas the others too)

Loïe Fuller

1904

Montevideo

June 29.

Author's Note

I first stumbled across the name Loïe Fuller while reading Ève Curie's biography about her mother, Marie Curie. Ève described how Fuller, the star of the Folies Bergère, approached her parents, Marie and Pierre, with the idea of making "butterfly wings of radium." She wrote, "The dancer was Loïe Fuller, a 'light fairy' whose fantastic inventions enchanted Paris," adding that "a picturesque friendship united her to the two physicists."

Radiant is the story of two brilliant women, spinning in distant orbits, who collided in Paris at the twilight of the Belle Epoque with an explosion of creativity and light. One can only imagine exactly what Marie Curie thought of Loïe Fuller, but Loïe's life and work were heavily influenced by their friendship. She kept meticulous journals chronicling her interactions with the scientist. Words inked in these notebooks and Ève Curie's biography of her mother, Marie, illuminate pivotal moments shared by the dancer and the scientist.

Radiant is a work of creative nonfiction based on the lives of Loïe Fuller and Marie Curie. Numerous documents indicate that Loïe and Marie met various times over the years—at their homes, in the Curie laboratories, in August Rodin's studios, and once at the theater. The dialogue in this book is mostly invented, inspired by extensive research, letters, personal memoirs, and biographies. When possible, I inserted Loïe and Marie's own words into the conversation. Loïe Fuller created her own legend, lied about her age, and often gave contradictory information, but the dates in this story are accurate, with the exception of Loïe's interview with the *Strand Magazine*, which actually took place in 1894.

It is also important to acknowledge that this book is set primarily in Europe at the height of colonialism. The story is told from the point of view of two women of European descent immersed in societies responsible for the enslavement, suffering, and death of countless people and cultures. Although many of the historical figures in the narrative were progressive thinkers, none of them were innocent of the prejudiced attitudes and unconscious biases ubiquitous at the time.

Both women were famous, and a tapestry of newspaper articles from the years when they lived weaves a background as colorful as one of Loïe's performances. While they were often drawn apart by circumstance—war, loves, and losses—the magnetic power of friendship and a luminescent blue light pulled them back together again and again. Their stories remind us of the duel nature of scientific discovery and demonstrate that in hard times, we must not only persevere but learn from our missteps and keep looking forward.

Act I

She evokes the otherworldly; materializes what is intangible.
She brings to our eyes what we would not see.

—Léo Clarétie on Loïe Fuller

Scene I

Electric Angel

1892

"Will someone put that light out?" Loïe whispered to a shadow behind the curtain.

With a sputter, the last gaslight was extinguished and it went dark backstage at the Folies Bergère. The five-foot-two American dancer raised her arms to extend the gauzy wings of her gown, gripping the smooth, light rods sewn into the folds of the dress as if her life depended on it. Her body hummed with nervous energy. She had to move.

Pushing her hands back and forth and rotating her wrists, Loïe created gentle undulations in the featherweight silk for a few moments before lowering her arms to maneuver the skirt back into place with a shimmy. She dropped her head, willed her shoulders to relax, and waited. It was impossible to wipe away the bead of sweat that tickled its way across her cheek down to the end of her nose, where it rested for a few moments before free-falling into blackness.

"Faker, Faker, Faker." The childhood taunt always haunted her at moments like these. She could still picture the faces of the boys who had teased her when she was a child, but they were grown men now. Maybe she was a faker, but fabricating the impossible from the ordinary was her greatest skill. Loïe might not be the most beautiful dancer in Paris, but she was by far the most inventive. Rather than depending on choreography or exposed flesh, she incorporated technology into her art to make it new and modern. Light, color, and nature were her muses, and she called on them to create dances so original that they crossed over into the realm of art. She only required an audience with the vision to appreciate what she'd done.

Loïe desperately hoped that Paris would be that audience. She'd fallen in love with the idea of the city and everything it stood for: art, beauty, modernity. Her own homeland refused to appreciate the importance of her work or credit her for it, and her ideas were being stolen almost as fast as she could manufacture them. Attempts to patent her costumes and choreography in the United States had failed miserably, and there was little comfort in the fact that none of her imitators had been talented enough to copy her special lighting and color effects successfully.

If no one in Paris was moved by her dances or recognized her talent for innovation, this would be just another failed stop on her endless quest for artistic and financial success. Still, she had a feeling that this city was her oyster. It had to be. Parisians appreciated art, or so she'd been told. Paris could make her dreams come true.

Thanks to Thomas Edison's recent invention of the lightbulb, the famous French capital had been transformed into the City of Light. For the first time, it was possible to walk the narrow streets safely after dark. Packed cafés and bars had become fertile ground for late-night conversations. Best of all, the city was a magnet for modern thinkers and the air was heavy with inspiration, full of ideas waiting to be plucked and formed by artists, writers, and philosophers.

New methods of depicting the world using language, line, and color were being born as fast as they could be jotted down. After years of portraying wealth, power, and religion, artists and writers had moved in a new direction and were now exploring the lives of working people, making them larger than life. Rather than representing royals and mythological figures, painters like Gustave Caillebotte and Camille Pissarro filled their canvases with revolutionary images of peasants scraping floors and gathering grass.

Naturalist writers like Émile Zola and J. K. Huysmans used starkly realistic descriptions to explore the life of the working class and the poverty-stricken. Zola's work, which occasionally wove myth into human experience and endowed ordinary objects with lifelike qualities, ignited a new school of thought called symbolism, whose disciples embraced dreams, the mythological and the spiritual, believing that truth was revealed in emotional reactions to words and visual experiences.

As an American, Loïe wasn't under the same constraints as French women, who struggled to pursue interests other than motherhood in a society that valued them primarily as vessels for bearing children. Despite the fact that they were legally and financially dependent on men, many women in Paris were searching for a way to move more independently into the future. They were studying every possible subject at the famous Sorbonne University, and a few paintings by female artists hung in the Parisian salons alongside those of male artists.

⌒

A deep, percussive clang indicated that the show was about to begin. As the last gaslight at the front of the stage was extinguished per Loïe's instructions, the murmur in the theater died down. The audience sat confused.

Stages were rarely if ever darkened, and Loïe had shrouded this one in black cloth, hanging a dark blue backdrop and ordering the orchestra to darken the pit as much as possible. When she'd peeked through the curtain earlier to remind the musicians to cover their music-stand lights, it had been obvious from the wagging heads in the reed section and the muttering cello player that they thought she'd entirely lost her mind. At first, they'd resisted following the orders of a woman, but the theater manager, Édouard Marchand, had told them to listen to Loïe.

A few shrill whistles echoed through the cavernous space and died away. Finally, with a creak of ropes and swish of fabric, the curtain rose, crinkling up layer after layer, like an enormous red Roman blind. Cigar smoke and beer-scented air rushed onstage to envelop Loïe in a stifling embrace. It was impossible for her to see the audience, but she could hear them shifting in their seats and murmuring in the dark.

The clear, sweet sound of a violin pierced the silence and sent a tingle of anticipation from her scalp to her fingertips. A second chill moved down her spine when the first beam of light appeared from one of the spotlights in the gallery, illuminating her dress like the first ray of dawn. Loïe could see the toes of her shoes now, but she remained as motionless as a statue as the music coaxed more light to the stage, little by little, making her dress glow like morning sun on a mountain peak.

"*C'est un ange!*" a low voice shouted in French. "It's an angel."

"Show us your legs," someone called out in heavily accented English. The comment was answered with laughter, and more whistles cut through the smoky air.

Loïe had trained herself to take slow, deep breaths while she listened for the chord progression that signaled it was time to bring her first dance to life. In those moments, she allowed her imagination to soar to the first row of the balcony, where she visualized herself onstage as a form draped in white; a dazzling apparition that had materialized in dusty electric beams; a far different creature from the corset-squeezed mannequin the crowd was expecting.

Only a few minutes before, she'd been shouting last-minute instructions to the twelve men on her lighting crew. Getting everything just right. Growing up on the stage had given Loïe an uncanny sense of the magnetic bond between the senses and human emotion. Atmosphere was everything. She absorbed technology like a sponge, noting every new special effect and the potential of each piece of equipment she encountered. She brought it all together in her original lighting system, which was far more technical and involved than anything the electricians at the Folies had ever seen. With electricity and her inventions, she could transform a burlesque club stage into a strikingly modern venue.

Marchand thought she was out of her mind at first, but he'd let her set the lighting using the special configuration she'd designed. In the week before the show, Loïe and her electricians positioned seven electric spotlights around the stage of the Folies: Two were visible on either side of the first gallery, two were hidden toward the back, with a pair in the wings behind the curtain, and the final light was hidden under a glass plate she'd had set into the floor underneath the spot where she would dance.

Once the equipment was in place, she'd taught the electricians to assemble each spotlight lens behind the special rotating disks she'd designed, which could be spun so that the light would shine through one of several holes that ringed them. Each round hole contained glass tinted a different color. Using dried gelatin and special combinations of chemicals she'd mixed and tested herself, Loïe had been able to create rich hues and patterns on the glass that would illuminate her dances.

She'd designed and choreographed her act so that as she danced, she could signal the men to rotate the disks to shine certain colors on her at certain times. The disks could be turned quickly to produce a kaleidoscope effect as the colors rushed and spun through the light onto Loïe's skirts and robes. Each time she danced, the performance was slightly different. Loïe relied on music and the audience for inspiration, but she left little to chance. Every detail of the performance had been gone over in her mind a hundred times, and she drilled the men over and over until they could manipulate the lights and disks with the exactitude of clockwork in response to her commands.

That evening, as she'd shouted and tapped her way through a series of signals one last time, Loïe had heard the hubbub rising from the crowd assembling in the lobby. There was always a robust audience at the Folies Bergère. The spectators were mostly working-class Parisians, but the upper classes had lately begun to grace the sordid dance halls too. Well-to-do women rarely made an appearance at the club, but famous beauties like Caroline Otero, who kicked and gyrated on the stage, were magnets for the wealthy married men who made a sport of collecting and keeping courtesans.

Writers, critics, and artists also frequented the club, and Loïe hoped that some might be there to see her dance. She knew that the diminutive M. Toulouse-Lautrec was a regular, carousing with dancers and courtesans while drinking himself into oblivion. Barely five feet tall, the artist was the premier poster artist of Paris and the starmaker of Montmartre, as famous for his cruel wit as he was for the stunning lithographs that turned night-club performers into celebrities. The famous sculptor Auguste Rodin was spotted at the Folies on occasion as well. These men wouldn't give her a second glance if they passed her on the street, but Loïe hoped she could capture their attention onstage. With a few words or brushstrokes, they could help her stand out from the crowd.

Familiar chords drifting up from the orchestra pit reunited her mind with her body and she was back onstage, squinting in the white spotlight. Inhaling deeply through her nose, she inflated her lungs to expand her chest and opened herself to the music, colors exploding in her mind. The vibrations of low, bluish notes coming from the string bass tingled in her fingertips, and gray beats from the tympani thrummed in time with her thumping heart. Loïe tensed her body in anticipation.

When the golden strains of her first musical cue finally reached her ears, she opened her arms and raised them to unfurl her fabric wings. Expanding her body like a butterfly into the dark open space around her, she became a canvas for light and movement. Using her entire torso as a fulcrum, she swung the fabric into motion, creating arcs by drawing giant figure eights with the wands attached to the silk. One arm descended as the other extended up in rhythm with the music to trace sweeping figures in the air.

The simple act of raising her arms repeatedly with the weight of the fabric was exhausting, and to survive the physical demands of her dancing, she'd learned to let gravity do some of the work for her. With each sweep of her arms, Loïe released her upper wand, accelerated into the downswing, and then rode the upswing, like a boat on a wave. As she moved the wands, Loïe twisted from side to side until her skirt writhed in a geometric serpentine swirl that extended from the floor to the space above her head. The delicate fabric was as treacherous as it was beautiful. If she let go of the wands, even for a fraction of a second, it would wind up and tangle.

She beamed as she danced, her face mostly obscured by the silken patterns formed by her motion. No longer a woman, she was a spirit of the atmosphere, radiating pure light and energy that was in turn absorbed and translated by the imagination of the audience. She could almost feel the light reflecting off her skin, her hair, and her dress.

Loïe was concentrating so hard on responding to the rainbow of sound coming from the orchestra as she spun that she was startled by the cries of delight that rang out when one of the colored spotlights flashed on, drenching her in yellow. She almost stumbled, but caught herself and tapped the next signal to the men controlling the lights.

With each passing moment, the cheers grew. Squinting and sweating, Loïe tapped signals and moved her wands in the well-rehearsed patterns. She swirled her robes to form more sinuous shapes, transforming herself into a wave, a flower, a butterfly—the geometry of nature. She was fire and water, earth and air. The audience roared.

When she'd finished her Serpentine Dance, the curtain fell and she changed her costume to perform the Violet Dance in a white robe she'd painted with flowers. The audience hooted and cheered through the Butterfly Dance, followed by the White Dance. Tapping her feet to signal the electricians perched throughout the theater, she blazed yellow, blue, violet, and red. With each successive dance, the enthusiasm of the audience grew, and fueled by their cheers, Loïe danced on with aching arms. Her eyes felt like they'd been held to a flame, but she didn't care. They loved her and she loved them.

Weary of half-naked cancan dancers and frothy Russian ballerinas, Paris had been primed for Loïe's radical magic. They'd never seen anything like her, and even the most jaded theatergoer became instantly obsessed. Every soul in the red velvet seats that night experienced Loïe differently, and she was multiplied infinitely by their imaginations.

As the symbolist Stéphane Mallarmé would write upon seeing her dance, "She lost the materiality of her body and became an idea."

When the curtain fell after the fourth dance, Loïe could barely raise her arms. The cheering was so loud that she could no longer hear the prelude that the orchestra was attempting to conjure over the noise, and Loïe was grateful for the chance to rest. She guessed that she'd been dancing without a break for about forty-five minutes. The electricians manning the spotlights in the wings looked exhausted, but they were smiling down at her from their perches. Marchand ordered the curtain to be raised again and again, but it was no use. Loïe couldn't hear the orchestra. Finally, after more curtain calls than they could count, she asked Marchand to think of a way she could get them to quiet down for the last dance.

"We don't need it. Don't you hear the cheering?"

He ordered that the stagehands open the curtain a final time, which proved to be a mistake. A drunken man climbed onto the stage shouting "La Loïe, La Loïe, La Loïe," and an enormous crowd followed him, swarming to surround Loïe. Someone grabbed her arm and dragged her through a sea of grasping hands as she attempted to protect her precious dress from trampling feet. She was lifted and carried to her dressing room and the door was slammed behind her to keep out the throngs who had trailed her backstage.

Elated and still somewhat terrified, Loïe collapsed into the shabby velvet couch that leaned against the wall in the small space. She dropped the wands she'd been gripping for dear life and put her hands to her hot cheeks. Her eyes ached, and pain shot from her shoulders up her neck to the base of her skull. The skirt she'd tried to shield was stained with black shoe polish and torn at the hem.

Loïe moved one hand to cover her mouth as her eyes filled with tears. Laughter escaped from the cracks between her fingers. In her life, moments of clarity had been few and far between, but at that instant, in a lowbrow theater perfectly situated under the Parisian sky, Loïe knew that her stars had finally aligned.

Scene II
The Folies Bergère
1892

Loïe had arrived in Paris for the first time with her mother only a few weeks before, hoping to secure a lucrative dancing engagement at the Paris Opéra. She'd immediately, and somewhat recklessly, checked into the Grand Hôtel. The luxurious accommodations were located just across the street from the opera house, which they were told had been nicknamed the Palais Garnier, after its architect. While her mother napped at the hotel and her manager, Marten Stein, spoke with the director of the National Academy of Music and Dancing, M. Gailhard, at the Opéra, Loïe eagerly explored the interior of the Palais Garnier.

In all her travels, she'd never seen anything so opulent. No expense had been spared and the result was a gilded riot of marble, mosaics, paintings, and sculptures. The light gray marble stairs of the grand foyer split from one staircase to form two, curving one way and then another. Every inch was adorned with dancers, gods and goddesses, and she discovered a pair of sinuous dragons hidden on a domed ceiling.

She sneaked past a maroon velvet rope to peek into the grandiose theater, but was disappointed to discover that a lushly painted curtain concealed the stage. The largest chandelier she'd ever seen dangled under the painted central dome, and Loïe guessed that the auditorium held a thousand plush burgundy seats.

Upon returning to the hotel, she learned that things hadn't gone well at all for Stein. M. Gailhard, a former opera star famous for singing the role of Mephistopheles in his youth, had informed Loïe's agent that he didn't find the written description of Loïe's dances nearly impressive enough to book her on a regular basis.

"In fact," he'd informed Marten in his famously deep voice, "her imitators have already arrived in Paris."

The Opéra had only offered her a few engagements a month, which was hardly enough to pay the bills, even at a much less glamorous hotel than the one they'd just checked in to. Loïe was well versed in rejection, but the news still stung, and they were dangerously low on money. The German tour preceding her arrival in Paris had been a complete disaster, and she'd ended up performing in a circus, bookended by an "educated donkey" and a musical elephant.

Loïe had written to M. Gailhard from Germany well ahead of their arrival in Paris, but it had clearly been naive to assume that she could secure an engagement at the Opéra. Now there was no time to waste. With imitators nipping at her heels and money running low, Mr. Stein suggested they visit some other venues in Paris, including the large music hall called the Folies Bergère. Following dinner at the Grand Hôtel, Loïe insisted that they bundle themselves against the cold October air and take a carriage to the Folies that very evening.

After opening as the Folies Trévise in 1869 and briefly masquerading as an opera house, the venue at 32 rue Richer had fully settled into its true nature as a burlesque theater and dance hall. Renamed the Folies Bergère, after the nearby rue Bergère, it retained some of the Trévise's acts, including gymnasts and musicians, but embraced a more hedonistic attitude.

An easy distance from the Gare du Nord train station, the Folies Bergère was a popular destination for twentieth-century Parisians hungry for the latest craze in entertainment. When Loïe arrived in 1892, Édouard Marchand had taken control of the theater and rebranded it as a British-style music hall that featured mostly female acts, including dancers, singers, and vaudevillians, which tended to be bawdy theatrical comedies.

Although it was considered the most important music hall in Paris, the exterior of the Folies Bergère was unimpressive. Unlike the Moulin Rouge, which stood less than a mile away adorned with a red windmill, or L'Enfer (Hell) with its enormous demon's-mouth door and facade of tortured bodies, the venue blended in with its surroundings. At street level, posters boasting dancing girls and acrobats were hung from one end of the building to the other, and the gridded windows were high enough to keep out prying eyes. Decorative ironwork bearing the dance hall's name hung in the center of five large second-story windows flanked by ornate columns, and there was a narrow sidewalk outside where one could study the placards without being run over by a passing horse and carriage.

It was chilly on the evening when they first visited the Folies, but being in Paris was exciting enough to warm Loïe up. The city was as beautiful as she'd imagined it would be, and the architecture was enhanced by October's golden trees. Tall buildings came together at intersections like the bows of enormous ships with ornate stone ornaments on their prows, and chestnuts littered the boulevards. It felt alive and civilized, with streets full of people drinking coffee and wine in small cafés, as if nothing were more important than a conversation with friends. She wondered what lay behind all the closed doors and courtyard gates they passed.

Loïe would soon learn that the city was as strange as it was beautiful. Novelist and critic J. K. Huysmans vividly described some of its haunts, including a café that was "a museum of natural history in which you can gamble and in which you can drink." It was populated with stuffed, painted birds, including "entire families of herons standing on one leg" and tables of old men, "their noses stuck in their cards, motionless as if preserved in this funereal atmosphere, of a jerry-built Versailles, of a bargain-basement Egypt, of a necropolis of fowls and men." He goes on to write about a boutique on the rue Legendre where "a whole series of women's busts with no heads or legs, with curtain hooks instead of arms and percaline skin, starkly colored in grayish browns, garish pinks, and harsh blacks, are aligned in a row, impaled on spikes or placed on tables." Referring to the Curtius mansion in Belgium, which housed a collection of archeological curiosities, Huysmans writes, "Looking at this expanse of busts revealed as if by low tide, this Curtius Museum of breasts, you think vaguely of the underground galleries in which repose the antique sculptures of the Louvre, where the same, eternally repeated torso brings joy to men who contemplate it, yawning, on rainy days."

At last, they pulled up to the Folies Bergère, and Loïe, with her bulky dancing skirt and veils concealed under a large overcoat, stepped out of the carriage first. Unable to control herself, she rushed to the front door of the Folies without waiting for her mother and Stein. What she saw stopped her dead in her tracks.

Directly before her hung poster after poster featuring a pretty blonde who was swirling the skirt of a revealing chartreuse-tinted yellow dress into sinuous curves, against a background that had been violently tinted black and pinkish-orange. Disgusted by the garish colors on the placards, Loïe didn't have to speak French to understand the words "Danse Serpentine." According to the posters, a woman named Mabell Stuart was performing Loïe's dance several evenings a week at ten thirty at the Folies. Whoever designed the printed advertisement even had the nerve to scrawl the words "L'Originale" in red across the lower left corner.

Heat rushed to Loïe's face. She wanted to scream, but instead she slowly turned to face her mother and Stein. They stood silently, but Loïe could see her own shock reflected in their faces.

"Well, here it is," she said. "My utter annihilation."

America was rife with showgirls doing bad imitations of her dances. It was the main reason she'd left for Europe. If dancers were already performing her Serpentine Dance at every big theater in Paris, she was ruined.

Her mother put her hand on her arm and Stein cursed. However, despite her moment of fatalism, Loïe's anger devoured her self-pity and spit it back out as determination.

"Follow me," she said, and soldiered forward with her mother on her arm. She grabbed the cold brass handle of the front door of the Folies, pulled the heavy door open, and marched to the ticket window. Suddenly recalling that she spoke barely a word of French, she asked Stein to demand to see the manager. Informed that they could speak to him only after the evening show, they silently took three balcony tickets and Loïe Fuller turned to step into the enormous lobby of the music hall that would change her life forever.

The appearance of the Folies Bergère had changed very little since 1879, when Huysmans wrote, "What is truly admirable, truly unique, is that this theatre has a real air of the boulevards about it. It is ugly and it is superb, it is in both exquisitely good and outrageously bad taste. It's also unfinished, like anything that aims to be truly beautiful...This theater, with its auditorium whose faded reds and tarnished golds clash with the brand-new luxury of the *faux jardin*, is the only place in Paris that stinks so deliciously of the make-up of bought caresses and the desperation of depravities that fail to excite."

Bejeweled golden statuettes of horses and women stood silent guard over the alcohol-fueled scene, where waltzes and polkas mingled with conversation and laughter. Usherettes in bonnets adorned with fluttering pink ribbons handed out advertisement-stuffed programs, and Loïe eagerly grabbed one to see what she could find out about her competition but was disappointed to learn nothing new. Besides the Serpentine Dance, the entertainment that evening included male gymnasts, sequined danseuses, and white-painted mimes called Pierrots.

A few men in top hats murmured "*Excusez-moi*" before pushing their way past, their dark suits vanishing into a sea of faces topped with the occasional ostrich plume. There were long galleries on either side of the lobby where people crowded around bars and sat at tables with their drinks. Small café tables flanked the floor of the main room as well, where most of the action appeared to be taking place.

Under an enormous golden chandelier, flocks of cancan dancers drifted through the room, while brightly costumed women with corseted waists and their male companions sipped on cocktails. It was easy for Loïe to pick out the painted prostitutes parading through the room, two by two, squeezing artfully through the groups of men, white petticoats flouncing. At the opposite end of the hall, two staircases funneled people up to the balcony level, which was ringed with white Moorish-style arches.

Stein suggested that they wait near the main bar, so Loïe and her mother maneuvered their way through the crowd, past more plaster sculptures and walls decked with ornate gold sconces sprouting red candles. The bar of the Folies Bergère, Stein explained, had been famously depicted a few years before by the controversial painter Édouard Manet. When she saw the enormous gilded mirror standing behind the bar, Loïe could see why the artist had been inspired. The entire room behind them was reflected in the silvery glass.

According to Stein, Manet's brushstrokes depicted a pretty barmaid in a wasp-waisted low-cut black dress trimmed with white lace, a lowborn beauty wearing a velvet choker while presiding over an army of Champagne, liquor, and beer bottles.

"Like that one," Stein said, gesturing at the woman behind the bar who was fearlessly arguing with a patron.

"And why, exactly, is a painting of a pretty woman controversial?" Loïe asked.

Stein explained that in the past, French paintings had mostly depicted the upper classes, biblical stories, and mythological figures. In Manet's painting of the bar at the Folies, however, a lower-class woman stares boldly from the canvas. On closer inspection, she appears to be looking at a man who is visible only in the reflection of the enormous mirror behind her. Stein went on to further describe the woman's reflection, which appears more animated than her physical body, and explained that the bowl of oranges on the bar signaled to the viewer that the woman is a prostitute who can be bought as easily as a tempting piece of fruit.

"Manet is controversial because he paints the demimondaines," Stein explained.

Demimonde, or "half world," referred to the pleasure seekers of the era, who lived on the fringe of polite society and overindulged in everything from intoxicants to sex and fashion. Women of this world, like the one in *A Bar at the Folies Bergère*, were a frequent subject of Manet's work. In his masterpiece *Le Déjeuner sur l'herbe*, a naked woman unabashedly picnics in the woods with two fully dressed men as a second scantily dressed woman splashes in the water in the background. Manet's *Olympia* confronts the viewer with a naked courtesan on an expensive couch, receiving flowers from her lover while staring frankly at the observer.

Manet did for art what a certain group of writers were doing for literature: magnifying the marginalized and confronting society with its double standards. The Naturalists, including Émile Zola, used literature to expose the double standards of the middle class—the bourgeoisie—who criticized the immoral behavior of the lower classes while freely indulging in the same behaviors.

A Bar at the Folies Bergère, Stein told them, transformed a lowly demimondaine into a modern Madonna presiding over a cathedral of sin. It displayed the hypocrisy of a Parisian society that looked the other way as men did whatever they pleased, including keeping mistresses, whereas women were almost universally classified as either faithful wives or widows or spinsters or whores.

Stein didn't bother to add that in the world of entertainment, both ballerinas en pointe at the Paris Opéra and burlesque performers at dance halls like the Folies were considered little more than talented prostitutes. Loïe was well aware of the stereotype, but as an American dancer in Paris who lived with her mother, she would prove extremely difficult for the

French to categorize, allowing her to live on her own terms. Even on that first night at the Folies, Loïe could sense that the world was changing. Later she would write that in certain places, "Everything seems to aspire towards a new life, towards new times. One feels oneself leap for joy, like the dog that precedes one in quest of the master of the house."

As Stein made his way to the bar to buy a drink, Loïe stared at the colorful array of bottles sitting on the bar, intrigued by the fact that the mirror allowed her to observe them from both sides at once. She considered how she might use reflective surfaces in her own act, imagining how a mirror would allow an audience to watch her dance from multiple angles at the same time. It was an intriguing idea.

When Stein returned, they decided to go upstairs to the balcony level and find their seats.

She led her mother, pushing through the noisy, fragrant crowd. As they approached the grand staircase, she peeked through the doors opening into the orchestra level of the theater, where she could just make out the lower half of the open stage curtains. Her view of the top of the stage was blocked by the mass of the overhanging balcony, but as they drew nearer, she could make out bows, bassoons, and the long necks of stringed instruments springing up like cat tails from the orchestra pit. The mustachioed maestro pumped his baton, while onstage an acrobat swung in lazy circles around a horizontal gymnastics bar.

Moving to one side, they made their way up the central staircase, following it to the right as it split and curved off to either side at the first landing. Handing their tickets to an usherette, they walked through the doors into the first balcony of the Folies Bergère and took their red velvet seats in the far-right corner. From the steep row where they sat, Loïe could now see the entire theater and imagined that if she were to spit, she could easily hit the stage.

The warm red of the shabbily elegant seats and walls coupled with gold highlights on the walls and the balcony front gave the theater a cozy feel.

Loïe counted fourteen seats in the front row and imagined that the brave souls who sat there risked being showered by droplets hurled from the lips of enunciating actors or thrown off of sweaty performers whirling close to the edge of the stage. In the orchestra seats below, bald heads and pomaded hair gleamed in the warm haze of gaslights and a garden of feathers and flowers sprouting from women's hats.

Wealthy ticket holders watched the spectacles onstage from gold chairs arranged in low boxes, which made up the front row of the balcony. Although she could study them easily from her balcony seat, Loïe didn't know anyone in Paris yet and couldn't identify the well-dressed Parisians. Onstage, the acrobat swung and spun so fast that he blurred, his legs, arms, and torso wrapped around a rope that descended from the ceiling like a boa constrictor. When he took his bow and applause shook the balcony, a knot of resolve formed in Loïe's belly. She wanted to be on that stage, in that theater. She studied the wings, the gallery, and the catwalk, imagining where she would position her spotlights.

"Here we go. The Serpentine dancer is up next," Stein said calmly. "Miss Mabell."

Loïe's heart began to race as she waited with her hands folded, dreading the appearance of her rival onstage. Trembling and starting to sweat, she squeezed her eyes shut and tried to distract herself by visualizing a dance she could create using a giant mirror, or several smaller ones. Her mother nudged her when the curtain finally opened, and she peeked through her narrowed eyelids to discover a very pretty woman doing a remarkably bad imitation of her Serpentine Dance.

Not only was the dancer inept at manipulating her costume, awkwardly throwing the large skirt around as if she were trying to fold a bedsheet, she was an old acquaintance from New York. The name had sounded familiar, but now Loïe was certain. In fact, the blond woman onstage had borrowed money from her at some point, and never paid her back. Leaning forward in her seat, Loïe focused all of her energy on the lovely

Miss Mabell Stuart, willing her to trip on the long, gauzy skirt and fall flat on her face.

However, the longer the dance continued, the calmer Loïe felt. Eventually, she relaxed, and when the dance concluded, she stood and rewarded her rival with the sincerest applause her hands had ever afforded any performer. She could have kissed poor, pathetic Mabell for the lackluster, ordinary performance she had just witnessed.

When the theater had emptied, she stood confidently onstage with her mother, Stein, and the Folies' manager.

"Mr. Stein, please ask Monsieur Marchand why he has engaged a woman who gives a feeble copy of my dances, when you wrote to him from Berlin to propose his talking with me." She glared at Marchand as she spoke to Marten Stein.

"We should be polite. He's probably already heard that the Opéra turned you down earlier today," Stein replied.

"That doesn't matter," Loïe said, determined. "Put the question to him. Besides, this man doesn't know anything. If I spoke French, I'd ask him myself."

M. Marchand calmly replied to Stein that he'd hired a Serpentine dancer because a competing club had hired one, but that the Folies audiences were underwhelmed by the dance.

Loïe snorted when Stein translated.

"Of course they're not impressed. She's horrible."

Marchand then offered Loïe the chance to show him how the dance should really look. She agreed, since she'd come prepared. Earlier, she'd removed her dancing robes to sit in the warm theater, but now she put them back on. With only footlights to illuminate her, she stepped onto the stage of the Folies Bergère for the first time. To the music of a single violin and without her lights, Loïe performed the original Serpentine Dance she'd created back in New York, confident that it was far superior to Miss Stuart's.

When she'd finished, Marchand gestured that they should follow him to his office, where he proposed to engage Loïe at his theater. She would have to agree to the condition of performing in a blond wig under her imitator's name until the end of the week, since he'd already paid for Mabell Stuart's advertising. It wasn't ideal, but Loïe agreed. She needed a job and had already made up her mind that she wanted to own that stage. Only later did she learn that Marchand spoke English, which seemed especially funny when she considered how he'd managed to keep a straight face while she insulted him.

Over the next week, Loïe finished out her imitator's contract and arranged an interview with the *Figaro* newspaper about her new dance. Then, Loïe began rehearsing in earnest for her debut at the Folies. Eight days later, her last dress rehearsal ran until four in the morning, at which point her exhausted troupe of electricians unceremoniously departed. She was disappointed, as they hadn't had time to rehearse her finale, which was to be performed over a square of glass illuminated from beneath, but relieved that they had gotten through the first four dances of her program: the Serpentine, the Violet, the Butterfly, and the White Dance.

Late the next morning, the day of her official Paris debut, the electricians showed up again and they ran through the lighting for the fifth and final dance. Loïe's eyes ached from the bright lights, and she knew she should be exhausted, but it felt like she was being fueled by pure electricity. Within days, everyone in Paris would be clamoring for a glimpse into the fantastical world of "La Loïe."

Scene III
Higher, Higher
1892

Marie tucked the small bag holding her gray copybook and pen case under one arm. She gathered her skirt in the same hand, wrapping it around her wrist to lift it higher, and with the other hand reached for the bucket of coal. A crease bisected the smooth skin between her eyebrows as she began her ascent up the worn stairs. It was already getting dark. She would have much preferred being in the warm, bright library of Sainte-Geneviève, but her classmates were worried that she might faint again, so she'd promised to go home to eat some dinner and study by the light of her kerosene lamp.

"Thirty-eight, thirty-nine," her lips counted silently as she trudged up the six flights of wooden stairs to her tiny garret apartment. Only seventy to go. Light-headed, she paused on each landing to set the bucket down and rest. Normally, she could climb the flights without stopping, but not today. Marie was grateful there was still water upstairs in her pitcher from the day before, so she wouldn't have to retrace her steps down the stairs to fill it at the tap on the first landing before ascending again.

She couldn't wait to take her corset off. When she'd first arrived in Paris, she'd had to hold her breath to squeeze into the rigid undergarment. Now, she had to pull the laces as tight as she could, simply to keep it in place, but it was just as uncomfortable. Although the heavy boning helped support her back through the long hours of standing at the oak table in the laboratory, she'd never gotten used to the cloth-and-bone prison binding her breasts and rib cage. The sweet days of her youth, when she'd run free through the countryside without the stifling undergarment, seemed like a lifetime ago.

When she reached the top of the stairs, Marie breathlessly set the coal on the landing and unlocked the door to her tiny room. With her head spinning, she brought the bucket inside and closed the door behind her, leaning on it for a moment until the room stopped tilting. She added a few pieces of coal to the stove, threw a crumpled piece of paper on top, and lit it with a match. Heat was slow to emerge from the small pile of fuel, but after a few minutes, smoke moved up the crooked pipe and she could rub her hands in the warmth emanating from the carbon chunks.

Although her stomach was telling her to eat a piece of bread, the sight of the flame bursting from the match reminded Marie of something her physics professor, M. Bouty, had mentioned in his lecture that morning. Completely forgetting to loosen her corset, she lit the kerosene lamp and put it on the white wooden table. Her chair made a scraping sound as she sat and pulled her gray copybook from the bag she'd had tucked under her arm, opening it to the page from that day's physics lecture as she scanned her notes for one particular equation.

There were still a few radishes left over from her lunch, so she nibbled on them to silence the sounds coming from her stomach while she flipped the pages. Peppery hotness burned her tongue, but she barely noticed. Picking up her pen, Marie started scribbling numbers. Soon the cold and hunger went away and there was only science. She was so intent on her lesson that she didn't hear the man entering her room.

⌒

The previous night had been especially frigid, and Marie had forgotten to buy coal. Because the stove in her apartment was too small to adequately warm her tiny attic space, most evenings she didn't bother to light it at all, unless her fingers got too numb to write equations. As usual, she'd studied at the tables of the warm, bright Sainte-Geneviève library until it closed at ten o'clock. Dizzy with exhaustion, she'd returned home to her apartment to finish her lessons, wrapping herself in a blanket and working on problems until three in the morning.

When she'd scribbled the last equation, in a routine that had become all too familiar, she'd squeezed into as many pieces of clothing as she could layer onto her thin body. Piling every other linen she owned on top of her covers, she crawled into bed with her teeth chattering. Marie rubbed her icy feet together in hopes that friction would warm them, but the effort proved useless so she curled herself up in a ball. Still cold and unable to fall asleep, as a last resort she'd reached for a chair to balance atop the pile of clothes.

It went against all logic, but no one was watching and the weight of the stack comforted her. When she was a child, her brother and sisters had played a trick on her, stacking chairs over her as she devoured a book, oblivious to the furniture balanced above her head. At the time, she hadn't found it amusing when the furniture crashed down around her, but now it was one of her fondest memories. Happy as she was to be studying in Paris, Marie was always a little bit homesick for Poland. She especially missed her father. Childhood memories of the games they'd played in his study made her feel safe and warm.

Marie had finally fallen asleep around three a.m., in a cocoon of wood-weighted cloth. As she slept, the water molecules in her pitcher snapped together like puzzle pieces, into a solid lattice of ice, so there were no ripples on the water's surface when the chair toppled from her bed and landed on the wooden floor with a bang. The crash was followed by the soft thud of a pile of linens, and Marie groaned. She had inadvertently triggered the avalanche by pulling one arm out from under her covers to block the morning light, which streamed through a small skylight in the slanted ceiling, directly into her eyes.

Shivering, she'd climbed off her thin mattress, straightened the bed linens, and picked up the chair. Lighting the tiny cooking lamp, she made herself a cup of tea to stop her teeth from chattering. Unable to bring herself to wash her face in the icy water, she pinched her cheeks to get the blood flowing. With numb fingers, she buttoned the threadbare dress she'd brought from Warsaw over her corset and bit into a piece of stale bread while she gathered her pen stand and copybook into her bag. She'd been taking one last sip of tea when a frizzy strand of ash-blond hair fell into her eyes. Exasperated, she scraped a comb through her hair, pulled it back and twisted it into a neat bun, which she secured with hairpins.

After all of her dreaming and saving, the life she intended to live had begun. The apartment might be small and bare, but it was quiet, exactly what she needed for an existence where science and math were the air that she breathed. In this tiny room, she could let herself be swept up by her passion for lectures on mathematics, physics, and chemistry. Material existence was secondary to her work. Equations and physical laws made perfect sense to her, and mastering them gave her a sense of control that few other things in her life offered.

When she'd first arrived in Paris, living with her sister and brother-in-law had seemed like an ideal situation. Just days after climbing off the train under the tall glass ceiling of the Gare du Nord, she'd begun to sign her name Marie rather than Maria, and settled into her new life, registering for classes at the Sorbonne at the first possible opportunity. Soon, climbing the corkscrew staircase of an omnibus in a long skirt and bumping past rows of limestone government buildings and apartments on her way to class became as routine as breathing. She loved the city, and even liked the fat gray pigeons that swooped in every time a crumb fell from the bread she nibbled on while walking between classes.

After an exhausting day of listening to lectures in French, Marie would come home to the familiar faces of her sister and brother-in-law, Bronya and Casimir, who greeted her with smiles and hot tea. Embraced by the easy warmth of her native language, she revived herself on familiar dishes like cabbage with mushrooms and cake studded with poppy seeds. Some nights, the bright-eyed, black-bearded Casimir would drag them to a concert or play, despite Marie's protests that she had to study, but she always ended up having a wonderful time.

At first, she'd thrown herself into Polish society in Paris, reveling in the piano concerts and parties in their neighborhood on rue d'Allemagne. The passionate copper-haired pianist Ignacy Paderewski had entranced them with his playing on more than one occasion, while Marie and Bronya laughed with a beautiful young woman named Mme. Gorska, whom Paderewski desperately loved. Many of the Poles in Paris had fled to the French city to escape their homeland's oppressive Russian occupation. One evening at a patriotic party thrown by a Polish sculptor, Marie had been delighted to play the role of "Poland breaking her bonds," in a performance of tableaux vivants. Draped in a tunic ornamented by long pomegranate-and-white veils, her blond hair loosed from its pins, she'd felt an almost unbearable love for her homeland.

That was before a cheerful note that Marie sent to her father, detailing her social adventures, resulted in a chiding from the man she loved most in the world. M. Skłodowski had responded to Marie that he was saddened by her letter because he feared that she was putting her future in Warsaw in peril. He wrote that "persons in Paris" were keeping an eye on the Polish community there and reporting back to Poland, suggesting that the information could be used against her one day, preventing her return to her homeland.

Marie had always been aware of the dangers of speaking out against Russia, even in Paris. But despite the risk of being arrested, she'd been participating in pro-Poland nationalist activities and organizations, which the Russians considered illegal, for as long as she could remember. Still, the fear hanging between the lines of her father's letter gave her pause.

Following her education at the Sorbonne, Marie planned to move back home and find a job in Poland in order to care for her aging father. He'd raised her to believe that if she worked hard enough, she would meet her full potential, and destiny would reward her. Sadly, under Russian rule in Poland, everything he'd worked for had been taken away, making Marie even more determined to succeed and to make him proud. She was convinced that education made a more desirable existence possible for everyone, and that it was her responsibility to do everything in her power to make the world a better place.

Perhaps it was her father's letter that changed her trajectory, or maybe Marie realized that every moment spent away from her studies was a moment keeping her from her true vocation. It had become clearer with every passing day that she didn't have time for social outings. Her French was passable, but she wanted to lose her Polish accent entirely. Her struggle to keep up with her work, two physician family members, and the engaging Polish community in their neighborhood created too many distractions. She loved her brother-in-law, but it seemed that he could never stop talking. In their apartment near the Gare du Nord, Casimir played the piano or chattered at her incessantly when he wasn't seeing patients. The doorbell was ringing day and night, and when Bronya wasn't rushing off to deliver a baby, she was mothering Marie, who didn't want to be told that she was staying up too late.

Day after day, Marie continued to climb the steps of the double-decker omnibus in the north end of Paris, but she found herself viewing her life through a new lens. Staring down at the backs of the horses that pulled passengers through the bumpy streets for the hour's journey across the Seine to the Boul' Mich' in the Latin Quarter, she started to wonder how much money and time she would save by not taking the omnibus at all. Finally, one evening, she gathered her courage, stepped into the apartment on rue d'Allemagne, and announced that she was moving out. She wanted to live within walking distance of the Sorbonne.

Marie refused to let Casimir change her mind, and Bronya, who was well aware of how determined her sister could be, didn't even bother to argue.

Though they were sad to see her go, Bronya and Casimir helped Marie secure an apartment and pack her belongings into a handcart. They rode the omnibus with her across the Seine to the Latin Quarter one last time, and her new life began in earnest.

Casimir had shaken his head when they dropped her off at the door of her new Parisian eyrie, warning her to beware of strange men and to be home before dark. The Latin Quarter was reputed to be a rowdy section of the city, full of young male students who were studious by day and boisterous by night. Marie was one of only 210 women enrolled at the Sorbonne, while more than 9,000 male students roamed the streets and frequented the sidewalk cafés. The area had become slightly more sedate since the arrival of the Sorbonne's small female contingent, but women still risked being surrounded and taunted as they walked down the boulevard Saint-Germain.

At the time, most Frenchwomen didn't leave their homes without an escort even during the day, much less after dark, lest they be considered prostitutes. But then, most Frenchwomen were not allowed an education beyond high school. Those few at the Sorbonne rarely studied anything but medicine. As a rule, Parisian society considered women a different species than men. To have a few female physicians around in order to assist these delicate creatures with menstrual issues and childbirth had been deemed acceptable, although even women doctors couldn't legally spend their own money without the permission of their husbands.

Following a recent military defeat by Germany in the Franco-Prussian war, French leaders had become painfully aware of the relationship between population and military might. While the populations of England and Germany were growing quickly, France's birthrate was relatively low. Nationalism mingled with sexism and influential men blamed French women for not having enough babies to populate their army with soldiers. They accused women of being socially and patriotically irresponsible by avoiding pregnancy and neglecting babies.

Few recognized or acknowledged the social issues underlying the low birthrate, but one physician, Henri Thulié, defended women against the charges being laid against them. He argued that, as the result of "the legal inferiority of woman, the Code's injustices toward her, and the absence of laws to protect her situation and that of her child," a high rate of infant mortality was in large part to blame for the lack of population growth.

The "Code" Thulié referred to was the French civil code, established by Napoleon in 1804. It gave men absolute authority over their families, depriving women of their individual rights. Napoleon, who famously said "Women ought to obey us. Nature has made women our slaves!" created a system of power where women were legally and financially helpless. The code ensured that men could only pass their wealth on to legitimate male heirs, keeping the social order intact.

There was no social or criminal hazard to men who strayed outside their own bedrooms, but a woman who committed adultery could be charged with a crime. French journalist and novelist Octave Mirbeau voiced the popular attitude when he wrote, "Woman is not a brain, she is a sex," and that those rare women who give the "illusion that they are creative…are either abnormal or simply reflections of men."

The sexist culture certainly wasn't enough to deter Marie from boldly striding into the cobblestone courtyard of the Sorbonne and registering as a new student to pursue her dream of being a scientist. Foreign women far outnumbered French ones at the university. While French women were generally considered tempting distractions to the male students, Marie and her fellow foreign students were stereotyped and mocked as bookish and boring.

This was an enormous advantage as far as Marie was concerned. As a Polish woman, she was able to move through the stone campus without harassment much more easily than her French counterparts. Although she sometimes drew admiring glances, she was lumped in with the Russian students, who were considered cold and sexless, which suited Marie just fine.

The famous university was Marie's new world, and there was nowhere she would rather be. Hours flew by in the chair-filled slopes of amphitheaters, where men with gray beards and chalk-smeared coattails elucidated the mysteries of math and science. M. Appell, one of her favorite professors, brought numbers and equations to life as he paced in front of the class gesturing and making wonderful proclamations like, "I take the sun, and I throw it." She always tried to arrive early, to sit on a bench near the front of the lecture hall, where she soaked up every word and devoured the details of scientific demonstrations.

Each day when she arrived in the Sorbonne's laboratory, a wide room with high ceilings, she would tie on a large linen smock to protect her clothing from acids and toxic chemicals. There, in a jungle of glassware, she explored the secrets of matter. Nothing broke her concentration. Camouflaged by her uniform and a common purpose, she moved among the male students unnoticed, belonging there as surely as they did.

If knowledge were food, Marie would have been plump, but science didn't fuel her body. Her increasing lack of attention to worldly things had started to take a toll, and after the long night of studying and a morning heralded by the crashing down of a chair, Marie fainted when she stood up at the end of Professor Lippmann's lecture. She'd tried to steady herself on the bench at the first sign of dizziness, but blackness invaded the edges of her vision, closing in until everything was dark.

Although she'd revived almost immediately, the students standing nearby couldn't help but notice. They took her outside into the fresh air and encouraged her to eat the cherries and radishes that she brought for lunch. Insisting that she was fine, she'd thanked them and promised to go home directly.

Marie's tiny attic apartment in the Latin Quarter was as stifling in the summer as it was cold in the winter, but she was poor. It was all she could afford with the money she'd saved for school, which added up to the meager amount of about three francs a day. Barely able to pay the rent, she'd furnished the room with a thin mattress she'd carried rolled up on the train from Poland. It now lay atop a folding bed frame made of iron, beside a little white table, where her washbasin and pitcher stood. At night, her kerosene lamp illuminated a single chair and an old brown trunk containing all her clothing and linens, which served as an adequate second seat, on the rare occasion that someone stopped by.

To prepare food, she had only a small alcohol lamp, but Marie didn't do much cooking or housekeeping. Food held no interest for her. She had exactly two pots, and when she did cook, the meals generally consisted of bread and a hard-boiled egg or two. Splurges like cheap steak or a piece of chocolate were reserved for special occasions. A few plates, one knife, one spoon, one fork, a kettle for tea, and three glasses rounded out her dining collection. It was a spartan existence, but she mostly didn't mind.

While many other poor students lived together and shared meals, Marie was determined to spend every moment of her new existence in the classroom, the laboratory, or the library. When she'd first started at the Sorbonne, she'd been painfully shy, but she made friends with a few other students who were as engaged in their studies as she was. It had been especially fun to join small gatherings with other Polish students, where they reminisced about home and talked politics. Unfortunately, she soon discovered that her diligent attempts to master the mathematics required for the university's physics classes hadn't been adequate, and she struggled to keep up. Realizing that she would have to spend every second of her time studying, she gave up her social life entirely to focus on math and science.

Although a little lonely, Marie soon learned that she didn't mind solitude all that much. Sitting around a dinner table talking for hours seemed like a waste when she could be working with her hands and her mind, observing the theater of science. It was satisfying to bring the equations she'd studied on paper to life in the laboratory, and she felt a Frankensteinian joy each time she stood before bubbling glass tubes, heating, cooling, and combining chemicals to transform them into something entirely new. The six flights of stairs leading to her room—the old servants' quarters—might be far from ideal, but it was only a twenty-minute walk to the Sorbonne and even closer to the laboratory, so it was well worth the climb.

Marie was finally feeling a little bit better and was deep into the numbers on the page when a strong hand clamped down on her shoulder. She was too surprised to scream. Jerking her head up, she twisted around, but her vision blurred and the room started to go black. She couldn't make out the intruder's face.

"For God's sake, Manya, take some deep breaths and put your head down on your lap," a familiar voice commanded. Sighing with relief, she obeyed and breathed deeply until the wooden floor came back into focus.

When the darkness abated, she sat up and looked into the disapproving black eyes of her brother-in-law. He took her chin and examined her face carefully.

"And how is starvation agreeing with you?" Casimir asked, half-joking, half-angry. "Bronya would have come too, but she's out delivering a baby."

Marie didn't have time to respond before he turned away to search her apartment. She held her tongue as she watched him clang through her things, holding up the clean plates, one by one, examining the empty stewpan, and finding only a packet of tea.

"What, exactly, have you eaten today?" he asked. "You're as pale as a ghost. Some of your fellow students showed up at our door this evening to report your fainting episode. Thank goodness someone is looking after you, since you're obviously not looking after yourself."

Bending her head at the scolding, Marie admitted to having eaten only cherries and radishes that day.

"But I nibbled on some bread this morning"—she sat up, defending herself—"and I'm sure that I only fainted because I stayed up very late studying last night."

"Gather your things," he said. "Bronya has ordered me to bring you home immediately. When you are well again, you may return to this little hovel you love so much."

Seeing how upset he was, and aware that her father had charged Casimir and Bronya with her care, Marie silently gathered her books, papers, and pens together. She finished chewing the piece of bread that her brother-in-law had shoved into her hand, insisting that she eat. When Marie felt better and Casimir proclaimed that enough color had returned to her cheeks, she put out the lamp and followed him out of her apartment.

As she closed the door behind her, a piece of paper covered with her neat writing fluttered off the table and landed on the floor beneath the skylight, where it lay in the cold moonlight awaiting her return.

> *Higher, Higher, up she climbs.*
> *Past six floors she gasps and heaves.*
> *Student shelter near the sky*
> *Up among the drafty eaves.*
>
> *This is no elegant abode*
> *The cold in winter chills the face,*
> *The room in summer's stuffy, close.*
> *But it's a tiny, quiet place.*
>
> *It sees the student's restless toil,*
> *The hours of work without a break;*
> *It's there when she returns from school*
> *To cook herself a leather steak.*
>
> *And when the time for sleep is come,*
> *When streets and shops are shut up tight,*
> *The room awaits her, quiet and calm,*
> *Libraries closed now for the night.*

But still she studies in her cell,
Spending long hours on lab or test
Before her cheap sheets cast a spell
And grant her a brief moment's rest.

How hard the life of her young years,
How rough her day till she retires
While, looking round, she sees her peers
Seeking new bliss with new desires.

Yet she has joy in what she knows
For in her lonely cell she finds
Rich air in which the spirit grows,
Inspired by the keenest minds.

Ideals flood this tiny room;
They led her to this foreign land;
They urge her to pursue the truth
And seek the light that's close at hand

It is the light she longs to find,
When she delights in learning more.
Her world is learning; it defines
The destiny she's reaching for.

Scene IV

The Invention Factory

1896

Loïe took a deep breath, enjoying the smell of fallen leaves. It was a crisp October day and the trees in Llewellyn Park blazed like torches heralding her arrival at the laboratory complex. She felt like skipping and spinning across the yellow blanket of leaves, but she willed her arms to stay by her sides and her feet to continue moving forward in a dignified manner. Hurrying past the gatehouse, she swept through the archway, feeling like a queen. Who would have imagined that a girl born in an Illinois barroom would be invited to visit a world-renowned inventor?

Sometimes it was still hard to believe that she was famous. At least she hoped that she still was. She wasn't sure. The last few months had been horrible, and her emotions were as fragile as her lungs. Loïe was lonely. She needed to be revived, both personally and professionally, and this excursion felt like exactly what she needed. Where better to get a jolt of inspiration than the laboratory of the man who perfected the incandescent lightbulb? And where better to get some free press?

After a rough ocean crossing on the steamer from Paris, she'd arrived in New York back in February, along with her lighting crew, her mother, and her brothers, Frank and Bert. The tumultuous journey across the Atlantic foreshadowed trouble to come, but the tour had started off triumphantly. After leaving the States as an unemployed actress who had been snubbed by the U.S. Patent Office, it felt impossibly glamorous to be returning to New

York as a famous dancer with an engagement at Koster & Bial's Music Hall, the best venue in the city. They'd put her up in a celebrity's penthouse in the Fifth Avenue Hotel, and the papers were buzzing that they were paying Loïe a thousand dollars a night for each of her ten performances. This was, in fact, true. She'd leaked the story herself.

About a week into her engagement at Koster & Bial's, Loïe had invited a reporter who called herself "Maid Marian" to spend an entire day with her. In return, the woman had written about her brilliantly in an article titled "One Day with the New Dancer from Paris: From Breakfast to Midnight with Loïe Fuller." Marian had arrived on Fifth Avenue at eight thirty in the morning as directed and was invited into the penthouse only to discover Loïe still in bed.

In a well-choreographed "flutter of blue and white and gold," Loïe had arisen to get ready for her morning visitors. All day, Marian followed Loïe through her routine, as she greeted callers and replied to stacks of correspondence. Finally, she accompanied the dancer to the theater for a behind-the-scenes look at what went into each of La Loïe's productions. Everything had gone smoothly, and Marian had clearly been charmed by her performance, both on the stage and off.

Her article described Loïe smiling and stretching her sore arms as she climbed out of bed, and detailed the lovely chaos of her hotel room where "heaps of roses" were "everywhere, vases, baskets, bowls, all full of them." Loïe, who was proud of the interesting friends she'd made, was glad that Marian mentioned her autographed photo of Alexandre Dumas. The reporter detailed how lovingly Loïe treated her mother, as well as the visits and piles of notes, telegrams, and invitations from American celebrities and millionaires.

Loïe, according to Maid Marian, underwent a transformation from a bright, charming American girl into a serious artist as she moved from her hotel room to the stage for her performance. She described six-foot-long boxes containing Loïe's carefully packed dresses, her well-practiced hair and makeup routine, and the precision of timing required to direct her electricians as she brought her famous dances to life.

Reporters had helped create the legend of La Loïe, and Loïe knew that they could destroy her as well. She spoke to them every chance she got, and the newspapers covered her performances extensively. As a result, New York's adoring throngs bought enough tickets to sell out each of her performances, blanketing the stage with flowers after each show as Loïe was called out for curtain call after curtain call.

She'd been grateful for the warm reception and bowed and curtsied convulsively, reaching down from the stage to grasp the hands of young men, blowing kisses and thanking her audience again and again. At every show, she received a number of suggestive notes from men looking for a tryst, but her brothers were adept at keeping unwanted admirers away.

The reviews had been mostly complimentary, and she'd saved one that she found especially amusing.

"Through it all the young woman is as distinctly visible as though she were in a bath," the journalist Hugh Morton had written. He continued by stating she was without a doubt a "mistress of electric effects" and recalled an amusing conversation he'd overheard nearby in the audience. "'But she doesn't dance,' said an envious *première danseuse* who was watching her one night. 'My dear,' put in someone who was sitting close by, 'do get her to tell you how she learned not to.'"

Morton conceded that "her feet do not meet and leave the stage with the rhythmic precision observable in almost every other dancer that has ever lived." He continued, the "beauty of motion that she displays and with which she amazes all beholders is produced by the marvellous trick of manipulating hundreds of yards of web-like fabric amid the fiercest glare of light that has ever been projected upon a stage," and he concluded that, "She is a spectacle that is scarcely equaled by rainbows, torchlight processions, Niagara Falls, or naval parades."

That article had been written nearly eight months earlier. Now, almost every cent she'd earned was gone. Although Loïe's salary was newsworthy, no one ever bothered to mention that most of the money was immediately consumed by expenses, which included transporting her equipment and covering the salary, room, and board for her large lighting crew, whom she paid personally. Following her New York performances and an impromptu tour of several cities, she'd had a complete physical and mental breakdown. Loïe had been forced to stay in bed between appearances at the Boston Theatre, only dragging herself out for performances.

Besides having a horrible cough, she'd been mentally exhausted to the point where she could barely walk without clinging to something steady. A constant stream of admirers flowed through her dressing rooms, but Loïe had to admit that besides being unwell, she was extraordinarily lonely. She told reporters that she was going to the mountains or seaside to rest and checked herself into a sanatorium for six months, where she recovered her health and her strength.

When she finally emerged, she told herself that she was ready to conquer the world again. That the American tour had, in fact, been worth the pain and stress. Still, she wondered whether she would have been better off staying in France. Her finances weren't good. In fact, they were terrible, but she knew that celebrity was all about optics. Despite its difficulties, her visit to the United States had reminded everyone in New York that she was shining brighter than ever.

On this particular crisp October day in New Jersey, sunlight filtered through the colorful leaves like a magic lantern, casting speckled shadows onto the ground beneath the trees. Loïe could see why Mr. Edison had chosen to live and work in West Orange. Positioned at an easy distance to New York, his complex was far enough away from the city to be embraced by open fields and flanked by trees.

Although she loved New York's buzz of activity and its theaters, the city itself was dim and dirty. Tall buildings loomed over narrow, crowded streets and blocked the light, and she'd started to cough almost from the moment she'd stepped off the ship into the hazy air. Here in West Orange, the leaf-scented autumn air reminded her of her childhood in rural Illinois. She inhaled deeply, rejoicing in the feeling of being able to expand her rib cage without coughing.

Thomas Edison's campus, which she had expected to be dull and gray, was quite the opposite. A rain shower had passed through that morning, leaving sky-blue mirrors of water everywhere. Damp red brick glowed all around her, saturated with light from the autumn sun. An enormous three-story laboratory building with arched windows dominated the lot, a cathedral of invention surrounded by rows of brick buildings and wooden ones painted to match.

From where Loïe stood, the lowest floor of the laboratory appeared to be twice as tall as the top two, with as much space taken up by glass as by brick. She imagined that the natural light inside must be wonderful. The doors and trim were painted a lovely dark green, and ladders ran diagonally from the top floor down, in case of fire.

A man bustled past her with a long metal bar, nodding to acknowledge her presence. She'd read that Edison's troupe of inventors, called muckers, came up with a minor new invention every ten days and a major one each month. Not only had he invented the modern lightbulb; Thomas Edison and his workers had created what was needed to put together entire electrical lighting systems, including power plants and the wiring that carried the electricity to streetlights and buildings, making it possible to illuminate the darkness with the flip of a switch.

Loïe herself had spent years working with all kinds of machines for producing rays of light, training crews of electricians to switch colored spotlights of her own invention on and off, illuminating her from different angles to achieve the effects she desired. She could hardly wait to talk to Mr. Edison about his electric advancements and discuss some new ideas that had been bouncing around in her head.

She wondered when Delia Davis, a newspaper reporter she'd invited on her outing, and Col. George Edward Gouraud would arrive. She imagined that the two of them must be hurrying toward Edison's compound now. Loïe had met Gouraud before. He was Edison's agent in Europe and had introduced the inventor's phonograph to the British people in 1888. The distinguished-looking Civil War hero was always happy to have a captive audience and was probably talking the ears off of Delia. He loved nothing more than a good story and was extremely proud of his friendship with Edison.

"To get Edison's attention, you have but to demand the impossible," Gouraud informed the reporter. Their carriage was now just a few blocks away from Llewellyn Park. "I prophesy for you an occasion of extraordinary interest," he continued.

Delia pulled out a small leather-bound book and started to scribble notes as Gouraud went on, "The combination of Edison and Loïe Fuller is something unique in the way of an interview. To begin with, La Loïe is distinctly a woman of brains and almost unlimited resources, with tremendous magnetic power to boot. You will see her propound the impossible to Edison and you will see how he will snap at it!"

Delia was certainly looking forward to watching the two larger-than-life personalities collide, and she told Gouraud as much as they pulled up to the brick gatehouse and stepped out of the carriage to find the dancer waiting.

Loïe turned to greet them with her famous smile. She grasped the colonel's hands, saying how glad she was to see him again, and gushed that she was delighted to have Delia on hand to document her meeting with Edison. Her blue eyes sparkled with excitement as the guard waved them in and they followed Gouraud onto the hallowed grounds of the invention factory. Unable to contain her curiosity, Loïe peeked into the windows of the first building they passed. It was full of motors, belts, and pulleys.

"That's the physics lab," the colonel said. "But Edison will probably be waiting for us in the library."

He led them into the main laboratory building on the right. After walking past a clock where some workers were punching in, they turned right and entered an enormous room that gleamed with hardwood paneling the color of burnt honey. The middle of the three-story room was open to the ceiling, and book-lined alcoves rimmed the walls above them. It was more theater than library, and sitting center stage at a rolltop desk stuffed with papers and stacked high with books was the star of the show.

Hunched over his desk, the inventor of the lightbulb and the phonograph hadn't seen them enter and was still fiddling with what appeared to be a small metal watch. Hearing Gouraud clear his throat, he looked up and unfolded himself from the chair to stand. As handsome in real life as he was in photographs, Edison stood almost six feet tall. Hurriedly tucking the apparatus into his vest pocket, he rushed to embrace the colonel enthusiastically, pounding him on the back.

"You look much better than usual," Gouraud joked. "There's no dust in your eyebrows and you've combed your hair!"

Delia rolled her eyes at Loïe as the men huffed and puffed their greetings for what felt like an eternity. When the male bonding rituals had concluded, Loïe moved forward toward the outstretched hand of Mr. Thomas Edison.

"Mr. Edison," Loïe said, "I am Loïe Fuller. So pleased to make your acquaintance."

He had broad palms, and she noted that his pinkie was almost as long as his ring finger. His fingers were cool but his grip was strong, and she shook his hand enthusiastically. While some men gingerly held a woman's fingers as if they were made of delicate porcelain that might be broken by the tiniest bit of pressure, Edison grasped her hand like an equal. The inventor wore a dark vest, suit coat, and bow tie, and his gray hair was parted to one side, crowning piercing gray-blue eyes. He smelled nice, like sawdust spiked with cologne.

Although his lips came together in a natural frown, the corners of his mouth turned up ever so slightly, giving him an expression of perpetual amusement. Loïe thought he exuded pale yellow energy as bright as one of his bulbs. She greeted him confidently, despite being somewhat starstruck. She had always been far more intimidated by a great mind than a perfect face or body.

The two of them had a good deal in common. Neither had much formal education, they had invented themselves to fame, and both were ingenious self-promoters. Loïe Fuller and Thomas Edison were the very definition of self-made Americans.

"It's the real me, in case you were wondering," she joked. "I know you spent some time with one of my imitators last year."

Edison was as fascinated with Loïe's work as she was with his. He'd wanted to capture her Serpentine Dance on black-and-white film, and the year before he'd sent a letter asking her to perform her famous dance in one of the new moving pictures he was making. Loïe had refused on artistic grounds, because the new medium was in black and white. Without the ability to capture her vivid and complicated lighting, she was certain that the new art form couldn't do her creations justice.

In her place, he'd used a Broadway actress and dancer named Annabelle Moore. The blond woman had done a rather pathetic imitation of Loïe's famous Serpentine dance, but in an attempt to replicate Loïe's lighting effects, Edison had hand-tinted the film to create the first color movie in history. Audiences were enthralled.

Loïe didn't mind the copycats so much anymore. Her imitators mostly served to make her more famous, now that she'd finally established herself as the creator of the Serpentine. Despite not dancing for Edison's film, Loïe's correspondence with him allowed them to become acquainted, which was how she had secured the invitation to his laboratories.

He laughed and took her hand. "Delighted to meet you, Miss Fuller. I'm always happy to meet a fellow inventor."

Loïe flashed her most winning grin. "I heard such nice things about your moving pictures that I almost wished I'd agreed to dance for you. Everyone in New York is crazy for them! When you can exactly capture the color of my lights, maybe I'll change my mind."

"When I figure out how to do it," Edison said, "you're the first person I'll tell. Did you see my moving-picture studio when you came in through the gate? The black building?"

Loïe nodded. She'd noticed the windowless building covered with tar paper as she waited in front of the complex but hadn't realized that it was for making moving pictures. Dotted with nails, the awkward structure looked like it had been assembled from dominoes. Edison explained that his film camera required ample light, and that the roof on one end of the building could be propped up by enormous wooden struts to let sunlight in. When she asked what happened when the angle of the sun changed, he looked pleased by the question and told her that he'd built the entire building on wheels, so that it could be rotated on a giant turntable as the sun made its voyage across the sky.

"Brilliant!" Loïe exclaimed, wishing that she had a spinning sunlit theater where she could hang a thousand crystals and dance in rainbows.

"I wanted to call it the doghouse," he said, "but everyone calls it the Black Maria, after the police wagons, since it's such a tiny space. It can be quite uncomfortable on hot days. Shall we move on?"

Loïe considered asking him to show her exactly how he made pictures move, but she was even more interested in his work with electricity, so she followed him through the door to the nearest laboratory. The colonel followed them, trailed by Delia, who furiously scribbled notes. Inside the cavernous industrial space, a rack hung with coats, hats, and umbrellas was the only hint of the outside world. In the midst of whirring motors, flashing bulbs, screeching belts, and alien-looking contraptions, muckers scurried around like mice, politely nodding to Edison and his guests as they walked by.

Loïe asked a million questions about every apparatus she hadn't seen before. They talked of dynamos, polariscopes, lenses and X-rays, polarized light and cellular systems as they moved from room to room. Delia and the colonel kept trying to steer the conversation away from technology and invention, but Loïe and Edison ignored them until they finally gave up.

Edison showed his guests a series of phonographs, calling the sound machines his "favorite invention." The earliest version, from 1877, consisted of a tinfoil sheet wrapped around a large cylinder connected to a hand crank. He pointed out a sharp needle fixed to a drumlike membrane, which he'd used to record the vibrations of sound by cranking the cylinder. As it spun, vibrations amplified by the membrane were transferred to the needle, which etched the foil, creating a groove whose depth depended on the individual vibrations. He attached an amplifier that looked like the bell of a trombone and played back the vibrations with a second needle that ran over the groove and reproduced the original sounds.

"Mary had a little lamb, its fleece was white as snow, and everywhere that Mary went, the lamb was sure to go." Edison's scratchy voice came from the bell, but he had already moved on to show them newer models with cylinders made from wax and enclosed in boxes.

Walking into the chemistry lab was, for Loïe, the equivalent of walking into Aladdin's cave. Jars filled with sparkling crystals, colorful compounds, and mysterious liquids lined the walls. Low lab benches traversed the long room, gleaming with glassware. White porcelain dishes sat suspended over blue-and-white flames on gas burners, and men stood bent over their work, scooping solids from small glass bowls arranged on long shelves and tables. Edison leaned over to pick up a bowl containing some crystals and handed it to Loïe. As she examined it, he told her that the chemists were preparing salts from acids to use in one of his new inventions. Despite the fact that she knew very little about chemistry, Loïe was spellbound.

Seeing the look of wonder on her face, Edison warned her that although it sounded exciting, the process of drying up liquids was a long and tedious one. They were testing hundreds of combinations of compounds, he said. The end goal was to discover which chemical compounds formed crystals that would produce light with very little color.

Loïe was incredulous. "Do you mean to tell me that these crystals glow in the dark? And that some of them emit colorful light?"

Reaching up for a lab notebook on a nearby shelf, Edison showed her a list of chemical names. When certain salts are exposed to a bulb that produces X-rays, he told her, they glow in the dark.

"Some of them are quite colorful," he continued, "but we're working to find a combination of acids that will produce colorless light to use in an X-ray image."

"Why in the world would you want colorless light when you could make colors?" Loïe asked.

"We want sharper images. I'll show you," Edison said. He led the group to a dark room near the chemistry lab.

"You are some of the first non-scientists to see our version of this apparatus," he explained to them, and gestured to a strange box that looked similar to a camera. It had a binocular eyepiece on one end and flared out like the bottom of a pyramid to a wider square on the opposite side. "We call it a fluoroscope."

"Ah yes," the colonel exclaimed. "You've mentioned this before."

Loïe examined the machine, turning it in her hands. "But the end is closed off and there is no lightbulb," she said. "How can one possibly see anything inside of it?"

The small box had a handle underneath like a stereoscope, but unlike a stereoscope viewer, which merged two images into a single three-dimensional one by using a binocular eyepiece, there were no photographs opposite the lenses. Instead, there was a solid wall of white with what looked like table salt pasted onto the surface. Outside of the box, and just behind it, was a tiny electrical lamp. Edison turned the lightbulb on to show Loïe that it glowed slightly green.

"That," Edison said, "is an X-ray tube."

The previous year, a German scientist named Wilhelm Conrad Röntgen had discovered invisible rays that glowed blue or green when they hit the glass at the end of a long glass bulb called a Crookes tube, which had no air inside and metal electrodes on either end. When the electrodes were wired to a high-voltage source of electricity, charged particles raced along the interior of the tube, gaining speed and energy until they crashed into the other end and lost all their energy very quickly to create the rays. Röntgen named them X-rays, for lack of a better term.

As he'd experimented with his Crookes tube in a darkened room, Röntgen had been shocked when his X-rays traveled through cardboard and lit up a screen coated with fluorescent chemicals sitting almost ten feet away. Six weeks later, he'd asked his wife to place her hand between the Crookes tube and a piece of photographic paper and taken the world's first X-ray image. Where the rays passed through flesh, their energy had turned the paper black, but where her bones and wedding ring blocked the rays, the paper remained white. The terrifying view of her own skeleton prompted Röntgen's wife to say that she'd seen her death. Crookes tubes were relatively easy to make, and soon scientists everywhere were experimenting with the inspiring new technology.

"So, this is a Crookes tube?" Loïe asked.

"Yes. Exactly," Edison answered, turning the light off again.

He asked Loïe to close the box she held and look through the eyepiece again. She couldn't see a thing. Through the binocular eyepiece, the interior of the fluoroscope was pitch black.

"Ready?" he asked, and Loïe nodded. She heard a click and a buzz as he turned the bulb on again, and although no light could possibly enter the closed box, the screen inside glowed with pale blue light. Edison explained that the wall in the box was covered with one of the phosphorescent salts he'd told her about, called calcium tungstate.

"The salts absorb the energy from the X-ray bulb, as sand does water, and become luminous," he told her. "Now, hold your hand between the light and the box."

Loïe eagerly complied, gasping as the bones of her hand came into focus. But it wasn't the shocking view of her skeleton that astonished her so much as the glowing light that danced around the dark shadows of her bones.

"The flesh around my bones looks like a veil!" she exclaimed, studying the image of her fingers. "It's beautiful!" She stood motionless for several minutes, fascinated with the curious glowing light thrown off by the salts.

The image blurred when she wiggled her fingers.

"We're working to make the technology portable, and to make the image on the viewing screen sharper," Edison said. "My assistant Clarence Dally has been testing different fluorescent and phosphorescent chemicals. Color interferes with the image."

"You are as bad as the astronomers, I believe," Loïe said, looking up when he switched off the light, "wasting perfectly good color. I have a workshop of my own in Paris, where I study light and color, although I never considered until today that puttering about with my research was science. I search for the beautiful in nature, the beautiful for the sake of the beautiful, and enlarge it so that the world can see it outside of the microscope."

Not long after arriving in Paris, Loïe had installed a workshop entirely dedicated to experimenting with her ideas. In addition to inventing new dance costumes and sets and playing with all kinds of electrical machines for producing rays of light, she was obsessed with trying to create fantastical new colors. For hour after hour, Loïe studied harmonies of shades, shifting forms and shapes, before combining chemicals on glass slides and gelatin and throwing light through them. While scientists like microbiologists and astronomers were working to eradicate the colorful halos formed in telescopes and microscopes by bending, bouncing, and interfering with light waves, Loïe labored feverishly to enhance the colorful spectra, seeking methods that would increase and augment the beautiful decomposition of light, rather than eliminate it.

Her favorite piece of lab equipment was a petrographic microscope. She owned a model very popular with geologists, which allowed them to study the composition of very thinly sliced sections of rock, to visualize colors and structural similarities they had never been able to see before. Thomas George Bonney, a geologist, wrote that these observations "dispelled many an illusion and reduced a chaos to order." After reading this, Loïe had promptly ordered a microscope of her own, to see for herself how color could be studied more closely through a lens. However, under the microscope, she discovered more chaos than order.

Loïe understood that light waves moved through space and transparent materials. Under certain conditions, the vibrations in these waves could be restricted to a single plane, called a plane of polarization, as though the light waves were moving between the parallel slats of a picket fence. Microscopes like hers contained one or more polarizers that could be stacked and rotated, allowing the user to illuminate objects by manipulating the angle of the light waves. These manipulations revealed structures and a deluge of colors that aren't normally observed under light from a bulb, or the sun. The riot of colors was almost enough to drive her mad.

Day after day in her workshop, Loïe spent hours studying dyed cotton fibers from a famous Parisian textile manufacturer. By looking at the samples without magnification, and then observing them under the microscope, she attempted to decipher which colors were visible in her favorite hues. This allowed her to attempt to re-create them by mixing pigments to tint new lighting gels for her projectors.

In her notebook she'd written, "There are 13,000 registered colors all with names existing in the fabrications of the Gobelins tapestries. But under the microscope—in polarized light—the colors are countless. They shift, changing, till the brain grows dizzy with only looking at them." She'd noted that the artifact displeased scientists, and that the colors were "the enemies of facts in nature because they conceal them and form a stumbling block in the march of science."

Loïe loved mixing new colors, drying them onto disks, and shining light through them. The hours she spent in her workroom made her a patient observer and an avid experimenter.

Now, Edison's explanation of how phosphorescent material absorbs light the way sand soaks up water gave Loïe an idea.

"Could I permeate a dress with those wonderful salts?" she asked Edison. "Are they very expensive?"

He started to say something, but she interrupted. "You compared the light from the salts to sand in water. I wonder if the salts would retain the light, as sand does water, and keep shining after the bulb was turned off? It would be impossible to dance with an electric bulb following me around."

Edison stared at her and reached up to tug on one eyebrow.

"I had not thought of that," he said, pulling out his pocket watch. "Shall we give it a try?"

He turned on the light, as Loïe looked into the fluoroscope. After a minute or so, he turned it back off, and Loïe continued to stare at the glowing screen. The brilliance of the salts lasted for a full two minutes, and then began to slowly fade away. As they waited, they discussed the possibilities of using Chinese silk for color research, checking on the salts for half an hour or more, during which time they still retained a faint light.

Finally, when the colonel had loudly cleared his throat several times and declared that he'd seen quite enough of the fluoroscope, they left it behind and turned their attention back to their companions. Back in the library, over pie and coffee, Loïe talked about her famous friends, and the colonel and Edison told stories from their days together in London until it was time to head back to the city. Delia commented to Loïe that she looked well.

"Thank you! Can you write that down?" Loïe asked, smiling. "That I look well? And please say that I'll soon be performing some entirely new dances on the stages of Paris."

When she bid the inventor good-bye, Loïe pulled a large silk scarf from her coat pocket and left it with Edison, who promised to have his assistant permeate the cloth with glowing salts. They agreed that she would visit again soon to spend a week in his laboratory, experimenting with color. For the briefest moment, Loïe longed to flee her lonely existence to become one of his muckers, tinkering her days away in his wonderful invention factory, but she knew that for now she would have to be content in her own small workroom in Paris. She made a mental note to order some fluorescent salts when she arrived back home. There was no point in waiting around for a man to do her work for her.

Scene V

The Atomists

1900

I began these researches by a study of the phosphorescence of uranium, discovered by Monsieur Becquerel," Marie began.

The doors to the lecture hall were open, but she was already sweating in the August heat. Mustachioed men in suits were stacked up on the slope of the lecture hall like a huddle of walruses on a beach. Pierre winked at her from the front row of the crowded room. Following his presentation, he'd folded his tall, lean body into one of the seats in the front row.

Although he appeared to fit in perfectly with the crowd of scientists, there was something different about Pierre, and that's why Marie loved him. Until he was fourteen, Pierre's parents had kept him from traditional school, realizing that their dreamy son, who learned slowly by focusing intently on his interests, wouldn't thrive there. He'd gotten his early education in forests and fields, by wading through streams and ponds where he gained a great love of nature through endless hours of observation.

When Pierre finally embarked on a more traditional educational path, studying with a professor, the shy chestnut-haired teenager proved to be particularly good at geometry. He and his brother Jacques had done groundbreaking research involving the symmetry of crystals, and in 1880 they'd discovered the piezoelectric effect, which allowed them to produce and measure electricity by squeezing or stretching certain types of crystals, including quartz. In 1893, Pierre went to work as the director of laboratory work at the School of Physics and Chemistry in Paris. Fascinated by invisible forces like electricity and magnetism, he continued to study crystals, but by then he'd shifted his focus to magnetic materials and how their behavior changed at different temperatures.

He was in no particular hurry to get his doctorate degree, and it was only around the time he met Marie in 1894 that Pierre gathered his work on magnetism into a doctoral thesis. Watching him present his work so beautifully was to become one of her fondest recollections. Later, she'd write:

> I have a very vivid memory of how he sustained his thesis before the examiners, for he had invited me, because of the friendship that already existed between us, to be present on the occasion. The jury was composed of Professors Bonty, Lippmann, and Hautefeuille. In the audience were some of his friends, among them his aged father, extremely happy in his son's success. I remember the simplicity and the clarity of the exposition, the esteem indicated by the attitude of the professors, and the conversation between them and the candidate which reminded one of a meeting of the Physics Society. I was greatly impressed; it seemed to me that the little room that day sheltered the exaltation of human thought.

Now, she and Pierre were partners in life and work, and after years of hard labor in a leaky shed, the two of them had given birth to a new science, which had made them minor celebrities among their peers. Everyone wanted to know what the French couple had learned from their meticulous study of the strange rays that had first been discovered coming from uranium four years earlier. While Becquerel and other scientists had abandoned the discovery to chase after X-rays, Marie had pounced on the new phenomenon. She'd started by testing every mineral she could get her hands on, searching for other rocks that emitted the mysterious energy, which she named "radioactivity."

While sweat stained their collars, the crowd of scientists sat spellbound in the stifling room watching Marie demonstrate her method for measuring radioactivity, using delicate equipment she'd transported from their lab. With steady, practiced hands, she showed the physicists the complicated technique she'd performed thousands of times. As she measured the electrical charge given off by her sample, using the electrometer she and Pierre had designed, she discussed their findings, including the fascinating discovery that emanations from the material they'd been working with had made everything in their lab mildly radioactive.

"The emission of the uranic rays," Marie told them, "is very constant, and it does not vary noticeably with time, nor with exposure to light, nor with temperature."

Her meticulous measurements had demonstrated that the power of the rays coming from each radioactive element depended solely on the quantity of the element being measured. The bigger the sample, the higher the reading on her electrometer would be. Marie's early work with uranium had also indicated that radioactivity didn't make any obvious physical or chemical changes to the element itself, which led her to believe that it was probably a property of the tiny building blocks of matter known as atoms.

When her research uncovered the existence of the entirely new elements radium and polonium hidden inside of mining ore, she and Pierre struck scientific gold. But to convince the scientific establishment that Marie's discoveries were indeed new and could be added to the periodic table, she would have to purify them. This was the work that now consumed her life.

"The preparation of the pure chloride of radium and the determination of the atomic weight of radium," she explained, "form the chief part of my own work. Whilst this work adds to the elements actually known with certainty, a new element with very curious properties, a new method of chemical research is at the same time established and justified."

Marie was determined to demonstrate that the idea of characterizing chemicals based on their radioactive properties had come out of their lab, and that the method would not be possible without the work she'd done using equipment invented by Pierre. They might not have positions or laboratories at the Sorbonne, but this groundbreaking new work belonged to the Curies. She wanted to lay claim to it here, in front of the most important physicists of the world.

The hall was unbearably hot, and when Marie wrapped up her lecture, she was sure that the attendees would bolt for the door, but after a brief pause, questions rocketed through the thick air, piling up on one another faster than she could answer them.

"Is it possible to obtain some of these radium salts?"

"Röntgen's X-radiation is produced by the addition of electrical energy. How do uranium and your new radioactive elements create their own energy from within?"

"Yes! What is the source of the energy?"

"Could Monsieur Curie please join you at the podium?" a voice from the back of the hall interrupted, halfway through one of her answers. "I'd like to hear his perspective on the matter."

"I am perfectly capable of answering any questions you might have," Marie said calmly in the general direction of the voice. "I realize that it's very warm in here, so you may feel free to leave at any time."

The inaugural International Congress of Physics was being held at the Hôtel de la Société d'Encouragement in Paris. Scientists from fifteen nations were presenting their research at the meeting, but the papers at the conference were given by French and German physicists, with the exception of one from Japan, another from India, and a few from the United States. Only two women, Marie and Isabelle Stone, the first woman to gain a Physics PhD in the United States, had registered for the conference, along with 789 men. Some of the participants were learning the details of the Curies' work with radioactivity for the first time and Marie and Pierre were the stars of the show.

The lecture they'd just delivered presented revolutionary data that seemed to contradict one of the most basic laws of physics, which states that energy can change forms but cannot be created or destroyed. These new radioactive elements appeared to be creating energy, and as Marie worked to purify radium, she and Pierre were also attempting to decipher whether its strange energy was being generated within or came from an external source. Was it possible that rays from the atmosphere or outer space had somehow been absorbed by certain earthly elements, causing them to become radioactive? They simply didn't know.

"As I stated earlier, we are still working to make known the nature of the rays emitted by radium," Marie said, reiterating some of the results in the paper she and Pierre had just published, titled "The New Radioactive Substances and the Rays They Emit."

That Monday, the mathematical physicist Henri Poincaré had given the conference's opening keynote address, making his case to the attendees that physicists are not decipherers of nature's laws but rather "librarians and catalogers of experience." New discoveries in magneto-optics, X-rays, and radioactivity had challenged old ideas and opened new avenues of inquiry in the physical and spiritual worlds. Scientists like the Curies stood firmly in the corpuscular, or atomist, camp. They believed that all matter was made up of tiny particles: individual building blocks, invisible to the naked eye. Other scientists stood solidly in the aether camp, imagining that the universe was cemented together by a mysterious, invisible substance that could propagate electromagnetic and gravitational forces.

"Are there any more questions?" Marie asked when the spirited discussion finally ceased. She was starting to feel faint from the heat.

"Does radium have commercial value? Have you found a practical use for it?" an American scientist blurted out, not even attempting to speak French. He said the word "radium" with a flat, drawn-out "r" that massacred the lovely word.

Marie tightened her lips and looked over at Pierre, who was shaking his head almost imperceptibly.

Everyone in the room knew that the American scientific community was constantly bickering over the merits of pure science versus research in the name of commerce, pitting the dollar, which was worth about 26 grains of gold, against the pursuit of knowledge for the greater good.

"That remains to be seen," Marie said in English, coldly but politely, returning her attention to the American. "Pierre and I hope that it will one day prove useful to society as a whole."

When she'd wrapped up the last of the questions and the meeting had been adjourned, Marie and Pierre went into the hallway and were immediately surrounded by a flock of scientists who fawned over Pierre, nodding and smiling at his every word. He tried again and again to throw the conversation to Marie, but before she could get a word in edgewise, she'd be interrupted by someone asking Pierre another question.

When they finally escaped and made their way out of the building, it was almost as hot as it had been indoors. It did, however, smell far better than a room packed with hundreds of sweating men. They'd decided to transport their equipment and samples back to the shed the following day, although leaving them in the hall made Marie nervous. Even a single day's work lost was a day when some undiscovered competitor might move ahead of her in the race to purify radioactive elements.

The physics conference was being held in conjunction with the Paris Exposition of 1900, which had gobbled up all the open spaces in central Paris, along with its riverbanks, and regurgitated them as eclectic international micro-cities containing buildings designed by almost every nation in the world to reflect their local architecture. On the way to the symposium, she'd seen boats cruising up and down the Seine filled with spectators gawking at the domes, towers, and palaces of glass.

Marie took Pierre's arm, feeling the lean muscle hidden under his sleeve, and they flagged down a carriage to the exposition's main gate, where a fifteen-foot-tall stone goddess called *La Parisienne* loomed over the entry with outstretched arms. Everyone in Paris detested the gate and the statue. It was common knowledge that the true symbol of the exhibition was the "Electric Fairy," who stood at the head of the Champ de Mars. Framed by a spiked halo that blazed white light at night, she gazed over the Palace of Electricity's waterfalls and fountains, a symbol of the shining technology that had transformed the world.

Science and technology had been moving forward at an unprecedented rate, but while scientists argued among themselves about conflicting theories and experimental results, a large percentage of the population worried that academic discoveries threatened religion. They believed that using science to explain and quantify the unknown endangered the souls of individuals and threatened the social establishment. Despite their discomfort with science, however, the public loved technology and rushed to the fair in droves to explore new inventions and learn about new ideas.

From where they stood, Marie could see the Eiffel Tower. Pierre wanted to explore the aquarium, so they walked toward the glass roof of the Grand Palais and along the rue de Paris to the gargantuan saltwater exhibit, which had been constructed just below the water level of the nearby Seine. As she'd expected, Pierre was captivated by the marine life, but as Marie watched projected mermaids frolicking among fish and coral, she couldn't help but think of the men at the conference. Even their postures suggested that they viewed her as some sort of strange creature that couldn't exist in the natural world, at least not without her husband's assistance. She might as well have been a mythical creature herself.

"Do you think they understand that I'm not just your laboratory assistant?"

Pierre looked at her in his usual serious way.

"Does it matter what they think? What the world thinks? All that matters is our work."

A shark drifted by, lazily following a school of small fish.

Pierre truly didn't mind being overlooked. He'd never fought for money or position and despised those who did. Still, it was much easier not to care what people thought when you were a man. Marie had learned a long time ago that she had to care, or she'd be trampled under the feet of unspoken rules based on gender, social status, and race.

"It matters to me," Marie said. "And it should matter to you. We need funding to do our work, and without recognition, there will be no funding."

"Nonsense. Everyone understands that you first discovered radium and polonium. That we conceived the methods to measure radioactivity and purify radium chloride. Our notebooks and publications are proof of your contribution which nobody can contradict."

Marie hoped he was right, but she knew better. Sometimes even scientists saw only what they wanted to see, despite the evidence right before their eyes. She had to work ten times as hard as any man and meticulously document her discoveries in order to get any credit at all. Still, she'd chosen wisely when she agreed to marry Pierre. He wasn't very helpful when it came to their two-year-old daughter Irène and the house, but when it came to science, he'd always treated her as an equal.

Blinking in the sunlight, they emerged from their undersea expedition and continued down the rue de Paris.

"Should we cross the river here, or continue on to the colonial villages?" Pierre asked.

While she found foreign cultures fascinating, Marie was appalled by the idea of people being put on display like zoo animals. Her experience under Russian rule in Poland had given her a tiny taste of what it was like to live under the fist of a foreign government.

"Let's cross," she said.

They marched across the Pont de l'Alma and hopped onto the electric sidewalk, which wound through the exhibition like a wooden serpent. When it curved to move away from the Seine, Marie and Pierre disembarked and began to make their way toward the Eiffel Tower, where they would meet up with the other scientists. Deep in discussion, they almost bumped into a short woman in a very large hat. Barely looking up, they mumbled an apology and continued on their way.

Late to an appointment with a painter, Loïe swerved to avoid the serious couple in dreary dark clothes who had nearly crashed right into her. She'd never heard of the young man who wanted to make a poster of Sada Yacco, the Japanese actress performing at her theater, but she assumed that, like every other artist in Paris, he was besotted with her. At any rate, he had clearly charmed the pretty girl who worked at Loïe's gift shop, who had insisted that she meet him. Loïe, who rarely missed an opportunity to scout for new talent, had agreed.

Since arriving in Paris, Loïe had been called the "Fairy of Light," but the exposition had given her a new moniker: the "Fairy of Electricity." As she walked the streets, she saw her own likeness and inventions reflected on every corner, from the flowing forms in the Art Nouveau building to the rainbow fountain of the Palace of Electricity and her imitators in the Palace of Dance.

She crossed the Seine at the Pont d'Iéna and walked along the river toward her theater. Initially allotted another location, she'd written at least a hundred letters and badgered the authorities to exhaustion until at the last minute she'd been granted a prime spot on the popular rue de Paris, where she was the only non-French artist. Once she'd secured her little piece of land, Loïe had fought countless more battles with her architect, Henri Sauvage, and the workmen, eventually taking the men she'd contracted to court for exceeding the budget. Thanks to her constant supervision, the theater had been built in six weeks, rather than the predicted six months, and it was making a nice profit.

The art critic Arsène Alexandre had kept close track of the goings-on at Loïe's construction site, writing:

> The ditchdiggers arrived on the eve of the exposition's opening, the carpenters later, and the masons after everything was open...People don't know Loïe's energy, her get-up-and-go. She is what is called *a very pushing woman*...During that time Miss Fuller was architect, painter, decorator, mechanic, electrician, manager, and everything else. There was nothing more amusing and charming than to see her on the construction site, running around to supervise the work or to correct a mistake, her plum-colored dress disheveled, her hair in wild disarray...Then all at once, she disappeared...She had gone off to buy material at some distant department store, or to contend with a ferocious prefect of police, or to mollify one or another stubborn functionary. She wore out two or three secretaries, though she wrote more letters than any of them...dancing at the Olympia in the evenings and also, I believe, in the afternoons.

All of the hassle had been worth it. The result of her labor was modern, beautiful, and functional. A stretched arch of stone ran the length of the structure and curled up at either end in a serpentine curve. Carved in rich relief, the plaster facade formed a draped, swirling veil. The theater was topped by a long, low roof punctuated with four stained glass windows and in the center of the building's facade was an arched door that opened like a cave's mouth beneath a large sculpture of the dancer with billowing robes.

An endless stream of diplomats, aristocrats, artists, and factory workers filled the two hundred seats to watch her perform four of her dances: the Light and Dark Mirror Dance, the Firmament, the Lily Dance, and the Fire Dance. Day after day, they went crazy for her Lily Dance as her long wands threw impossible volumes of silk twenty feet into the air to create a spinning white vortex that concealed her figure completely in a funnel of fabric.

Her Fire Dance was equally popular, drawing on her acting skills as she danced to the dramatic music of Wagner's "Ride of the Valkyries." Standing over a glass trapdoor that allowed her to be lit from underneath, she burned red, yellow, and blue, lit by brilliant spotlights that turned the silk of her robes into flame against a black background.

The critic Jean Lorrain wrote:

> Molded in the middle of ardent embers, Loïe Fuller does not burn; she filters and oozes light, she herself is the flame. Erect in glowing coals, she smiles, and her smile seems a mocking grin under the red veil in which she is wrapped, the veil she moves and waves like a smokescreen down her lava-like nudity. It's Herculaneum buried under ashes, it is also the Styx and the infernal shores, and it is also Vesuvius with its half-opened mouth spitting the earth-fire; this immobile nudity which is still smiling in the embers of a fire from heaven, with Hell as a veil.

Loïe's work with the astronomer Camille Flammarion had inspired her Firmament dance. Surrounded by light-scattering crystals, Loïe would catch the moon from the sky and bring it to Earth, projecting it on her robe. Her last creation, an original mirror dance, split and multiplied her image in a myriad of configurations. The more science-minded in the crowd noticed that her work reflected the modern technology they'd seen in the Palace of Optics, where visitors could peer at the moon through a 200-foot-long telescope, dive into the microscopic world of Louis Pasteur, and study X-rays, crystallographic polarizations, and chemical incandescences.

She weaved her way through the crowd until she arrived at the front door of her theater. Few people noticed her when she was offstage, and she moved unobserved between the figures of dancing girls on either side of the arch to smile at the young woman at the counter, who motioned toward a dark-haired young man in a cap. He had his back to her and was studying one of the Larche sculptures of her dances that were on display. The room was a sort of temple to Loïe, filled with both real art and cheap souvenirs mirroring her dances.

"Bonjour, Monsieur," Loïe said.

The young man turned to face her. He took his hat off and held it in both hands as he studied her. Probably in his late teens or early twenties, he stood only a few inches taller than she, but the confidence of his gaze added height to his presence. His penetrating black eyes were mesmerizing. She raised her chin and studied him more carefully. He had a powerful, barrel-chested physique, a prominent philtrum above his upper lip, and wore his black hair brushed off to one side.

"Je suis Loïe Fuller," she said.

"La Loïe. *Encantado.*"

He gave a small bow and introduced himself very seriously, stating in heavily accented French that he liked her dances very, very good.

Loïe laughed. His French was even worse than hers. She was happy enough to meet him, but immediately decided that he was far too young and poor to add to her collection of friends. Loïe had to admit, however, there was a magnetic quality about him.

The young man smiled, sculpting the smooth olive skin on either side of his mouth into parentheses. He gestured for a similarly dressed man on the other side of the room, who spoke only slightly better French than he did, to join them. Loïe called her own shop employee over to help translate. Although Loïe had been in France for almost eight years, she still struggled to understand the language when it was spoken too rapidly or with an accent.

Her shopgirl fluttered over like an eager butterfly, beaming at the attractive young Spaniards in their black corduroy jackets, odd cloth hats, and bright ties. It seemed that the charismatic young artist was in Paris to see one of his own paintings, which was hanging in the Spanish Pavilion at the exposition. He'd been to Loïe's theater on more than one occasion, he said, and was a great admirer of both Loïe's dances and Sada's acting. Pulling a few rough sketches from his pocket, he told her that he wished to make a poster of Sada Yacco's famous death scene. Although the drawings had obviously been made quickly, she was impressed by the skillful arabesque lines.

"Ah yes, everyone loves Sada," said Loïe, smiling at him.

The French were absolutely wild for the Japanese actress. They'd never seen anyone die so beautifully. A woodcut print come to life, the lovely Sada posed, danced, and gracefully expired on her theater's stage exactly twice each day.

Fascinated with everything that came from Japan, Loïe had read about the actress and her troupe when they were appearing in America for the first time. A visionary as always, she recognized the enormous potential of the talented, beautiful woman who could bring popular Japanese art to life on the stage. Loïe booked Sada and her troupe immediately and, upon their arrival at the fair, designed their sets and lighting using her own special effects and equipment.

In addition to her unique lighting, Loïe played to the bloodthirsty French public by adding samurai seppuku to their performances. Loïc had laughed when Sada told her that shortly before they came to Paris, someone in the American audience had fainted at a beheading in the play. "But in France," Sada continued, "things are different: The more bloody, the more glad the audience will be...Under their grace and beauty all the French people are hungry for blood and tears."

As Sada had predicted, the audience went mad when men fell on swords and Sada's character committed suicide by cutting her own throat. It was historically incorrect and unbelievably successful. Sada's expressive face would distort, sweat, and grow pale during her death scenes, as Loïe's lights tinted her lips blue. Sada Yacco's acting and Loïe's lighting were a marriage made in heaven.

Word had traveled quickly, and crowds flocked to the theater to see the Electric Fairy and the Japanese actress perform. Drama critics, writers, actors, and artists rushed to the little theater on the right bank of the Seine. It was even rumored that the famous actress Sarah Bernhardt came to the theater disguised in a veil to watch Sada Yacco perform. Young dancers from around the world sat in the audience as well, including a few memorable young Americans. A swan-necked dancer named Isadora Duncan had been especially noteworthy, showing up again and again at Loïe's theater.

Now this young artist, who had been charmed by Sada, would be disappointed to learn that his request was all but impossible to grant.

"I'm so sorry, Monsieur. Sada Yacco is very busy. She will not even pose for my good friend Auguste Rodin," Loïe said. She told him that he was welcome to decorate the rooms of the Japanese actors, who were staying in her house in Passy, if he wished, although she couldn't afford to pay him anything.

"Thank you, Mademoiselle Fuller. I hope that we meet again."

Loïe nodded.

"I believe that we will."

She could see the disappointment in the artist's eyes, but he smiled again and nodded at Loïe before bidding her au revoir. The young man went to collect his friend, and just before they stepped out into the sunlight, he whispered something into the shopgirl's ear, making her giggle.

"Pablo Ruiz Picasso." Loïe repeated his name so that she'd remember it. In fact, she had no idea whether she would see the artist again, but there was something special about him. Perhaps he would show up on her doorstep with his paints, but she doubted it. Loïe envied his youth. As she headed to the dressing room to prepare for her dances, it occurred to her that besides managing her theater and directing the productions there, she would soon be making her thousandth appearance on a Paris stage. She hoped the French weren't growing bored of her.

Scene VI

The Letter

1901

Loïe yawned and sat down at her desk. The London tour had been completely exhausting, and it was good to be back home in Paris. She squinted at the paper and the salutation she'd scrawled at the top. This was one of hundreds or maybe even thousands of notes she'd written in her lifetime, but it was special. On this particular autumn day, she hoped that the lines she wrote would connect her to the most fascinating woman in the city.

She had a love-hate relationship with the mail. While letters, invitations, and notes from admirers were always welcome, bills and legal summonses had a nasty habit of showing up as well. Her work had an annoying tendency to drag her into debt, and she wasted far too much time scrambling to find funds to pay everyone. Luckily, Sada Yacco and her troupe were back in Paris performing with her at the Théâtre de l'Athénée, and money was flowing in faster than it was leaking out. Still, she knew all too well that she would spend every franc before long.

Loïe needed to make something new, better than the Serpentine, more interesting than mirrors or crystals. When she wasn't at the theater, she was always working in her lab, mixing colors and making lighting gels, but lately her eyes had been bothering her. Her vision was so blurry that she couldn't see through her microscope. She'd begun to worry that her spotlights were literally blinding her and knew that she should probably visit a physician.

Taking a sip of her coffee, she blinked in the bright morning light and peered through her window at the people passing by on the boulevard below. Its palette of soft yellow, gray, blue, and green fed her soul. Compared to the rough wooden buildings of her birthplace back in Illinois and Chicago's gritty streets, this city felt monumental and immortal. She wasn't exactly embarrassed about where she'd come from, but simply being in Paris made her feel like she'd moved up in the world.

Reconstruction of the city in the 1850s had opened Paris up to the sunlight. Dark narrow alleyways had been replaced by grand boulevards lined with chestnut trees, and since the turn of the twentieth century, pagoda-inspired glass-and-iron entrances nicknamed "dragonflies" protected stairs that descended into the subterranean burrows of a new underground metro system. It was a thoroughly modern city, fringed by the old-world charm of neighborhoods like Montmartre, where streams still ran down pastoral tree-shaded streets.

When Loïe craved inspiration, she always returned to Notre-Dame to experience the rays of sunlight that passed through the sumptuous rose windows and vibrated in the church. She loved to stand in color-drenched beams, painting herself with light. Soon after arriving in Paris, she'd taken a white handkerchief from her pocket and waved it in a sunbeam tinted by the rose window to study the play of color on the moving fabric. That experiment had changed her world.

Since then, she'd been kicked out of the cathedral more than once by patrolling vergers, who thought that she was crazy and found her habit of fluttering handkerchiefs offensive. They would seize her by the arm, lead her out of the church, and deposit her on the pavement outside. Loïe almost felt sorry for the old men with their swinging silver chains who were so bound to tradition that they seemed blind to the beauty of the place. She had long since decided that if there were a God, he was in the process of revealing nature's truths to humanity through science and would most definitely approve of her experiments with color and light.

For her entire life, Loïe had attached a hue to everyone she met. Her mother was cornflower blue, and her dear friend and companion Gab, who was always dressed in black, had a violet aura. Color was art, science, poetry, and music. Loïe dreamed that someday, someone would invent an instrument for performers to play colored light rather than music, and she loved to imagine an orchestra performing a composition of pulsing, rhythmic light waves. She saw herself as a sunshine-yellow thread running through the brilliant tapestry of humanity.

Although she loved color, Loïe was also obsessed with the absence of light. She was fascinated by the positive and negative images she could create on a darkened stage and had been the first dancer in Paris to stand in pitch black as the curtains parted. To complete the effect, she'd designed covers for the orchestra lights, after the musicians rebelled against the black paper printed with white notes that she'd tried first. Darkness was essential to her transformation into fire, spirit, flower, and water, until the lights went out and she disappeared again into utter blackness.

Now, a new dance had imprinted itself in her mind, and she was determined to bring it to the stage. As always, she would first appear in total darkness, but this time there would be no electric light. Like the image on Thomas Edison's screen, her costume would glow in the darkness. She hoped to be the first dancer in the world illuminated by a new kind of light, a new discovery. In her vision, when she opened her arms to allow the extended sleeves of her black costume to fan out, the audience would see a ghostly butterfly glowing faintly blue, like a creature of the spirit world. With radium-lit wings, she would appear to defy gravity as she fluttered and floated through the darkness: a personification of art, science, and dance.

Loïe's coffee-fueled daydream was interrupted when a man in a black overcoat paused in front of her house. She didn't recognize him and couldn't discern his expression, so it was a relief when he continued down rue Cortambert. After a recent traumatic experience, she'd grown wary of strangers. Paris had a dark side, which she'd been exposed to when two masked robbers broke into her house and knocked her unconscious, leaving her sore and adorned with a choker of brown-and-blue bruises. She'd barely recovered in time to perform in her little theater at the Paris Exposition.

On the street, almost no one recognized her as the famous dancer whose image had been plastered around the city for the last nine years. When she went out, she often wore a long coat and a veil and was mostly able to move around the city without drawing attention to herself, but parties she threw for her celebrity friends sometimes made the news, and it was well known that she resided in the Passy district.

After the attack, she'd taken in a stray dog and kept the ground-floor windows tightly locked, even on the hottest evenings. Loïe was especially grateful for the electric lamps that populated the avenues like lilies. The city came to life after dusk, when Paris began conducting a current of humanity through its grid of boulevards.

In 1829, long before Loïe arrived, modern streetlamps had begun to appear. The flammable-gas-expelling fixtures were ignited every evening by lamplighters and put out again the next morning. By 1857, natural gas had been piped to all the boulevards and monuments, and the city glittered after dark.

With glowing streets and a busy nightlife, Paris had been dubbed the City of Light, and soon the most famous city in France was shining even brighter. The first electric streetlamp in Paris, called a "Yablochkov candle," flooded the Avenue de l'Opéra with white light in May of 1878. Soon electric arc lamps were all over Paris, their sputtering, fluctuating light produced by an intense electrical discharge struck between two charged carbon rods. Arc lamps were more like stars than fireflies, throwing off intense white light that far outshone the beams produced by their predecessors, and by the time Loïe designed her theater at the Paris Exposition of 1900, smelly, dangerous gaslights were on the way out.

Loïe found arc light glorious, but it was far too harsh and blinding and noisy. She much preferred the possibilities offered by softer, safer incandescent light. Although her friend Thomas Edison hadn't invented the incandescent lamp, in 1879 he'd filed a patent for the first commercially viable one. Edison's invention contained a tiny filament made from carbonized thread or bamboo, housed in a glass bulb evacuated of air. As electricity was forced through the thin filament, it became so hot that the fragile thread glowed with visible light. Edison also figured out how to marry power production, wires and bulb in order to create the first electrical grids.

Loïe had become fluent in the language of incandescent light, specifically how current flowed from a power source through conductive materials while electricity raced around a circular track called a circuit. The language of electricity and light allowed her to communicate efficiently with her team of electricians while designing, choreographing, and executing her performances. When everything was going as planned, the spotlights worked in concert to intensify certain colors or create new ones, avoiding combinations that would ruin the visual effects she worked so hard to achieve. Ever the "faker," Loïe relied on technology of her own design to achieve her spectacular performances.

At that moment, though, Loïe was intensely interested in the work of someone else. Smoothing the paper again, Loïe tried to focus on what she would say to the brilliant woman she had come to admire so much. The scientist was the key, but Loïe wondered whether she had ever heard of her, or was familiar with her dances and inventions. Perhaps she spent every waking hour in the laboratory and despised art.

Loïe certainly hoped that wasn't the case. She'd become obsessed with the idea of getting her hands on a little bit of the glow-in-the-dark element that the reclusive researcher had discovered. After reading about radium in the newspaper, she was desperate to see it with her own eyes. Of course, she hoped that it wouldn't be too horribly expensive, but it might be worth buying at almost any cost, since it would surely draw enormous crowds to the theater. She was certain that the mysterious "radioactive" substance would soon be all the rage in Paris, and she wanted to be the first performer to have it. The critics would go wild.

It was Loïe's mind, rather than her face or body, that made her shine brighter than the other dancers in Paris. Her true talent lay in her creativity and ideas. She was a blue-eyed shape-shifter who could turn science into art, an alchemist creating dreamlike images that no one had ever before synthesized onstage. Loïe painted fabric with light, like her friend Rodin sculpted figures from clay.

She started writing to the scientist in French, but almost immediately shifted to her native language, hoping that she knew some English.

"*Voulez vous* be very kind and tell me if you can give me a little bit of radium to light up a new dance I'm working on?"

Loïe added a note about the work she'd done with fluorescent salts and asked for more information about the marvelous substance radium, revealing her plan for creating glowing butterfly wings. Looking over her letter one more time, she folded and addressed it, scrawling on the back "24 rue Cortambert," and sent it off to the house of the scientist.

That evening, in a little stucco house on boulevard Kellermann hidden by trees, Marie Curie kissed her little girl goodnight. Inhaling the clean smell of her daughter's curls, she tucked her into bed and sat beside her cot until she heard soft, steady breathing. She was five years old now, but Irène still refused to go to bed without a kiss from Marie.

Before falling asleep, she'd asked Marie whether she was going to that "sad, sad" place in the morning, and Marie had answered that yes, she and Pierre would be going to the lab as usual. Despite their best efforts to convince Irène of the importance of their work, the little girl couldn't help noticing that the mothers of other children in the neighborhood stayed at home all day long.

There were so many strings pulling at her that some days she could hardly bear it. Radium, Irène, and even Pierre fought for her attention.

More often than not, Pierre was as jealous of the time that Marie spent with Irène as Irène was jealous of the lab. He'd get annoyed at how long it took her to put Irène down at night, despite the fact that she'd been at the lab with him all day long. Pierre wanted her at the lab or at his side, Irène wanted her at home, and Marie wanted to be in both places at once.

She never said it out loud because she loved Irène so much it hurt, but if she had to choose, she would prefer the lab. The radium called to her, day and night. She was determined to be the first to purify it. Still, as a wife and mother, she was expected to manage the cooking and other household matters, and she did like to put Irène to bed at night. Sometimes she wondered if she'd ever be able to reach her scientific goal, with all the demands on her time. Without Pierre's father, who had come to live with them and watched Irène during the day, it would have been even more difficult to accomplish anything.

Marie crept down the stairs, praying that Irène would stay asleep, and collapsed next to Pierre on their worn green velvet sofa. As usual, he was engrossed in a scientific journal, but he smiled when she plopped down beside him, right where he wanted her. They had an understanding. Science, which had brought them together, might as well have been sitting on the couch between them. It was a third entity in their relationship. Without looking up, he held out a letter addressed with loopy right-slanting handwriting. She looked at the envelope and then at Pierre, who raised his eyes to her, arching an eyebrow.

Marie still treasured the memory of the first time she'd seen Pierre, standing in front of a French window at a gathering thrown by one of her professors. She was twenty-six years old, and he was thirty-five, but he looked ageless that day, surrounded by a halo of light. Deep in thought, he was staring outside and didn't hear Marie approach. Not wanting to interrupt his reflections, she'd waited, studying his profile. Finally, when it became apparent that he wasn't going to notice her anytime soon, Marie cleared her throat, startling the tall, slim man.

"I beg your pardon." He stared at her. "I was just contemplating the possibility of…Ah, never mind."

She immediately liked his voice and had the strange feeling that they'd met before, although she was sure they hadn't. A thick shock of hair standing on end like freshly cut grass dipped down at the center of his forehead, giving Pierre's angular face the appearance of a heart. His nose was almost a perfect triangle, and dark brows arched confidently over intelligent eyes. As he studied her face in turn, his pale blue eyes had the reflective look of a daydreamer. She liked his grave and gentle expression, and when he met her gaze, something in Marie's chest lurched, just the tiniest bit.

Trying to ignore her physical response to him, she stepped forward. She'd vowed to reject such feelings. "Bonjour, je suis Marie Skłodowska."

"Ah, yes. It's so nice to meet you. Monsieur Pierre Curie, at your service."

Pierre's cheekbones rose slightly, and the corners of his mouth turned up as his clear gaze took her in. He had a certain abandon in his attitude that she found completely disarming. After a few awkward attempts at small talk, they finally got down to the business of science. Marie needed lab space. She asked M. Curie about his lab and the work she'd heard that he was doing with crystals. What he did next took her entirely by surprise.

Pierre looked her in the eye and spoke to her as an equal. He wasn't a professor who had witnessed her excellent academic performance and probably only knew that she was a Polish student studying at the Sorbonne. But he was absolutely unlike most of the other men she'd spoken with about physics and chemistry. Rather than assuming that she knew nothing, he spoke to her like he would talk to a colleague. And not only did he seem genuinely interested in her work, Pierre followed up his questions with more questions. Before Marie left the party to go back to her apartment, she'd promised to see Pierre again.

They met frequently, and before long, Pierre told her about his dream of an existence entirely devoted to science, which was so similar to her own. He wanted to marry her, but to say yes to him would mean abandoning her family and her country. When she was finally able to return to Poland for a visit, Pierre flooded her with letters begging for her quick return to Paris. Eventually, the grave young physicist unlocked her heart and she agreed to marry him.

They vowed to make their wedding as simple and purposeful as they were, with no gold ring and no church. On that July day in 1895, Marie wore a navy suit with a light blue striped blouse. She and Pierre rode on the top of an omnibus through the streets they knew so well, past the Sorbonne and on to the village of Sceaux, to make their vows at the city hall and then in the garden at Pierre's parents' house. Marie's sisters were there, along with her dear father and some of their close friends as she and Pierre promised to love each other as husband and wife.

They began their life together biking through the French countryside, and then devoted their days to the goal of unearthing scientific knowledge that would improve the overall well-being of society. They'd found a little apartment with a garden view, where Marie managed the household and made all the meals, in addition to keeping up with her research work. Although they were poor and endlessly busy, Marie loved their life, and they spent almost every moment of those first few years together. When the university was in session, Pierre was often the only person who stopped by the old shed where she spent most of her time. Her days revolved around lab benches and experiments, with occasional forays into lecture halls. Their evenings were devoted to reading scientific journals or having animated discussions with scientist friends.

She missed those days. Lately Marie had the uneasy sensation that their idyll might be coming to an end. Since the article about radium had been published, more and more letters were arriving, and uninvited visitors were knocking on their front door and arriving unexpectedly at their laboratory. Reporters had gone so far as to write about Irène and their cat. She hated it. Not only did the attention make her nervous, it made it impossible for them to get any work done.

Breaking the seal on the envelope, Marie read the note inside. She reread it. Only her raised eyebrows betrayed her thoughts, but Pierre was deep into his reading and didn't notice. She nudged his arm and handed him the letter. When the corners of Pierre's lips started to turn up, she laughed.

"Imagine, Pierre. La Loïe Fuller is interested in our discovery!"

The star of the Paris Exhibition and the Folies Bergère had written to them with a charming but impossible request. Marie knew that everyone in Paris was in love with the American, who used the geometry of an enormous swirling skirt to hypnotize audiences by drenching the undulating fabric with rainbows of electric light. However, she wasn't the type of person to be impressed by celebrity, unless of course that celebrity was a well-respected scientist.

Marie could have simply dropped the letter in the trash, or kept it as a souvenir, but she decided to respond. The note intrigued her. Mlle. Fuller had mentioned her own work with sulfur of zinc and that she'd become interested in glowing substances after visiting Thomas Edison in his New Jersey lab. The idea of a dancer who was familiar with phosphorescent salts was appealing. Who was this woman? Maybe it was something less tangible that attracted her: the artistic curve of the extra curl the dancer had added to the "M" in "Madame," or the way Loïe determinedly moved between French and English, as if trusting the force of her idea to translate itself.

At any rate, Marie went to the table and picked up her pen, thanking Loïe for her inquiry. She tried to use simple words, since the dancer obviously didn't speak French very well, writing as neatly as if she were writing in a lab notebook. Marie told Mlle. Fuller that she'd heard from some colleagues that her dances were very interesting and said that she'd like to hear more about her visit to Thomas Edison. She wrote that the dancer's idea, although delightful, was fanciful, and it would be quite impossible to share her newly discovered radioactive element with anyone other than scientific colleagues. Everyone wanted to get their hands on radium now, and despite what the newspaper may have said, it was very, very rare.

Marie's gray eyes lit up as she penned the word "radioactive." She loved the idea that she'd made up a word everyone was now using. As she wrote, laboratory dust that had accumulated in her hair from the day's work showered down on the paper, impregnating it with minute traces of the element Loïe desired. Marie pointed out that purified radium could cause burns on flesh and that it was far too precious to use as glowing paint for a costume. It was, she wrote, a very interesting idea to make glowing clothes from radium salts, but perhaps the same effect could be achieved using other luminescent salts.

"Precious" was an understatement. Marie's back ached. She was absolutely exhausted from three years of unrelenting physical labor in her quest to purify enough radium to allow the measurement of its atomic weight. But nothing would stop her. Not her declining health. Not Pierre.

She hadn't so much as paused in her mission since 1896, the year she'd figured out how to measure Becquerel's mysterious rays and started to search for them in every rock she could get her hands on. Marie's life changed forever when she placed a chunk of brownish-black mining ore called pitchblende in her apparatus and the readings went off the scale. Further work revealed that pitchblende contained minute amounts of a substance much more powerfully radiant than uranium or thorium. Soon she realized that she'd found not just one but two entirely new elements.

Pierre quickly abandoned his own research to join Marie on her quest to isolate and characterize the new metals. They named the first element polonium, after Marie's homeland, announcing the discovery in July of 1898. The following September, they introduced radium.

That's when her race against time started. Science is built on measurable data, and before the existence of radium could be proved, the pure element had to be observed, weighed, and chemically characterized. In addition, its atomic weight had to be determined, which could only be accomplished by using enough pure radium to move the dial of a scale. To make matters more complicated, the scientific community didn't understand spontaneous radiation. It contradicted fundamental theories that scientists had depended on for centuries to explain the makeup and behavior of matter. With Marie and Pierre's discoveries, the worlds of physics and chemistry were turned upside down.

Radium was as elusive as a piece of dust on a needle in a haystack, and to verify her discovery Marie would have to purify the element from mountains of pitchblende mining waste. It was mind-numbing, health-killing work, requiring her to carry large, heavy containers, pour off liquids, and stir boiling pots of mining waste with a heavy iron rod. Her lungs were raw from choking on the hot, toxic smoke of chemical compounds as she fractionated and crystallized elements, but she'd already managed to process nearly a ton of ore. With the end finally in sight, it was clear that her years of labor would yield a fragment of pure radium smaller than a grain of rice, but Marie never looked back. She'd made it her mission to ensure radium took its rightful place in the periodic table of elements, with the Curie name attached.

Marie was drawn to her lab at night like a moth to a flame, and some evenings after the sun set, she and Pierre would sneak off to the lab to stare in wonder at the glow radiating from their discovery. Although they didn't yet know what the pure metal would look like, when the lights in the shed were extinguished, the beakers and flasks of radium precipitates emitted soft blue light. In the midst of their isolated labor, they dreamed of the mysteries that radium in its purest form would reveal: nature's art laid bare.

"I wonder what it will look like. Pierre, what form do you imagine it will take?"

"I don't know," he would answer. "I should like to think it would have a very beautiful color."

Marie smiled. She was grateful for Mlle. Fuller's letter. It reminded her of the beauty behind the drudgery. Sometimes she wished that time would slow down so that she could simply bask in the radioactive glow of what they'd found and contemplate all the possibilities. Maybe tonight, when she drifted off to sleep, her discovery would take flight, and she'd dream of a butterfly gliding through the night on radium-lit wings.

Act II

Out of the night, the apparition escapes;
She takes form, becomes alive.
Under the caress of electric beams, she breaks away
from the background of mourning,
Abandons the dazzling whiteness of a diamond
To don all the colors in a chest of precious stones.
—Roger Marx on Loïe Fuller

Scene I

The Old Tavern

1901

"I've had a cold for practically my whole life," Loïe said. "It started on the day I was born. It was so cold that water froze in dishes two yards from the stove."

Loïe loved telling Europeans about her childhood in Illinois. They all seemed to think that anyplace beyond New York City was the Wild West, so she played it up for all it was worth. Mrs. M. Griffith, who was from London, had almost certainly never experienced anything like an Illinois winter.

She continued, opening her eyes wide for effect: "Fortunately, the harsh circumstances of my birth, along with a sturdy ancestry on my father's side, has given me a certain power of resistance, although as I said, I've never been able to shake the cold I caught on that day." Removing her glasses, she rubbed her eyes. Now they hurt. She squinted slightly to focus on the woman sitting across from her.

"Are you quite alright?" Mrs. Griffith asked.

"Yes, it's from the stage lights," Loïe said. "But it's not serious."

When she heard a knock that morning, she'd raced to the door, hoping that it was the mail with a reply from the Curies. Instead she found the reporter, who she'd completely forgotten was coming. Seeing the surprised look on Loïe's face, the woman introduced herself as Mrs. Griffith from the London *Strand Magazine*. Loïe made an excuse for her forgetfulness and

79

ran upstairs to close the dog in a bedroom while the reporter waited on the front steps. She collected a few things and stopped in front of a mirror to pin down her unruly hair before returning to invite the woman into her home.

Loïe was always glad to be interviewed, and the *Strand* was a popular magazine. It would give her yet another chance to cement her reputation as the creator of the Serpentine and her other inventions. She led the reporter through her modestly furnished house, past the large marble bust that the sculptor Édouard Houssin had made of her, pointing out miniature models of stages that she used to experiment with new ideas and techniques. When they emerged into the courtyard, she offered Mrs. Griffith a chair in a shaded spot on the patio. Loïe's eyes still ached from the previous night's performance, so she put on her tinted glasses and a hat before sitting down across from the reporter, who pulled out a pen.

Upstairs, she'd grabbed copies of her patents, along with a copy of *Scientific American* to show the reporter. The American publication had been established in 1845 as "The Advocate of Industry and Enterprise, and Journal of Mechanical and Other Improvements" and within five years had founded the first branch of the U.S. patent agency. Thanks to the journal, over 100,000 inventions had been patented by 1900. Its pages included detailed illustrations of new technology, and readers of *Scientific American* were often the first to learn about inventions such as Edison's phonograph.

By 1896, when Loïe heard they'd written an article on her stage lighting techniques and Serpentine Dance, the magazine called itself "A Weekly Journal of Practical Information in Art, Science, Mechanics, Chemistry and Manufactures." Naturally, Loïe had been thrilled, and when she finally got her copy of the magazine, she flipped through the pages eagerly, past a glowing article titled "Patience and Perseverance in Invention," an article on "Low Temperature Research," drawings of new innovations—among them a letter filing cabinet and a combined bed and sofa—and an article on the "Ravages of the Bicycle Craze," which complained that the public was destroying the economy by biking rather than drinking, smoking, and going to the theater.

"Instead of sitting idle and smoking most of the day," it claimed, "hundreds of men now ride, and smoke only when they are resting."

Finally, on page 392, she found the article titled "The Skirt Dance," featuring a stunning illustration of her lighting designs and including a detailed drawing of a Serpentine dancer with her arms extended by rods, standing on the glass platform Loïe had invented. It accurately depicted one of her spotlight configurations, showing the spinning color filters she'd invented for the lights. In truth, she would have preferred less detail, since it would be simple for anyone who saw the drawing to copy her effects, but her heart leapt with the idea that she would finally get some recognition from scientists and inventors, a community she was desperate to join.

Loïe's elation had turned to disbelief, and then something akin to grief, when she read the article. It mentioned her name only once, in the first paragraph, to say that "This dance was made famous by Miss Loïe Fuller, whose reputation is now world wide." She'd read on, somewhat optimistic that the author would give her credit for her innovations, which he described in great detail, but the next paragraph began, "Our illustration is designed to show the methods adopted to produce the wonderfully beautiful effects which have characterized the dance. The performance is executed in a darkened theater." There was no mention of *who* had adopted the methods.

The article reported on every aspect of Loïe's inventions without once naming her as the inventor and concluded by describing her famous Fire Dance. "One of the most startling effects is the flame dance. The filmy veil is pure white, but as the dancer approaches the opening in the stage floor the veil turns to a fiery red and the flames wave to and fro as if they were being blown by the wind. Shadows are then thrown onto the veil which produce an exact reproduction of heavy black smoke, which suddenly changes to an ardent flame again, as if the fire had broken out anew."

Loïe vividly recalled sitting there staring at the fruit of her imagination

and hard work laid naked on the page, the words "Scientific American N.Y."
scrawled across the lower right-hand corner. U.S. patent number 518,374
was evidence that she'd invented the wands, staging, and movements for
her dances, but the magazine dedicated to inventions and patents hadn't
bothered to cite it. She'd flipped back to the article on "Patience and
Perseverance in Invention," which spewed out praise for a string of men like
Edison and included a cautionary tale of a brilliant inventor who lost credit
for his idea due to his lack of perseverance.

> The obvious moral to be drawn from these reflections is that where
> the inventor has good reason to believe that the root idea of his
> invention is sound and useful, he should never become discouraged
> by failure in the minor details. Patience under the sting of failure
> and perseverance in new lines of search will often secure to the first
> inventor those fruits of his toil which are now too often gathered
> by other hands.

If she hadn't been so furious, she would have laughed out loud.

"They're hypocrites. If I were a man, they would have given me credit,"
Loïe said to Mrs. Griffith, as they looked at the *Scientific American* article
together.

"Can you imagine?" Loïe said. "They only mentioned my name once."
It was nice to speak English to someone besides her mother. "They didn't
bother to say that I invented anything in this drawing, let alone that I
invented all of it. And look what they write about Thomas Edison." She
paged back and read in a serious voice, "Invention, in the case of Mr. Edison,
is a search, and the search is prosecuted along multitudinous lines with a
perseverance which may have been equaled but has never been surpassed in
the history of the world."

"He's a friend of mine, you know," Loïe told Mrs. Griffith. "Edison is
brilliant, obviously, and I like his saying that genius is one percent ingenuity

and ninety-nine percent hard work, but he has plenty of money and hordes of men helping him do his hard work and patent his inventions. If only I were so lucky!"

Although Loïe never expected to be examined on the same plane as the man who invented the phonograph, it was disheartening that from the beginning, the press gave her shockingly little credit for her work. With a few notable exceptions, the scientific community she admired so fervently paid her no attention at all. This might have been an inevitable response to the fact that she had little education, but Edison had little education, and they called him a genius.

Fortunately, a handful of writers, artists, and scientists recognized Loïe as the wizard behind the curtain of her popular creations, and some of them had become her most treasured friends. The public adored her, Loïe told Mrs. Griffith, but there were plenty of other dancers, and certain critics, who didn't understand her and lambasted her physical technique as either too free or too mechanical.

Mrs. Griffith nodded sympathetically.

"You must ignore the critics," she said, "and keep doing what you do. People hate change. They are not yet used to women inventors, or female reporters for that matter. You're a harbinger of the future, like a supernatural being sent to teach us the poetry of light and motion. Last century, in all probability, you would have been burned as a witch!" Mrs. Griffith raved.

A modern witch! Loïe smiled, wickedly delighted at the thought. Perhaps she could work that into a dance somehow. She already had a dance of fire.

"I have only revived the forgotten art of the ancients," Loïe said with false modesty, "for I have been able to trace some of my dances back four thousand years."

"And your garments of ever-changing tints?" Mrs. Griffith asked. "Those are illuminated by the lights you invented, the ones in the illustration, correct?"

Loïe reiterated that all the colors and lighting that painted her dances were original, modern, and of her own creation.

When Mrs. Griffith asked about her childhood, Loïe ran upstairs again to retrieve some old photos from her bedroom. In addition to popular stories by authors like Sir Arthur Conan Doyle, the *Strand Magazine* was well known for its liberal use of photography. She handed the reporter a black-and-white image of two buildings surrounded by a split-rail fence and tall grass.

"This is the farm where my parents lived when I was a baby, but I was born in a dance hall on that freezing January day," she explained. "And back then they called me Marie."

Marie Louise Fuller made her grand entrance into the world in the Old Tavern, which sat in the village of Fullersburg, Illinois. With temperatures registering 40 degrees below zero, Loïe's mother and father had fled their freezing-cold farm near Chicago to settle in the public house until their baby was born. The saloon, in the Brush Hill settlement of DuPage county, had been transformed into a sleeping room for the Fuller family by a relative who managed the building, but on that numbing January day in 1862, the barroom where Loïe was born had been so cold that even an enormous cast-iron stove couldn't warm the space.

Built around 1835, the tavern sat on the Chicago-Aurora stagecoach road at the crossroads of two Indian trails. It was a two-story structure with a gable roof, built on a foundation of rubble stone, and the barroom where Loïe was born was attached to a hall leading to two parlors and a stairway. A long dining room with an adjoining kitchen flanked one side of the building, and upstairs the Old Tavern opened into a ballroom, four more bedrooms, and a room marked on the building and elevation plans as "unfinished." Before and during the Civil War, the building had been used as a safe house on the Underground Railroad, aiding slaves escaping from the South into free states. Abraham Lincoln was said to have been an "occasional guest" in the years before Loïe was born.

Loïe explained to Mrs. Griffith that it had been far too cold to heat the entire building when her parents arrived, so they'd converted the bar into a bedroom for about a month, which inflicted considerable hardship upon the villagers, who were deprived of their entertainment for more than four weeks. She described the foxes and wolves, prairie chickens, wild turkeys, sandhill cranes, mink, and squirrels that populated the area around Fullersburg, throwing in the delicious detail that the wolves had proved such a menace after the coming of the settlers that the government offered a five-dollar bounty for them. By the time Loïe was born, the Potawatomi people had already been forced out of their grassland, forest, and river homes.

Her grandfather Benjamin Fuller and his family had arrived in DuPage county from the East Coast, by covered wagon and boat. They'd built a farmhouse in 1840, and Ben had started several businesses in town. By 1850, planks had been laid on the road that ran through Fullersburg, and hundreds of horse and oxen teams traveled through the intersection each day. Loïe's mother recalled that herds of cattle heading to Chicago regularly passed through the area, and by 1860, Fullersburg was one of the leading communities of DuPage county, boasting twenty houses, two hotels, three taverns, a post office, a blacksmith shop, a school, a cemetery, and a grist mill. Her parents, Reuben and Delilah Fuller, had been married in 1850, when she was nineteen and he was twenty-two.

"My father always had big plans," Loïe said.

Not long after the wedding, Reuben caught gold fever and left Loïe's mother to join the gold rush in Panama, coming very close to being killed when his ship caught fire on the return trip. Upon arriving home, he bought a farm a few miles from his family's settlement, but Delilah never forgave him for leaving her alone those first few years of their marriage.

Reuben was never happy running the farm. He was much more interested in breeding and raising horses than crops, and he raced his trotters at the DuPage County Fair every year. A talented dancer and fiddler, he some-times managed the Old Tavern in Fullersburg when things were slow at the farm, but whether playing jigs or dancing, Loïe's father was always the life of the party.

A few weeks after Loïe was born, the cold spell broke and her parents headed home. Icicles dripped and golden sunlight poured through every window in town, as if setting the stage for Loïe's debut. As her mother told it, during a party at a house near their farm, six-week-old Marie Louise had been unceremoniously scooped up by two gentlemen who had discovered her in a dressing room wrapped in yellow flannel and waving her tiny hands and feet in every direction. They'd carried her into the ballroom where her parents were dancing.

"According to my mother, one of the women at the party said, 'She has made her entrance into society,'" Loïe said. "And I proceeded to charm everyone until the last of the dancers swirled home that night."

"How old were you when you began performing onstage?" Mrs. Griffith leaned forward.

Loïe explained that she'd first stepped onto a platform when her family moved to Chicago. Her father had been disappointed when a new railroad was slated to be laid down a full mile from Fullersburg, just far enough away to keep Fullersburg from thriving. A new town sprang up closer to the tracks, and when Loïe was around two years old, the Fullers sold the farm and moved to the city, where Reuben bought a boardinghouse.

"This is how Chicago looked around the time we moved there," Loïe said, giving Mrs. Griffith an old newspaper with a grainy snapshot of a dreary-looking cityscape. "Before the big fire."

In 1867, Chicago was the fastest-growing city in the United States. The Civil War was over, and the front page of the August 15 edition of the *Chicago Tribune* related stories of battles from the "Indian War" as white settlers continued to displace Indigenous peoples from their lands. "Base ball" fever was sweeping the country, and there were reports of marine disasters, falling bridges, and outbreaks of deadly cholera. A whirlwind of cattle yards and commerce, Chicago set the stage for the next chapter of Loïe's life, and in the blink of an eye, the little girl with huge blue eyes and a button nose took to the spotlight.

She handed Mrs. Griffith a photograph of a round-faced child in a striped dress sitting on the lap of a tall man with light eyes. The bows on the top of each of her elastic sleeves appear to have been pushed down to create an off-the-shoulder look. It's difficult to decipher whether her father looks amused or annoyed in the strange portrait, even though he appears perfectly in focus, whereas Loïe's image is blurred, as though she couldn't stop moving.

"Everyone called me Louie back then. You can see that I've never been very good at sitting still."

The picture, she explained, had been taken a year or two after she made her first appearance onstage, at a meeting of the Progressive Lyceum in Chicago. The American Lyceum Movement was an adult education movement outside the university system, started by a Yale graduate named Josiah Holbrook in the nineteenth century.

At the time, many American academic institutions were church-affiliated and focused on teaching traditional subjects, like natural philosophy and classical languages, which allowed them to focus on training clergy. It also helped them avoid broaching topics that might challenge long-held religious beliefs. Holbrook started some community clubs where members could discuss applied science, history, and art. An avid rock collector, he lectured on modern scientific subjects, including chemistry and natural history. Eventually, the idea evolved into the American Lyceum, whose purpose was to educate communities so that they could apply science and various branches of knowledge to domestic and practical arts such as farming and manufacturing. The movement thrived.

"Thousands of clubs were formed around the United States," Loïe explained, "and at the meetings women were expected to stand at the podium and contribute their voices on equal terms."

Outside lecturers were regularly brought into the meetings as well. Among the Lyceum's most famous lecturers were Henry David Thoreau, Ralph Waldo Emerson, educational reformer Horace Mann, and Nathaniel Hawthorne, author of *The Scarlet Letter*. The movement was partially responsible for the establishment of land-grant colleges in the United States, which offered educational opportunities for women and the working class.

Chicago's Progressive Lyceum, which Loïe had attended, offered a recitation period for children, who sat each Sunday morning with their parents to watch invited speakers. Loïe's family went to these meetings rather than church, and it was on one of these mornings that she made her speaking debut, dressed in yellow. She claimed to have been only two years old when she surprised everyone by scrambling up onto the stage to recite her bedtime prayer before bumping back down the steps until she reached the floor of the house.

"They laughed at me," Loïe told the reporter. "But I wasn't discouraged, and the following Sunday, I recited 'Mary Had a Little Lamb' in front of the same audience. According to Mother, my voice resounded throughout the hall and I didn't stop even once. That time no one made fun of me."

In 1866, when she was four years old, she'd gotten her first real role on the Chicago stage, playing a boy named Reginald in the comedy *Was She Right?* which starred the well-known actress Henrietta Chanfrau. Next, she played Willie in the drama *East Lynne*. Her family spent several years in the boardinghouse they owned, and Loïe was nine years old on the infamous October day in 1871 when a cow allegedly kicked a lantern over in a Chicago barn. By the time the fire was put out two days later, it had destroyed the business district of Chicago and killed more than three hundred people.

"Lucky for us," Loïe said, "the wind pushed the fire east of our house."

Her father grew restless once again and moved the family to the town of Monmouth, Illinois. Soon, Loïe was onstage again. Not long after their arrival in the town of a few thousand residents, she'd been cast in an anti-alcohol drama called *Ten Nights in a Bar Room*, which led to a stint as a temperance lecturer at the tender age of eleven.

"Before long," Loïe said, "they called me the Western Temperance Prodigy, and I was in demand all over the state. I made enough money to earn my own living doing that, but we moved back to Chicago again when I was fifteen. Back then, I was willing to take on any role, you know, big or small, and devoted myself with ardor to the study of every detail of my work. That's when I started going by the name Loïe."

After doing a few plays at the Chicago Academy of Music, she'd departed on a nine-month tour with an acting company. Loïe landed in New York for a few years following the tour, taking roles in burlesque shows, comedies and dramas until 1883, when she got her first big break as the banjo-strumming waif in William F. Cody's production of *The Prairie Waif*.

"You probably know him as Buffalo Bill," she said.

Loïe's tour with the rifle-shooting company famous for reenacting scenes from the Wild West had ended abruptly when she came down with small-pox. She'd continued acting, taken up voice lessons, and finally made it to Broadway starring as Jack in a burlesque called *Little Jack Sheppard* at the Bijou Opera House. After performing in several more melodramas, she was cast in a production of *Aladdin*, which gave her an insider's view of the latest theatrical lighting techniques, including colored lights projected on water through a prism, and light projected on steam. Although many of the plays weren't all that successful, she'd had a good run as an actress.

"By the time I was twenty," Loïe told Mrs. Griffith, "the public and the theater world knew my name, but my path wasn't always strewn with roses." She'd actually been closer to twenty-five, but who was counting?

"There were many difficulties and discouragements," she continued. "I worked all the time and didn't have a penny to spare. I played Ustane in *She* at Niblo's Theater and was in the production of *Caprice* at the Royal Globe Theatre in London."

Hopefully, Mrs. Griffith didn't know what a fiasco *Caprice* had been. Loïe certainly didn't want to get into the details of her unsavory circumstances at that time, so she jumped straight to the story of the Harlem Opera House's production of *Quack M.D.*

She loved to tell friends and reporters alike that the creation of her light-drenched, swirling choreography was an accident, a fluke. Loïe was well rehearsed at telling the story, but sometimes she'd change it ever so slightly to craft an intriguing version of many truths, a compilation of experiences, into a single narrative. Whatever the story, the outcome was the same. After years as a moderately successful actress in the American theater, she'd invented a dance so unusual that every newspaper in New York published articles and illustrations of her "wonderful creation." What began with a few swirls of a Hindu skirt in *Quack M.D.* transformed her from an actress into a dancer.

The tale of the Serpentine began with a gift: a soft, silky skirt that some young British officers had given her at a dinner party. The gauzy garment was at least half a yard too long for Loïe, so she'd pinned it up to create an Empire waist. During the play's hypnotism scene, set in a garden "flooded with pale, green light," Loïe had mirrored the motions of the doctor character. When he raised his arms, she copied him, following him around the stage as if in a trance. To avoid tripping on the long skirt, she'd been forced to hold it with her arms raised high as she flitted around.

The audience was much more interested in Loïe's appearance than they were in the mediocre play. Someone yelled out, "It's a butterfly." Another audience member shouted, "It's an orchid." When the play was over, they called for twenty encores of the scene. The play failed, but Loïe had begun her metamorphosis into something new and wonderful.

In her room, she recalled, she put the skirt back on and stood in front of a full-length mirror opposite a window, as sunlight flooded the room. Amber light enveloped her, illuminating her costume and giving a translucent effect. "Golden reflections played in the folds of the sparkling silk, and in this light my body was vaguely revealed in shadowy contour.

This was a moment of intense emotion. Unconsciously I realized that I was in the presence of a great discovery, one which was destined to open the path which I have since followed."

She'd then set the silk in motion to create her new dance. Practicing hour after hour, day after day, Loïe swirled her skirt in front of a sunlit mirror, perfecting her movements. She performed the Serpentine for a few friends, asking them which motions were the most interesting, until she had choreographed a dance unlike anything the world had ever seen.

"How does this sound?" Mrs. Griffith asked, scribbling in her notebook: "Hours passed, yet still she flung the snowy fabric round her, and pirouetted about, registering in her mind for future reference the effect of each position and step."

"Perfect!" Loïe replied.

There were other "skirt dancers" in theaters at the time, who created swishing fabric shapes, but their dancing exposed flesh to showcase their legs and bodies as objects of desire. Rather than making her body the focus of her dance, Loïe used it as a fulcrum whose motion helped her arms rhythmically sculpt fabric into beautiful shapes. She crafted colored spotlights to illuminate her form as she spun, creating shifting undulations in the fabric to form spirals, organic shapes and patterns.

"Finally," she said, "I reached a point where each movement of the body was expressed in the folds of silk, in a play of colors in the draperies that could be mathematically and systematically calculated."

Calling on her muses, Loïe incorporated color, light, and music into twelve movements. One dance would be performed in blue light, another in red, and a third under yellow. Her final dance would be performed in total darkness with a single ray of yellow light crossing the stage. Loïe may well have been a synesthete, which means "sensation together," and she associated certain colors with different musical sounds. Her idea involved projecting electric lights through colored glass onto fabric, and because such technology didn't exist, she created it herself.

Soon her artistic vision was realized. Under her spinning discs of color, she could become a fluttering moth one moment and an ocean wave the next. Spinning in the center of her gowns, she was so obscured by the patterns she created that she became unrecognizable. No longer human, she was form, light, and color. Sadly, no one cared.

Theater managers weren't prepared for Loïe's modern interpretation of dance, and she couldn't convince them that their audiences would be interested. They'd primed their patrons for a glimpse of thigh, bloomers, or cleavage, and the lack of overt sexuality in Loïe's act was akin to profanity in their eyes. Manager after manager sent her away, saying that they only engaged star dancers, that she'd been away from the theater too long and that the public had already forgotten her.

Although cut to the quick by their dismissal, she persisted, only to be turned away again and again. She'd been so poor that she was forced to leave her home and move in with friends. Still, Loïe wouldn't give up. In her heart, she knew that she had created something special, and that she only needed one chance to show people what she could do. Finally, her perseverance paid off, and she got an audition.

Loïe bundled up her silk robe and ran to the theater. Slipping the robe on over her dress onstage, she looked out at an empty theater to see the stage manager seated in the orchestra section, looking as if he'd rather be almost anywhere else.

"There was no dressing room. No music. No lights," Loïe told the reporter.

Undeterred, she'd hummed a tune and started to dance, feeling her long, light skirt catch the air and move. From the corner of her eye, she'd seen the manager stand. He moved closer and closer. Finally, the man ascended the stairs to watch from the side of the stage until she collapsed at his feet, exhausted.

When she looked up, she found the manager's eyes were glistening. He told her that he'd never seen anything like her dance before. Loïe couldn't decipher whether his eyes were glistening with emotion or greed, but he hired her on the spot. Excitedly explaining that he had the perfect music for the dance, he'd led her to his office, where he played a popular tune for her called "Loin du Bal" on the phonograph. Within the week, Loïe set out on a six-week tour of the countryside with his theater.

"In the end, he did not turn out to be a very good manager," Loïe said. "But I do give him credit for recognizing the importance of what I'd created. And that," Loïe concluded, "is how I created my Serpentine Dance."

When Mrs. Griffith left, Loïe checked with the housekeeper to see whether any mail had arrived. Tearing through the stack of letters, she was disappointed to find nothing from the Curies. Rather than admitting that perhaps they would find an uneducated burlesque dancer too uninteresting to even pen a response, she imagined that the scientists were at work in their laboratory, far too busy to read all the letters they received. If they didn't answer, she'd have to find another way to contact them.

Taking a fortifying breath, she charged out the back door to spend the hours before rehearsal in the small workroom behind her house. Hopefully, she'd be able to focus her eyes well enough to use the microscope. A visit to the doctor was inevitable now. Loïe couldn't lose her eyesight. There was far too much to do.

Scene II

Bright Start

1901

"Please tell me the stories about Poland again," Irène begged. "Tell me about Grandpa Skłowdoski's electoscope!"

"Electroscope," Marie corrected her. "El-ec-tro-scope."

"Electroscope. Please, Me!"

"I suppose I can, but I have to get to work soon." Marie sat down and Irène settled at her feet, leaning her head against the black dress Marie wore to the lab every day.

"You smell like smoke."

"I know, my little mouse." Marie smiled at the eager little face and leaned down to kiss the top of Irène's head. She loved to talk about her beautiful homeland, even if it made her homesick, but there were so many things she couldn't tell her little girl. Not yet. Her mind moved back to the Poland of her childhood.

"You call me Me, but my mother called me Manyusya," she told Irène.

"Was she nice?" Irène asked. "You look so sad."

Marie nodded. "Yes, she was very nice, and she loved us very much."

The painful fact was that, although she'd loved her mother more than anything in the world, she couldn't remember ever having been kissed by her. Back when she was Irène's age, she longed for nothing more than her mother's embrace, but she had to be content with a loving smile and the occasional touch of thin fingers gently brushing her forehead.

94

"She would stroke my forehead so gently," Marie said, running her fingertips across Irène's forehead. "Like this."

"That tickles!" Irène giggled.

Marie put her lips to Irène's soft, fine hair again and kissed her cheek.

The cruel interloper between her frail, beautiful mother and her five-year-old self was a highly infectious disease. Also called consumption and nicknamed the "white plague," tuberculosis was a brutal killer that had left a wake of dead bodies, orphans, and grieving parents in its path for as long as anyone could remember. Passed from person to person, or contracted by drinking contaminated raw milk, the infection killed indiscriminately, but was especially cruel to the poor, taking advantage of crowded living conditions.

Scores of artists, poets, and musicians had famously died of tuberculosis, and scores of tragic novels had been written about it, giving the deadly disease a reputation as a "romantic" illness. Five years before Marie was born, Victor Hugo published his novel *Les Misérables*, which begins with the story of Fantine, a beautiful young woman who perishes from tuberculosis in a darkly heroic attempt to provide for her illegitimate young daughter. For a time, fashionistas powdered their faces white and donned bright spots of rouge to give themselves the appearance of having the disease, which had become associated with heightened sensitivity and spiritual purity. Unfortunately, tuberculosis was anything but romantic. Although it was possible to contract the infection and not show symptoms for years, the full-blown disease could appear at any time to sicken the victim with fever and weight loss and ravage lungs with a persistent blood-spewing cough.

Marie knew all too well that children were especially susceptible to tuberculosis and that the disease was often fatal for them. Some nights, she'd lie awake fighting a knot of panic in her chest. What if she carried the disease and passed it along to Irène? Marie didn't have any symptoms, but how could she know for sure? What if the dry cough she attributed to chemical fumes was actually tuberculosis?

Following the invention of the microscope, an invisible world had come to life, and scientists were just beginning to understand that the creatures they saw under their lenses could make people sick. A field of science called microbiology had been established by the French scientist Louis Pasteur, whose "germ theory" stated that many diseases are caused by organisms too tiny to see without magnification. Near the beginning of his career, Pasteur stated that "In the field of observation, chance favors only the prepared mind," a motto that Marie had come to live by.

Pasteur had made an astonishing number of important discoveries with the potential to greatly improve people's lives by protecting their bodies from microscopic invaders, including a vaccine for rabies. Around the same time, a German scientist named Robert Koch postulated a method of determining which microorganisms cause specific infectious diseases. In 1882, he infected animals with tuberculosis bacteria, observed the symptoms of the disease in the animals, and recovered the bacteria from their blood, demonstrating that tuberculosis was caused by the tubercle bacillus, a rod-shaped microorganism. Unfortunately, there was still no vaccine and no cure.

Marie's mother had contracted the horrible disease around the time Marie was born. At the time, many people still believed that tuberculosis was hereditary, but she had been wise enough to keep a safe but heartbreaking distance from her little ones. Mme. Skłodowska only used dishes that she'd reserved for herself and would never embrace her son or her little girls. Although she tried to hide her illness, they all knew she was sick. Marie and her siblings were haunted by their mother's coughing, which echoed from one room to the next. Their father always looked worried, and the short phrase "Restore our mother's health" had been added to their evening prayer.

"Grandma Skłodowska loved to sing, didn't she, Me?" Irène prodded Marie.

"Yes. They say she had a beautiful voice," Marie answered.

Before she got sick, Marie's mother sang and played the piano, but

Marie never heard her Polish folk songs. Their beloved homeland had been recovering from a second failed uprising against Russia and its czar. Marie had been the last of five children born to the Skłodowskis in the years between 1862 and 1867. Four years before her birth, the Polish people had mounted an insurrection against their Russian oppressors, in what came to be known as the January Uprising. They'd suffered a crushing defeat, which sent tens of thousands of Poles to work camps in Siberia, where many died. Thousands of other well-educated Poles fled the country, many of them settling in Paris.

One of Marie's uncles was exiled to Siberia, while another fled to France. A third uncle, who was sick with tuberculosis, came to live with the Skłodowski family a few years before Marie was born. No one ever said it out loud, but everyone suspected that his illness may have been the cause of Mme. Skłodowski's infection, despite any precautions she might have taken.

As Marie grew older and her mother battled the disease, Poland refused to surrender its soul. Russian police and spies patrolled the country under orders to silence writers and journalists, and choke out the national language. Poles like the Skłodowskis, who remained in their homeland under the rule of the czar, maintained a silent resistance, wearing black and pushing back on attempts to destroy their culture. Booksellers in Warsaw refused to carry Russian books, and music sellers shunned Russian compositions.

The czarists cracked down on schools in a campaign to destroy the Polish language. This directly affected the Skłodowskis, who were a family of educators. After attending a private school in Warsaw, Marie's mother, Bronisława, had become a professor and then a director at her alma mater. She'd met an equally accomplished man named Władysław Skłodowski, a biologist by training who worked as a teacher and school administrator. They married and together took up arms in the secret battle against their Russian occupiers. Marie's father belonged to the intelligentsia, a group who believed that educating and training people was Poland's only hope. Poland's new heroes were the intellectuals, the artists, priests, and schoolteachers.

Officials watched over schools like hawks, often stopping by unannounced to make sure that Polish teachers were complying with Russia's curriculum. Sick of the pressure and ill with tuberculosis, Marie's mother finally quit her post as school director to stay home with her five children, but she never stopped being an educator.

"My mother was a teacher before she got sick," Marie explained. "When she stopped working, she taught me and my sisters and brother."

"You're lucky to have brothers and sisters," Irène said. "What did they call you? I forgot."

Marie laughed. "You didn't forget. You never forget anything. They called me Manya, back then"—Marie smiled at Irène—"and they still do."

"And what games did you play?" Irène never grew tired of the stories.

"We played hide-and-seek and made mud cakes that we dried in the sun, and built a tree fort where we hid snacks, like gooseberries, carrots, and cherries. When it rained, we stayed indoors and built continents and tall towers from wooden blocks," Marie said. "We had great battles!"

"Who won?" Irène prodded.

"Well, I'm sure that it wasn't me," Marie answered. "I was the smallest one. But I loved to read. Grandpa Skłowdoski read to us each night."

At home, Marie, along with her siblings Zosia, Bronya, Hela, and Jozio, had grown like weeds in a household bursting with intellect and creativity. They loved learning and did physical exercises before bed. As an adult, Marie realized that, as he read, her father had impressed upon his children a love of literature along with hatred for the czarist regime.

Zosia, the oldest Skłodowski child, was a brilliant backyard actress and writer, while Marie, the baby of the family, had astonished everyone by teaching herself to read at a very young age. More than anything else, though, Marie had been fascinated by the scientific instruments her father kept in the workroom of their house. One of her dearest memories was watching her father take apart his barometer, which used delicate springs connected to long gilt pointers glistening against the white dial to measure the rise and fall of atmospheric pressure, for the occasional cleaning.

"And I loved to look at Grandpa's scientific equipment."

"Does he still have his bara...?"

"Barometer," Marie said again.

"Barometer," Irène repeated with a serious expression.

"I'm sure that he does," Marie said.

When she was young, their family workroom had been sort of a formal study, containing a long desk where the older children gathered to complete their schoolwork. Every chance she got, Marie would sneak over to a glass case in the room that held Professor Skłodowski's scientific equipment like fish in an aquarium. Since the government crackdown, the objects of her fascination had been woefully underused at the school where he taught. Her father told her that the equipment was called "physical apparatus," a name she never forgot. A treasure chest of science, the case contained graceful instruments, glass tubes, small scales, specimens of minerals, and a gold-leaf electroscope.

"Electroscopes," she explained to Irène, although she knew the five-year-old wouldn't understand most of what she said, "are simple devices that allow an electrical charge to travel from a single point into two very thin metal strips, causing them to repel each other like magnets and move apart."

Marie held her hands in front of her a few inches apart with her palms facing each other.

"Now touch my head with your hand," she told Irène.

Grinning, Irène stood up, held out one hand, and gently set it on Marie's hair, just in front of her bun. Marie moved her hands apart a little bit.

"Like this," Marie said. "Now take your hand away."

Irène complied and Marie returned her hands to their original position.

"The more electrical charge an object carries, the further it will push the metal strips away from one another," she explained. "This allows scientists to make measurements. Your Da and I use a similar instrument in our laboratory to measure radioactivity."

"I hope that someday I can see Grandpa's electroscope," Irène said.

"If you work hard on your studies," Marie said, "perhaps one day you will have an electroscope of your own."

"Do you miss Grandma?" Irène asked.

"Very much," Marie said softly. "And I miss your Aunt Zosia."

"It's OK, Mommy." Irène put a hand to Marie's cheek and settled by her feet again. "Now you have Da and me. We'll take care of you."

Marie blinked away tears. The pain of losing her sister and mother within a two-year span had dulled but never disappeared, and she had struggled with bouts of depression ever since. She still blamed the Russians for her sister's death. After doing away with science classes in the school that her father ran, the town's Russian overseer reduced his salary, took away his title, and kicked Marie's family out of the home associated with Professor Skłodowski's previous job. They'd moved several times and finally settled in a corner apartment where they took on boarders, whom her mother fed and her father instructed in academics. Up to ten students lived with their family at a time, and Marie and her siblings had to get up before dawn every day so that the boys could have breakfast in the dining room, which served as their bedroom at night.

Besides noise and chaos, the boarders brought another unwelcome guest into the house. Russians nicknamed the parasites "clothes lice," because they hid out in unwashed clothing and bedding. The bloodsucking body lice, capable of carrying fever-causing typhus bacteria, thrived in conditions like the Curie household where people lived crammed into tight quarters.

When a body louse bit a person infected with typhus, it picked up the infectious bacteria and carried them from person to person, shedding more bacteria in its feces. Victims scratched itchy bites, and their fingernails could break the skin, offering an entry point for the microbes. If another louse bit the infected person, the cycle continued. A week or two after scratching typhus bacteria into a louse bite, most victims came down with fever, headache, and a rash. Some of them died.

In the first of several tragedies that Marie would endure in her lifetime, her sisters Bronya and Zosia were both infected with typhus that had been brought into the house with the boarders. Bronya recovered, but after tossing with fever for weeks, beautiful Zosia succumbed to the disease in January of 1876, when she was only fourteen years old. Dressed in a black coat, little Marie had followed her sister's coffin down the street, while Bronya and her tuberculosis-weakened mother watched from the window above.

A devout Catholic, Marie's mother had never blamed God for her misfortunes, but Zosia's death had been the final blow to her health. Despite long sojourns in fresh mountain air to help her recover, she died of tuberculosis less than two years after losing her daughter. Bidding her husband and remaining children farewell from her deathbed, she'd sketched a cross in the air and murmured, "I love you," before closing her eyes for the last time. Marie remembered wishing she could go with her mother. Back then, she still believed in heaven.

"How old were you when your Me died?" Irène asked.

"Only nine," Marie said. "But I still remember her big heart."

Marie fell into a deep depression following her mother's death. Fortunately, her father didn't give up, but rose to the new challenges. Taking over his children's education, he slowly but surely brought light back into their lives. Marie emerged from the darkness to take refuge in literature, languages, mathematics, and science. Although her father no longer had a laboratory where they could experiment, he patiently answered all her questions and encouraged her curiosity. There were quiet evenings at home reciting Polish prose and trips to visit relatives in the countryside.

"After my mother died," Marie told Irène, "my Da helped me to feel better. Sometimes he took us on trips to the mountains and the sea. I still recall how my heart leapt at my first view of jagged mountain peaks, but the ocean impressed me even more."

"You're not going to die, are you?" Irène whispered.

"What? No. Not anytime soon," Marie reassured her, smoothing her hair.

"But your fingers are cracking!" A fat tear rolled down Irène's cheek. "Are you sick?"

Marie turned her palm up and studied the tips of her fingers, which were unusually hardened and cracked from her work. She was used to the unsightly wounds and didn't think about them much. Pierre suffered from the same symptoms. They'd learned early on that radioactive materials, and especially the very active ones that gave high readings on their equipment, could burn the skin and the tissue beneath. Holding tubes and capsules of highly radioactive material without protection caused wounds to form, which made the skin peel off her fingers and took weeks to heal, leaving phantom pain. It was excruciating when chemicals worked their way into the raw fissures, but Marie was certain they were nothing to worry about, although she could see why the cracks might look alarming. That Irène might worry was something she'd never even considered.

Pierre and their friend Henri Becquerel, who had first discovered radio-activity, liked to joke about the time Henri had carried in his coat pocket a box containing a glass tube of radium salts that the Curies had given him. After about six hours he'd removed it from his pocket, having forgotten it was there. The next day he'd discovered a mysterious burn on the skin of his torso beneath where the pocket had been, in the exact shape of the test tube. He'd been both delighted and bothered by the experience, saying that he loved radium but bore it a grudge. Marie loved the story, because Becquerel's burns were testimony to the power and potential of their discovery.

"Ah! No tears." Marie stood, pulling Irène up with her and swinging her around in a circle, smiling. "Those are beautiful cracks in my fingers. Your Da and I are working very hard in the laboratory to make pure radium and find a use for it. Radium can burn the skin a little, but we are perfectly fine. Don't you worry about a little thing like that!"

Irène looked up at her and smiled, the tears forgotten.

"Dance with me!"

They circled around the room as Marie hummed a Polish folk song, wishing that her father lived closer and that her mother could see Irène. Breathless, she wiped her eyes and gave Irène an enormous hug. "I love you, but I must go to the laboratory now. Go find your grandfather. You can run along to the garden and pull some weeds."

Marie called up to her father-in-law that she was heading to the lab. She didn't know what she'd do without him. There was always so much work to do.

Scene III

Little Star of the West

1901

Loïe was in a yellow mood as she climbed out of the carriage in front of her house on rue Cortambert. She loved her neighborhood. Besides being fashionable, the Passy district of Paris, in the 16th arrondissement, gave her a certain freedom that she didn't have in the city proper.

A village since the thirteenth century, the area had gone from poverty to affluence in a relatively short period of time. Bridging city and country, Passy stood adjacent to the Bois de Boulogne, a forest crisscrossed with formal avenues and paths. While many Passy residents sought the shade and society of the woods during the week, they avoided the area like the plague on weekends, when the general population of Paris poured into the Bois to promenade and picnic.

The French playwright and novelist Georges Lecomte wrote: "I prefer my corner of Passy to any other district. With its villas, its gardens and its quiet population, it gives me the impression of being a picturesque Parisian village on the threshold of tumultuous Paris, because like the Bois de Boulogne, which is close to my house, it is like a private park, where, in addition to majestic trees and the calm waters of its lakes, I can enjoy meditating as I walk."

Liaisons were sparked daily on the Bois's tree-lined boulevards, where society men and women paraded up and down on foot, on horseback and in carriages, draped in the latest fashions. For wealthy men, courtesans were as abundant as birds and butterflies, and depending on what one was looking for, eye contact, feathered fans, or even particular breeds of dogs signaled availability.

A number of well-to-do Parisians had established homes in Passy, allowing them to be within easy distance of their city offices while their wives and children enjoyed the fresh air of the countryside. Long before Loïe moved there, the impressionist painter Berthe Morisot had been documenting the invisible world of Passy domestic life on canvas. She and her friends established the Passy district as a sort of safe space, where women could move freely and even step into the woods when they wanted to escape the walls that confined them. Loïe was grateful for a neighborhood that offered her a respite from the noise and chaos of the city. Despite the nighttime incident with two masked robbers when they'd first moved to the area, she felt perfectly comfortable leaving her mother there alone during the day while she was at the theater.

Humming to herself, she mounted the steps to the front door and looked up from rummaging for the keys in her bag to find herself staring into the stormy eyes of Mademoiselle Gabrielle Bloch.

"Now what did I do wrong?" she asked.

Pink blotches appeared on Gab's cheeks, and Loïe instantly regretted her impudence.

"Did you forget that you're hosting a dinner for the Flammarions tonight?" Gab demanded. "There are forty people on their way here right now. Forty. Some have already arrived, and your mother has gone up to bed."

Loïe gasped. "Oh, Gab, I'm so sorry! I ran into some students from the Beaux-Arts."

"I am going upstairs," Gab announced, marching back up the front steps. On the top step, she turned to glare at Loïe like an angry schoolteacher. "The chef is waiting for you in the kitchen. And he is not happy either."

Loïe knew that Gab would forgive her. At least she hoped so. The two of them had been together long enough that she was fairly certain that her dear companion had become accustomed to her lapses of attention when it came to anything other than work.

Gab was the extreme opposite of Loïe, who was an irrepressible extrovert, and she hated forced social situations. Try as she might, Loïe couldn't comprehend how a strong, intelligent woman like Gab turned to stone and fled under the gaze of a visitor. But Gab had no patience whatsoever for small talk, and few people besides Loïe lived up to her impossible expectations.

As a child, the serious girl's mother had ascribed her daughter's antisocial behavior to shyness, but Gab had confided to Loïe that she was neither shy nor timid. She simply found most people to be horribly annoying and didn't want to be forced to see them. Although Loïe doubted very much that Gab had been chatting with tonight's guests, she knew that the dear girl probably felt obligated to face them and make excuses for the dancer's tardiness at her own dinner party.

There would be time to apologize to Gab later, but more guests would be arriving at any moment, and Loïe had a party to arrange. She rushed to the kitchen to find the chef shaking his head. He explained that the tables and dishes had arrived around six. Unable to reach Loïe, he'd tried to pay the men from his own pocket, but didn't have enough money, so at seven o'clock they'd left, taking everything with them. In a panic, he'd rushed to the neighbors' houses and they'd been kind enough to bring over an assortment of tables, chairs, dishes, and glassware to furnish the party. Now, everything was piled up in the parlor and she would have to figure out how to organize it.

A knock at the door gave Loïe the opportunity to escape his disapproving gaze, so she thanked the cook as she retreated, promising to have everything set up by nine. She instructed her housekeeper to invite guests in as they arrived and raced up the stairs to change into her favorite yellow dress, which had a skirt that practically floated on air. Gab was nowhere to be found, so Loïe went into her mother's room to check on her.

Delilah sat in bed like a granny from a fairy tale, spectacles and all, reading a book. Her skin was crinkled like an apple that's been ignored for too long and has gone soft. She hadn't been feeling well for some time and suffered one battle with bronchitis after another. Loïe put a hand on the frail woman's cheek and leaned over to kiss her forehead, which felt slightly warmer than it should.

"I'm sorry you'll miss the party," she said.

"I don't mind," her mother said. "I'll have a delightful time listening to all the fun from up here, and I won't even have to get dressed up."

"I'm sure that Gab will check on you," Loïe said.

"She already has," her mother replied. "I heard that you were late to your own party again."

"Ah, yes. I lost track of time. I'll come kiss you goodnight later." Loïe stood and fled before her mother could give her a second scolding.

Arriving at the bottom of the stairs, she discovered that some of her guests had taken it upon themselves to organize the furniture in the dining room into an arrangement that would seat everyone. Some tables were short and others tall, with a mismatched assortment of chairs. It would definitely be a unique affair for her famous friends.

She loved few things more than spending time with fascinating people, and as it turned out, many celebrities were quite interesting. When she and her mother had first signed the lease and moved into the house on rue Cortambert, she'd thrown a housewarming party for a hundred people, including critics, artists, writers, and scientists. Among the most famous were her dear Auguste Rodin, the novelist Anatole France, and the soprano Emma Calvé. After dinner that evening, Loïe had enchanted everyone by changing into a gauzy dress and dancing in the garden, illuminated only by moonlight and the soft glow of Japanese lanterns.

Even dear Gab had braved the crowd to watch her dance on that magical night. It had been nine years since Gab, whose mother had always called her Gabrielle, had seen Loïe dance at one of her first matinee performances in Paris, and Loïe knew the story well. M. Marchand, the Folies Bergère manager, had spotted Gab's famously beautiful mother from across the theater and came running to tell the two of them more about the American called La Loïe.

He'd assured them that Mlle. Fuller was a perfectly proper young lady who lived just upstairs with her mother. In fact, he told them, he'd cut a door into the wall of an apartment attached to the Folies, so that Loïe could go home without facing her crowd of admirers on the street. After each evening's show, two men would carry Loïe, exhausted from her forty-five-minute performance, up the stairs and lay her on her bed, where she would ice her aching arms and shoulders until she fell asleep. Marchand called Loïe a strange sort of girl who seemed to think of nothing but her work, but said that she was of the highest moral character.

Gab, fourteen at the time, had giggled when he told them that Loïe didn't know a word of French but smiled all the time and said "bong-jour." Gab's mother bought two tickets to the matinee. Not only had La Loïe managed to make it fashionable for women to attend her shows at the Folies, the near absence of the female form in her performances made it socially acceptable to bring children to the burlesque club on weekend afternoons as well.

What Gab had seen that afternoon in 1892 changed her view of art and dance, and eventually it would change her life. Transfixed by the shape-shifting dancer, she'd gasped each time new colors exploded onto the billowing silk of Loïe's gown. She'd added her voice to the audience roar demanding repeated curtain calls, and clapped until her palms were bruised. Arriving home, she'd rushed to retrieve her journal and scribbled page after page about the "dream pantomime" of the dances, concluding with adoring words: "She is the butterfly, she is the fire, she is light, heaven, the stars."

In those early days at the Folies Bergère, Loïe had autographed a photograph for Gab, who at the time was just another person in a long line of admirers, but the starstruck teenager eventually got a formal introduction to La Loïe. An older cousin happened to be married to the wife of the dancer's dear friend the art critic Roger Marx, whom Loïe had met when she first moved to Paris. One of the dancer's most ardent admirers, Marx wrote beautiful reviews of her performances, and his wife and boys often attended Loïe's matinees. In 1893, he'd written: "Out of the night, the apparition escapes; she takes form, becomes alive. Under the caress of electric beams, she breaks away from the background of mourning, abandons the dazzling whiteness of a diamond to don all the colors in a chest of precious stones."

Just before introducing Loïe to Mlle. Bloch, Roger whispered to the dancer that the young woman's father, a wealthy banker, was mostly absent from her life. In his absence, it seemed that Gab's mother had insisted that her daughter have an exceptional education. At first, Loïe was slightly intimidated by the serious girl's intelligence. Her mother bragged that her daughter had been reading the philosopher Schopenhauer when she was nine years old and was now studying ancient Indian literature. However, Gabrielle was quiet and unassuming, and because of her relationship to Roger and obvious passion for Loïe's work, by conversation's end the dancer had invited the young woman to come work as her assistant.

From that day forward, Gabrielle was by Loïe's side at every opportunity. She was about the same height as Loïe and made a perfect body double for the dancer. The young woman would patiently stand onstage, posing for hours on end wrapped in soft crumpled paper or yards of silk, modeling costumes and veils, while Loïe flooded her with a rainbow of light and tested her special effects and color combinations. Soon Gabrielle became "Gab," and the two of them were great friends.

"Ah, I have a look in ze glass," Gab would say, running to the mirror each time she put on a new costume, making Loïe laugh.

Gab's mother died after a trip to India when she was only thirty-seven, which sent Gab into a deep depression. Her friendship with Loïe suffered when her absentee father hired a strict governess, and she was no longer able to help the dancer design her lighting schemes. At one point, Loïe heard that the heartbroken girl had scraped together enough money to publish her dead mother's manuscript *Au Loin*, which the critic Jean Lorrain called the most beautiful book on India that he'd ever read. Sadly, Loïe had been far too busy with her engagements to keep tabs on her young assistant, and they fell out of touch for several years while she cultivated new friendships with artists and scientists. But Gab had come back into her life, and now Loïe couldn't imagine spending a single day without her.

However, it looked as if she would have to do without her tonight. The dinner party, which she'd planned and then almost forgotten to attend, was in full swing. Loïe stepped into the dining room, which was bustling with activity, to greet her guests and help them set up for the party. She found it quite amusing that some of the most well-known personalities in Paris were doing work normally reserved for their servants. There were no tablecloths or knives to be found and only a few glasses had been collected, but everyone seemed to be enjoying themselves all the same.

When all was set, Loïe sat down to savor the wonderful food her chef had made and watched as her friends sipped wine from coffee cups and bottles. Rodin was there, which made her very happy, along with the Norwegian painter Fritz Thaulow and many other actors, writers, artists, and critics. She knew most of the people seated around the room fairly well, but she was always courting new acquaintances who were either very fascinating or very rich, so she'd added a few new names to the guest list as well.

After dinner, she stood on a chair and clanged her fork against a glass dish to get everyone's attention and began to speak in French as well as she could.

"I've gathered you all tonight to celebrate my friends Sylvie and Camille," she said. "What few people understand about Monsieur Flammarion is that he is not content with being an eminent astronomer. Besides having the finest head of hair in Paris and dressing as unconventionally as I do, he is fascinated by psychic forces and writes science fiction novels. Madame Flammarion has proved herself to be a worthy partner for this great man, although she is tormented by his great head of hair and has to trim it so often that she's stuffed a divan cushion with his locks."

Her friends laughed.

"And he is the only man I've met who is as rabid about the subject of color as I am."

In fact, at the time they met, M. Flammarion had been studying whether color influenced the behavior of living organisms, and they'd bonded immediately over their mutual fascination. Flammarion had built conservatories of different colored glass to study the effect on plants contained inside. Depending on the glass color, some plants had grown tall but fragile, while others were small and thick, or had no leaves. Even the plants surrounded by clear glass were not quite normal, which suggested that glass itself affected growth. He'd done a similar study on humans by putting them in a room with windows of colored glass and concluded that yellow light excited people, while red light made them sleepy.

He and Loïe had talked at length about her idea of using luminescent salts to illuminate cloth, and they discussed the visual similarities of certain objects seen through a microscope and a telescope. The influence of their conversations had been evident during the 1900 Paris Exhibition, where Loïe's projected images of the moon in her dance "The Firmament" brought to mind globes of algae as revealed by microscopy and Flammarion presented "phosphorescent dancers" in the Palace of Optics, their dresses lit by small dots of Edison's salts. At the time, Loïe was still not satisfied enough with the results of her work with glowing chemicals to use the shimmering salts in her own dances. They made her expanses of silk far too stiff and she wanted more than a dull shine in the darkness. She wanted color.

They'd continued to discuss their findings at every opportunity, and Loïe had since become a member of the French Astronomical Society, which Flammarion had founded in 1887. Loïe thought the society's castle at Juvisy-sur-Orge was one of the loveliest natural spots in France, and she adored peering through its powerful telescope at celestial bodies.

Loïe beamed. "The Flammarions have a great love story, as they began their life together by ascending to the heavens in a hot air balloon! Madame Flammarion, would you do the honor?"

Sylvie nodded and rose from her chair. She wore her hair fashionably piled on her head, showing off a beautiful profile.

"I would live in a hot air balloon, if I could," she began quite seriously, "if not for the practical impossibility," and the story unfolded.

Sylvie told the guests that before their wedding day, she'd never set foot in a balloon but had always wanted to. When the ropes were released, they'd made a dizzying climb into the atmosphere, along with Camille's brother and the aeronaut M. Jules Godard. As the sun set, they rose to 1,900 meters (6,000 feet) and peered down at a mountain of clouds until air currents pulled them into the monstrous masses of vaporized water and tossed them about before they emerged unscathed into the moonlight.

"We felt," she exclaimed, "we saw in action, the powerful, incessant, prodigious forces of the atmosphere while the Earth slept below."

Everyone was listening raptly, Loïe happily observed.

Sylvie described how they watched the moon shadow of the balloon race across the landscape below until they spotted a thunderstorm in the distance and rose back up to 3,000 meters (10,000 feet) to avoid it. With Sirius glittering above them, they wrapped themselves in furs and continued to rise to 4,000 meters (13,000 feet), where it became more difficult to breathe. Wine inside the picnic basket froze in its bottles—a shame, as Sylvie could have used a glass of it. Camille used his barometers, telescopes, and thermometers to take measurements. Finally, they'd descended, after spending thirteen hours floating through the atmosphere.

"I would be glad to make a thousand aerial voyages," Sylvie proclaimed, "but thus far I have only been up two more times."

Everyone clapped at her delightful retelling and she sat down, her cheeks flushed from the attention.

Loïe rose. "And now I have a story about Camille. You may have heard it before, but please indulge me. It's one of my favorite stories, which also features the great Alexandre Dumas fils."

There was no need to explain to her guests who Dumas fils was. The son of the *Three Musketeers* author, the younger Dumas had written *La Dame aux Camélias*, a tragic story involving tuberculosis that had been adapted into the opera *La Traviata*. Loïe had been introduced to the famous writer by a Haitian prince. She'd since kept a photograph of Dumas in her dressing room as a memento of the treasured friendship.

"One night after dancing at the Athénée, Monsieur and Madame Flammarion and Monsieur Dumas appeared in my dressing room following the performance. They'd been admitted," Loïe told her friends, "along with the usual crowd of admirers, and I wondered why two great men like Camille and Alexandre were not speaking to each other. When Sylvie told me that they'd never actually met, I pulled them together and asked how in the world it was possible that they were not acquainted."

She looked out at the roomful of faces, pausing for effect. Her career as an actress still came in handy at times.

Loïe continued dramatically. "'It is not so remarkable,' joked M. Dumas, 'for, you see, Flammarion dwells in space, and I am just a cumberer of the Earth.'"

Everyone laughed, including her friends who had already heard the story. They were very patient with her, and she loved them all the more for it.

"And then what did Flammarion say?" Rodin called out from halfway down the room.

Loïe grinned from ear to ear. "Flammarion replied, 'Yes, but a little star come out of the west has brought us together.'"

Everyone cheered and she raised her glass. "To Camille and Sylvie!"

Glasses clinked and Loïe beamed. Bringing great minds together was one of the greatest pleasures of her life. Surrounding herself with genius fed her creativity like nothing else could. To sit at a table with Rodin and Flammarion was to be immersed in passion and inspiration. Sylvie's story had left the image of floating clouds with lightning flashing below imprinted in her mind. What a dance that would be!

When the last guest had departed, Loïe looked out over the wrecked dining room. She felt sorry for the cook, the housekeeper, and probably Gab, who would spend the next morning sorting through furniture and dishes, so they could be returned to the neighbors. Loïe would try to help, but she knew herself well enough to admit that she probably wouldn't last long before finding an excuse to leave most of the cleanup behind. People like her were much better at inventing new messes than tidying up old ones.

She climbed the stairs on tiptoe, humming under her breath. The evening had been a lovely success despite her forgetfulness, and she was grateful that it had all come together so well. Loïe peeked in at her mother, who was sleeping soundly. Her breathing sounded raspy as usual, but it was deep and even. Continuing down the hallway, she opened the door of her own bedroom to find her dearest Gab sitting on the bed, reading.

Gab always dressed in black and preferred to wear suits tailored with a masculine sensibility. The color complemented her raven hair, which she parted over her forehead and gathered in a tight bun at the base of her neck. A poet friend of Loïe's had once commented that Gab's voice, skin, hair, and eyes all seemed to be made of velvet, and that her name ought to be Velours, which made Loïe laugh because it was absolutely true. Even the way Gabrielle moved was slow and sensuous, as though she were moving through a thicker atmosphere than the earthly beings around her.

It wasn't until Loïe had returned to France from her second American tour that they'd found their way back to each other again. By that time, Gab was eighteen and living on her own in a small, dark apartment in Paris. Loïe had been thrilled to meet up with her old friend. She'd invited Gab to accompany her and her mother to Nice, where they were staying while Loïe performed at villages up and down the coast of the French Riviera.

Those months by the sea in the spring of 1897 held treasured memories of their blossoming romance. One day, Loïe had convinced a reluctant Gab that they should go horseback riding in a pine forest along the seashore. Loïe dressed in white, while Gab abandoned her usual head-to-toe black for a cheerful white blouse and boating hat. A city girl through and through, poor Gab had been absolutely terrified when the men at the stable plopped her on the back of a horse, and gripped the reins so tightly that her fingers turned white.

Loïe, who was entirely in her element, found it all very funny. Having grown up around horses, she'd easily climbed up onto the horse's rump to sit behind Gab, and she clowned when a photographer took a photo of the two of them. Her mother had been there too that day, sitting in a chair in the shade of the pines, laughing at their shenanigans.

Gab had managed to smile for the picture, although she didn't loosen her grip on the reins until Loïe took them from her. Later that day, as the two strolled along the shore in golden summer light, shy, serious Gab finally revealed her true feelings to Loïe. They'd taken shape, she confessed, the very first time she'd seen Loïe dance.

"I never see you exactly as you are," Gab had said, "but as you seemed to me on that day."

Loïe had been giddy with happiness at the revelation, but she was sure that, despite her romantic proclamation, Gab could see her perfectly well as she was in that very moment. The beautiful young woman loved her, despite the fact that offstage, she was always something of a mess.

Because Gab's English was much better than Loïe's French, they usually spoke to each other in Loïe's native tongue. Gab had beautiful handwriting, so she often translated for Loïe, and she took care of all the French business correspondence. Keeping track of Loïe's contracts, commitments, patents, and correspondence was enough to drive anyone mad. Somehow, though, her "little friend," as Loïe called Gab, managed to wrangle the loose ends of her hectic life into order, day after day. Although they didn't live together, they were never far apart. Loïe told anyone who asked that they were as close as two sisters.

"Have you forgiven me yet?" Loïe asked.

Gab looked at her but didn't answer. Instead, she stood up and went to the dresser to retrieve an envelope.

"You got a letter," she said, holding it out. "I would have given it to you earlier, but you seemed very busy."

"What? Let me see!" Loïe grabbed it from her hand and turned it over. On the back of the envelope were the neat initials M.C.

"Rascal! You should have told me," she scolded Gab, tearing it open.

"You never asked," Gab replied smoothly.

Loïe read the letter inside, reread it, and handed it to Gab, who scanned the neat writing.

"How kind of her to write in English," was all she said, unflappable as always.

"You are impossible!" Loïe laughed. She took the letter from Gab and threw it on the bed. "I've been invited to meet the Curies! You know how much I admire them!"

She caught Gab's hands and swung her around, humming "Clair de Lune" until Gab's cheeks flushed and she finally smiled.

"Quiet!" Gab reprimanded her breathlessly. "You'll wake your mother."

"Fine," Loïe said. Still holding Gab's hands, she leaned in close enough to feel Gab's breath on her cheek. "Now, will you please help me get out of this dress? It's absolutely strangling me."

Scene IV

The House of Cadavers

1901

Marie had barely slept, and she'd made her way to the lab even earlier than usual that morning. She'd made the mistake of reading an article on radium from an American newspaper. Amusement had turned to incredulity as she translated.

"Madame Curie, the French woman physicist, is the only experimenter so far to separate radium absolutely from its compounds. She discovered the process two years ago."

It was the next sentence that haunted her.

"The first scientist to discover the substance without getting it in free quantities was Prof. Henri Becquerel of Paris in 1896."

"Don't worry," Pierre had said. "Reporters make mistakes all the time, and everyone in France knows it was you who discovered it."

Marie *was* worried, though. And re-energized.

Cool autumn sunlight poured down through the paned roof of the shed, reflecting off glassware and making things feel somewhat less dismal. Marie plopped down on the cane seat of the old chair beside the stove. She opened her bag and pulled out a piece of sausage, nibbling on the cold meat. Sipping tea between bites, she stared at the pine table across the room where her precious white evaporation dishes sat waiting. Ringed with concentric circles of dried crystals, they were the result of months of backbreaking toil.

When her hands started shaking, Marie had forced herself to take a deep breath. Carefully setting the dishes down, she stopped for lunch. She was getting so close. It would be stupid to have an accident.

It felt like she'd done ten years' worth of hard labor in the twenty months that had passed since the first heavy wagon had pulled up in front of the shed on rue Lhomond, but the memory was still fresh in her mind. At the sound of hooves clattering up the cobblestones, they'd raced out to greet the driver without bothering to change out of their laboratory gowns. Pierre had stood calmly as the heavy sacks were unloaded, but Marie had been unable to contain her excitement. She'd run to the first burlap bag that the man hoisted into the shed's courtyard and cut the strings.

Austria's trash was Marie's treasure. The dull brown mining waste spilling from the sack was the most beautiful dust she'd ever seen, and they'd paid almost nothing for it. She sifted the grains, letting them fall through her fingers, trapping pine needles that had been scooped up along with the ore. The soft dirt had felt so wonderful on that first day. She had no idea that soon dust would permeate every fiber of her clothing, coat every hair on her head, and clog the fine pores on her face.

Marie almost laughed out loud. None of her chemistry classes at the Sorbonne had taught her how to remove pine needles from a solution. Everything about the project was unconventional and unexplored, which made it almost more wonderful. If things went as planned, she would be the first person in the world to extract the element she'd discovered from this dusty mess, working not in a neat, well-furnished laboratory but in a hangar-like shed.

It had been torture to wait while they unloaded the rest of the bags. Marie was absolutely desperate to test the activity of the dust and hoped that it would be even more radioactive than the pitchblende rocks she'd been testing in the lab thus far. Radium and polonium were just specks of dust in these mountains of mining waste, but they carried with them an unmistakable signature: mysterious rays that electrified air and spun the mirror in her apparatus slightly or dramatically, depending on how active they were. Marie still couldn't believe how lucky they'd been to get the cast-off dirt.

After her research revealed that minuscule amounts of highly radioactive radium and polonium could be found hiding in pitchblende, Marie had despaired at the expense of the rocks. Despite people's excitement about their discoveries, the Curies had no influence in the academic world. Many of their colleagues had asked for and been given laboratory space at the Sorbonne, but when Marie and Pierre made a similar request, they were unceremoniously turned down. They didn't even bother to ask for research money from the government or the University of Paris, who would have laughed at them.

Pitchblende was mined in Bohemia. At the time, uranium salts were extracted and used to tint colorful glass. It would be impossible for two poor scientists to acquire even a fraction of what they'd need to purify a measurable amount of the elements. Luckily, one of their colleagues, an Austrian geologist named Eduard Suess, knew the director of the mine at St. Joachimsthal. He learned that by some stroke of luck, the mine's processed waste hadn't been thrown away but had been heaped up on the floor of a pine forest in Austria, near the uranium plant.

Marie and Pierre received permission to have the mining waste collected. They'd scraped together their entire savings to come up with enough money to buy that first precious load of dust. Pierre then asked Baron Edmond de Rothschild to fund the transport of the pitchblende residue to Paris. The banking family baron, who was a great philanthropist, agreed, and the wagons of brown dust made their way to France.

Besides their lack of funding, the shed that had been provided as a research lab, something of a consolation from the Sorbonne, was barely fit for the cadavers that had once inhabited it. After it had been abandoned by the medical students who performed dissections there, the School of Physics and Chemistry, or EPCI, had acquired the space and left it to fall into disrepair. When Marie and Pierre requested space for their work on radioactivity, the director of the School of Physics felt sorry for them and gave them the use of the old shed. As she set up her equipment in those first days, Marie tried not to think about all the cold, dead bodies that had lain on the worn pine over the years.

Just across the courtyard from their original laboratory, where Pierre still had an office and workroom, the miserable, leaky building was Marie's heaven and hell. Inadequate in so many ways, the old wooden room with its walls of windows and glass roof had become her second home. She and Pierre had arranged the tables as well as they could to keep their samples and equipment safe from the water that dripped through the glass roof every time it rained. When it was hot outside and the sun beat through the panes, they baked.

In winter, the small stove standing at one end of the room wasn't much better than the one she'd had in her tiny apartment in the Latin Quarter, and this one had a cavernous space to heat. Standing next to it warmed her slightly for a few moments, but it was impossible to work beside a stove all day, so most of the time she froze.

When it wasn't raining, she stirred masses of mining waste in pots outdoors in the courtyard. Otherwise, she had to move her chemicals into the shed. Even outside, the work produced horrible vapors that filled the courtyard and drifted into the indoor workspace. They'd open the windows in the shed year-round to keep the air moving and lessen the fumes, which blew dust around. By the end of each day, when she went home to eat dinner and put Irène to bed, she was almost broken with exhaustion.

Despite the hardships of her labors, it was in this miserable old space that she'd spent some of the happiest days of her life. It turned out that the mining waste was wonderfully radioactive, even more active than the pitchblende Marie had first tested. Ecstatic, she went to work immediately, testing her chemical methods on the precious bags of dust.

After some experimentation, she discovered that following the tedious large-scale washes and extractions, she could use a precipitation reaction to begin to separate the radium from the other waste. Radium clung to the element barium, so a simple chemical reaction would cause the barium and radium to form a solid precipitate, which sank to the bottom of the chemical solution.

Marie found that radioactive radium could be separated from barium far more easily than her other radioactive element, polonium, could be separated from its coprecipitate. Determined to collect a pure sample as soon as possible and lay claim to her discovery, Marie had chosen to focus on extracting pure radium from the mining waste.

Since then, she and Pierre had worked incessantly, absorbed by their common mission. Faced with the seemingly insurmountable task, Pierre had abandoned his other research to help Marie with her work. Day after day, they'd wake, Marie would dress Irène and feed her, and they'd leave for the shed around nine. They saw almost no one but each other with the exception of Pierre's former student André Debierne, whom Pierre had hired to help Marie. It was a dreamlike existence, with both working so hard that they fell into a dead sleep every night before waking up to do it all again.

She was grateful their health was not bad, but it could be better. Pierre suffered from rheumatism, which he blamed on the damp environment of the shed. He insisted that his leg pains weren't serious, but Marie recognized the mask of pain that covered his face continually. Thankfully, Irène was growing well. Marie kept a record of every tooth that popped in, what Irène ate and how she grew, as though her daughter's health could be tracked and controlled like an experiment, though she knew from experience that she had no control at all.

As Marie charted Irène's growth and noted that the little girl's cheeks were getting plump, her own face had grown gaunt. People started to comment on the fact that Marie had gotten noticeably thinner since embarking on her mission to extract radium. Although she suspected that the decline in her weight was due to breathing toxic fumes and constant exhaustion, her doctor was concerned that she might have contracted the disease she dreaded most: tuberculosis. Her dresses, which she'd filled out beautifully when she and Pierre were first married, were beginning to hang loosely on her frame again, much as they had during her student years at the Sorbonne.

She always gained some weight back in summer, as they were forced to stop working when the university closed. Leaving Paris behind, they'd spend long days bicycling and picnicking their way through the French countryside. Pierre loved hiking, swimming, and exploring nature as much as she did. While Marie lay in the grass daydreaming, he would explore nearby ponds and streams. Since childhood, he'd been drawn to the observation of living things, but one day when he casually dropped a live frog into Marie's hand, he'd learned that she didn't care for amphibians quite as much as he did.

For all of Pierre's genius, he lacked Marie's ambition and tenacity and had been ready to give up on radium on more than one occasion. When he'd suggested to Marie that she abandon her quest, she'd been furious. Unperturbed, he'd calmly explained his worry that they would never accomplish the seemingly impossible task. Although he too dreamed of pure radium, he envisioned a less torturous path to scientific glory. They could already achieve great things using the impure radioactive salts. Marie ignored him and soldiered on.

Accidents in the lab were regular occurrences, but even small setbacks felt like disasters. When glassware was dropped and samples were lost, Pierre was convinced that the stress of it might kill Marie, so she hadn't told him about the heart palpitations she'd been experiencing. He'd tried to comfort her on one horrifying day when she'd spilled distillates that she'd spent three months purifying onto the shed's porous floor, but she couldn't be consoled and could barely drag herself out of bed the next morning.

Most days were better, though, and Marie continued to line the laboratory with flasks, tubes, and vials of ever-purer radium distillates. Fellow scientists dropped by on occasion to visit and talk physics and chemistry and scribble equations on the blackboard. Every day, she and Pierre drank tea together by the tiny stove, and sometimes they shared their lunch break in the shed, if the timing of their experiments permitted.

Marie started to imagine that Pierre knew her thoughts before she even spoke them. He stroked her hair when he passed her in the laboratory. They jotted results one after the other into a single lab notebook, as united in their work as they were in their marriage. She'd never imagined that it would be possible to find someone who would so entirely share her passion for discovery. It was here, in this dingy shed, that she'd gone from feeling that she'd chosen the perfect companion to falling head-over-heels in love with her daydreaming physicist.

To reach their common goal of obtaining and characterizing pure radium more quickly, within the first year of their work they'd decided to divide their focus. While Marie labored in the courtyard and shed, stirring vats of acid and performing precipitations, Pierre worked indoors to study the properties of their radioactive subjects.

Getting rid of the contaminants in the pitchblende waste in order to obtain pure radium required multiple, mostly miserable steps. Like calcium, Marie's radium compounds could be combined with acid or washing soda (sodium carbonate) to produce radium-laced salts and carbonates. She would dump sackfuls of precious mining residue into a vat of boiling sulfuric acid and stir the concoction with an iron bar. It made her feel like one of Macbeth's witches. More purification steps would follow, and the products would be moved into progressively smaller containers to undergo further chemical treatments.

Day after day, Marie would return to the vat in the courtyard to start working on a new batch of mining waste. Before long, the tables and shelves of the shed were full of glassware that contained liquid and solid radium salts at different steps of purification.

The most delicate work came at the end of the process. Marie's new system for extracting radium from pitchblende culminated in a method called fractional crystallization. She'd adapted the technique at the suggestion of the EPCI's laboratory director, Gustave Bémont, a master chemist who was interested in her work. By boiling and cooling solutions containing radium, she took advantage of the fact that different elements form crystals at different temperatures. This final crystallization step allowed her to separate the purified radium from the last of the contaminants.

Because they'd created a new branch of science, researchers around the world were increasingly interested in obtaining samples of radioactive substances for their own work. After about six months of watching Marie work obsessively, Pierre persuaded the Central Society for Chemical Products to undertake some of the initial processing of the mining waste for them. They treated the discarded mining ore with acid, salts, and fifty tons of rinse water per ton of waste, and then the factory sent Marie the concentrated bromide they'd recovered from the residue. The society paid the salary of her laboratory assistant, Debierne, to supervise the factory processing, and for their investment in the project, the factory received some of the radioactive distillates to sell.

Although the pretreatment saved Marie an enormous amount of time and backbreaking labor, she was still processing an immense volume of radioactive material. She'd start working with about twenty kilograms at a time, about the same weight as a small bale of hay. The radium-laced bromide that was now delivered to her shed was twenty times more radioactive than an equal amount of uranium, but each kilogram still contained only the tiniest amount of the precious element she desired.

She'd take the factory-purified bromide and continue with the purification process, able to focus on the steps that required her unique expertise and every ounce of her concentration. Fractional crystallization was delicate work, and her fingers were cracked and numb from the chemicals. Despite the fact that she'd hung a heavy curtain up in the lab in an attempt to protect her samples, the shed was a dusty, dirty place. Every day, Marie cursed the iron and coal dust that floated freely through the air, tainting her samples again and again.

In addition, everything in the lab had become contaminated with radio-activity. Although it was an interesting phenomenon, which they'd named "induced radioactivity," it was a nuisance and muddled their results. In the two years since the first wagon arrived, she'd treated well over a ton of the waste and had yet to collect enough pure radium to determine its atomic weight and convince other scientists that this was, indeed, an entirely new element.

"Marie!" Pierre strode into the lab with his long legs swinging unevenly, like a pendulum slightly out of balance. He kissed the top of her head and stroked her hair. "I'm glad you stopped working to eat some lunch. You don't take care of yourself."

She smiled, wanting to comment on his limp, but she bit the words back and swallowed them with her next nibble, changing the subject.

Pierre shook his head. "I'm on my way to a meeting, but I just received word that another experiment with radium therapy has been successful, so I wanted to share the good news."

Pierre had been studying the heat emission from radium for a while. The concentrated radium salts and solutions that Marie gave him produced enough energy to melt ice very quickly. In fact, radium could melt its own weight in ice in an hour, while its own appearance remained unaltered. It defied all scientific explanation.

As their fingertips bore witness, radium could burn the skin as well as it melted ice. After learning that the German chemist Friedrich Giesel had strapped 270 milligrams of radium salt to his arm to study the effect of radium on skin, Pierre replicated the experiment by wrapping some of Marie's radium salts in cloth and tying the small bundle to his arm for several hours before removing it to observe, day by day, the changes that occurred.

At first, the exposed skin was only slightly red, but after a few days a lesion resembling a burn appeared where the radium had been. The sore had developed slowly, and it wasn't until twenty days after the radium exposure that a scab finally formed. After a month and a half, the wound finally started to heal, and almost three months after the radium burned him, the skin finally closed, leaving only a gray scar. He and Henri Becquerel had recently published their own paper on the phenomenon, and Pierre, who had always been interested in biology and physiology, saw the potential in radium's ability to destroy human cells. He teamed up with some physicians to test its ability to destroy skin cancers by burning them off and letting new skin heal.

"One of the skin tumors that they've treated by applying radium salts appears to be completely gone. So far, it's not growing back, so our radium seems to have killed all of the abnormal cells. Imagine"—Pierre leaned forward on the table, his intense gaze drinking Marie in—"that our discovery may cure cancer one day."

Their dream of making scientific discoveries for the greater good was beginning to come true. This new branch of science that they'd opened held the potential to unlock the secrets of matter and cure a horrible disease. Still, Marie wouldn't be satisfied until she held a vial of pure radium in her hand.

"You didn't forget about tonight, did you?"

Pierre gave her a look that indicated he had no idea what she was talking about, so she put her hands on either side of his face and looked at him very seriously until he smiled.

"Loïe Fuller is coming. How could you forget?"

"Ah yes," he said. "The dancer. I'm still surprised that you invited her. It's not like you."

"Perhaps it was a mistake, but it's too late to call the whole thing off now." Marie had been second-guessing her invitation all day. The chances that she'd have anything at all in common with Mlle. Fuller were infinitesimal, but she hoped that the dancer and her art would be amusing.

Pierre nodded. He closed his eyes and inclined his head so that she could kiss his eyelids, the left one and then the right, as she always did. Marie bade him au revoir and made him promise to be home early. When he'd gone, she went back to her evaporation dishes with steady hands, worrying about the arrival of the dancer and praying to the gods of science that there would be no accidents in the laboratory that day.

Scene V

The Exploding Dress

1901

Loïe stared up at the three windows on the second level of the small house. With shutters cracked open, they peeked over a vine-blanketed stone wall onto boulevard Kellermann, where she stood. The stucco dwelling was simple and rather pretty, with a row of trees ornamenting the front, but the house begged not to be noticed. Had they heard her carriage? Were they peeking out the windows?

Imagining herself standing in full view of the scientists' gaze made her nervous, so Loïe straightened her hat and moved forward. She preferred not to linger under their microscope for too long. Motioning to her electricians to follow, she pushed open the small door in the wall and marched briskly up to the two-story fortress.

Desperate for the Curies to like her, especially Marie, Loïe felt her lack of education keenly. She hoped that the time she'd spent with Camille Flammarion had prepared her to talk to her new idol without making a complete fool of herself. Despite developing thick skin after years in the limelight, bad opinions could still cut to the bone.

Loïe had been mocked by critics more times than she could count, but even the men who called her plump, sweaty, or made fun of her "dumpy" street clothes invariably concluded that despite her imperfections, onstage she always transformed herself into something spectacular. Hopefully, tonight's performance would demonstrate to Marie and Pierre that there was more to her than met the eye. Surely, they'd be more interested in her artistic inventions than how many years of school she'd finished or the outfit she'd chosen to wear to their house. Sucking in a deep breath, she straightened her shoulders and knocked.

When the door creaked open, Loïe found herself staring into the gray eyes of a woman slightly taller than she was. In her narrow black dress, Marie Curie looked exactly like the photograph Loïe had seen in the newspaper, but light and life breathed color into the image she'd carried in her mind. Marie's high cheekbones were flushed pink as though she'd run to the door, and a spotlight of late-day sun poured through the doorframe, turning the unruly blond hair that had escaped her bun into a golden halo.

Although she looked like an angel, the scientist studied Loïe with the chilly, penetrating gaze of a suspicious schoolteacher. Rather than shrinking under the intense scrutiny, Loïe stood a little straighter in the spotlight of Marie's intelligence. For once in her life, she was determined to impress the teacher, so instead of blurting out something impetuous, she stood quietly.

"Miss Fuller?" Marie finally broke the silence in accented English. Her voice was as serious as her expression, but it was pleasant, and Loïe sensed curiosity in her tone.

"Madame Curie," Loïe murmured, suddenly embarrassed by her bad French, *"c'est une* honor *grande...grande* honor?" She sighed. It was hopeless. "I am honored to meet you. *Je comprends français, mais je ne parle pas très bien.* I understand French much better than I can speak it. *Vous comprenez?"*

The corners of Marie's mouth turned up ever so slightly and she nodded, but her focus had shifted to the men that stood behind Loïe. The scientist observed Loïe's electricians with a wary eye as they approached her front door, weighed down with lighting equipment. Loïe had asked permission to bring them along, and Marie had agreed, but the presence of so many strangers was obviously making her uncomfortable.

"Then you must speak in English and I will *parler en français,"* Marie said. *"Ça va?"*

"*Parfait!*" Loïe agreed with her brightest smile, hoping that her blue eyes were sparkling. She was determined to charm Marie. "And thank you for letting my technicians accompany me." It was rumored that very few strangers ever entered the Curies' private sanctuary.

Marie and Pierre had their own small colony of intimates who gathered regularly in their workroom, around their dining table, and in the garden behind the house. Fewer than ten of their friends held an open invitation to the house on boulevard Kellermann, although one or two of Marie's favorite students from the school where she taught in Sèvres were welcome there as well. Those in the inner circle of the Curies had one thing in common: They were all scientists, or they were married to scientists.

Opening the door wider, Marie led Loïe and the men into the simply furnished house. There were books everywhere, and a cheerful vase of daisies stood on the table by the front door. She showed them into a long, narrow dining room, where Loïe would dance. It was an impossible space, but Loïe told Marie that it would be just fine.

The petite scientist nodded and rather brusquely informed Loïe that she and Pierre had to go to the laboratory, but that they would return in an hour or two. Loïe bit her tongue to keep herself from blurting out a request to tag along. To catch a glimpse of radium, or even to be in the same room with it, would be a dream come true. However, she knew it would take her at least two hours to set everything up for her dances, and it was obvious that she'd have to treat Mme. Curie very carefully in order to win her approval.

With a worried look back at the men, Marie exited, leaving Loïe and her electricians to set up. When they heard the front door open and close, Loïe and her team went to work. Her ability to get a job done quickly had become legendary during the 1900 Exhibition.

The shape of the Curies' dining room made it difficult to arrange the equipment, but Loïe tackled the problem with her usual determination. As always, the men scrambled to follow her instructions as she experimented with different combinations of light, arranging the curtains and rugs as well as she could in order to reconstruct her enchanting spectacle. When they'd tested the generator and the electric lights positioned at either end of the room, the men started to hang a curtain.

As she rushed around, Loïe noticed the curious face of a little girl watching them. She seemed amused by the noisy chaos that had invaded their home and studied Loïe as she whirled in every direction, pitching orders at the lighting technicians. An older man briefly appeared in the doorway to take the girl's hand and lead her away. As they turned the corner, Loïe heard him whisper to the child that she must not get in the way.

They'd just finished when Marie and Pierre returned to discover their dining room completely transformed into a theater. Pierre looked a bit taken aback, but Marie seemed pleased. Loïe rose from a needlepoint chair where she'd been resting, delighted to finally meet Pierre.

"I see you've brought your own generator," Pierre said. "Excellent."

M. Curie had a shock of short hair that bristled up as if electrified, and streaks of silver at his temples punctuated his intense blue gaze, amplifying the effect. He spoke and moved slowly and deliberately, as though his youthful flesh veiled the skeleton of an old man, and he projected an aura of ageless intelligence. Loïe took his extended hand, expecting a jolt, but felt only warm skin. She liked him immediately.

The older man she'd seen earlier entered with the girl in tow. She noted now that he looked like a shrunken version of Pierre.

"This is our little Irène," Marie said to Loïe, "and Pierre's father, Monsieur Eugène Curie. Say hello to Mademoiselle Fuller, Irène."

Loïe noticed that the scientist was smiling, but her voice was cool rather than inviting.

"Bonjour, Mademoiselle Fuller," Irène said politely.

"I'm delighted to meet you both," Loïe said. Despite Marie's apparent indifference, she was absolutely thrilled to meet the entire Curie clan.

Eugène had kind azure eyes like his son, and he greeted Loïe warmly in

French, grasping her hands and kissing each cheek. He was clearly a beloved presence in their home and had a smile as warm as a sunset. Four-year-old Irène hid behind him, studying the dancer with huge eyes as the adults conversed.

Marie told Loïe that they didn't frequent music halls like the ones where she performed, but once or twice a year they escaped the confines of their laboratory warehouse to attend a concert or play.

"I see. I imagine most scientists don't go to the Folies," Loïe replied. She wasn't sure whether Marie was simply stating a fact or insulting her. "Although Monsieur Camille Flammarion and his wife Sylvie have attended several times to see me dance. Do you ever go to see the great Sarah Bernhardt perform at the theater?"

She learned that while the Curies appreciated the famous French actress Sarah Bernhardt, they preferred the great Italian actress Eleonora Duse, a darling of the intellectual crowd. Bernhardt was a representational actress, big, bold, and flamboyant, and Duse her polar opposite, famous for her quiet, reserved presentational style. Eugène confided to Loïe that he enjoyed mocking Pierre and Marie when they returned from the theater, depressed by an Ibsen play or another dark production favored by the university crowd.

Marie laughed, her face relaxing for the first time. "Yes. He always says to us, 'Don't forget that you went for pleasure.'"

"I'm a great admirer of Sarah Bernhardt," Loïe admitted. "But Mademoiselle Duse is very good as well. One day, Mademoiselle Bernhardt came with her little daughter to watch me dance at the Folies."

"And were you very nervous?" Marie asked. She sounded more curious than impressed.

Loïe grinned. "Very nervous!" she said. "It was so strange to think that my idol had come to see me! That day I brought my dances to life only for her, although she, of course, had no way of knowing it. And when the performance was over and she rose to applaud during the curtain calls, it felt as if I were the audience, as I watched standing in that box. It was like a dream."

There was a knock on the door and Eugène went to answer it.

"Ah, I must go change out of my work clothes," Marie said. "Please excuse me."

The Curies had invited some friends to join them for the evening's spectacle. Before going to greet their guests, Pierre informed Loïe that she was welcome to eat with them on the back patio before her performance, if she wished. While her men went out to the street to smoke, Loïe pulled her gown out of the box.

Irène peeked around the corner, staring at the white silk.

"They said that you're a fairy of light," she whispered to Loïe in French, as if she knew what she said might get her into trouble if she was overheard, "but you seem rather plain to me."

Loïe laughed.

"It's true. I am not extraordinary at first glance," Loïe whispered back in poor French. "But I am an inventor, and I discovered how to make darkness and light change me into something more than what you see now."

Irène studied her with a serious expression.

"Like Me's radium salts?" she asked. "They look like ordinary salt until you put them in the dark, and then they're very beautiful. Me says they look like fairy lights."

"*Exactement.*" Loïe nodded at the precocious child. "Will you show me where the garden is?"

Irène led her through the kitchen and out the back door. Loïe had no desire for children of her own, but she did enjoy their company. A child's honesty was cruel at times, but just as there was truth in art, there was art in truth.

They emerged into a small garden behind the house. While the front was like a fortress, the space behind their home was a refuge of green, dotted with flower beds and fruit trees. Loïe had heard that the Curie household was a magnet for scientists. A group of intelligent-looking men and women sat around a small table engaged in energetic conversation, with

Marie holding court in the center of the debate. Their discussion came to an abrupt halt as Loïe approached.

Motioning for her to sit, the scientist introduced the dancer to the people ringing the table. She learned that dark-haired Henriette Perrin was one of Marie's closest friends and that her husband, Jean-Baptiste, studied negatively charged particle beams. André Debierne, who worked in the Curies' lab, had arrived with Pierre's former student and close friend Paul Langevin, an attractive man who studied magnetism. Loïe found them all quite amusing, and they seemed interested in her as well. The scientists didn't often cross paths with figures from the theater.

Loïe conversed with Marie and her friends, soaking up information as the conversation jumped from politics to physics and back again. Marie was absolutely charming around her friends. Loïe nibbled at some bread, but it took all of her concentration to follow the rapid-fire French. After half an hour, she excused herself to go change into her costume, leaving Marie, Pierre, and their friends to finish their meal.

When the sun had set and the stars appeared, Marie shooed everyone into the dining room and hurried up the stairs to retrieve Irène and her father-in-law. Once they were all seated in the makeshift theater, one of the lighting men put out the lights and after a hushed minute, Loïe appeared. As she danced, Loïe wondered what the scientists saw: magnetism, strange energy, radium? For a moment, Loïe glimpsed Marie and the scientist was smiling. When she'd finished, everyone applauded loudly and Marie brought Irène to say goodnight.

"Did you like my dances?" Loïe asked, and Irène nodded. "What did you see?"

"I saw a flame, and a lily, and a goddess and a witch!" Irène exclaimed with wide eyes. "You really are magic!"

"No fairy?"

"Even better than a fairy!" she whispered. "Thank you, Mademoiselle Fuller!"

When everyone had departed and she'd said goodnight to Eugène, Marie motioned for Loïe to follow her. Leaving the electricians to restore the dining room to its original condition under Eugène's watchful eye, she led the dancer out of the front door, calling to Pierre that they were leaving. Passing the stone wall, they dissolved into the dark night, moving in unison down rue de l'Amiral Mouchez.

Pierre followed a few yards behind. Although Paris was lit at night, it still had enough dark corners and strange characters that women couldn't safely walk alone.

"*Ça va bien?*" Marie inquired when Loïe rubbed the back of her neck. "It is a half-hour walk to our destination."

"I'm fine." Loïe reassured the scientist that she was always sore after performances. It was an unpleasant side effect of her job as a performer, but worth it, she said.

"My eyes are bad too," Loïe admitted.

"Then you must let me take your arm. It's very dark."

It was as though a door had been opened between them. Marie confided that Pierre was vulnerable to being overly fatigued, and the heavy lifting and chemical fumes often left her sore and sick as well.

Loïe nodded empathetically. "I've been called a 'very pushing woman' because I can work for days on end to accomplish the things that I'm interested in." She raised an eyebrow and glanced at Marie, and then back at Pierre. "I've never heard anyone called a 'very pushing man.'"

"At least you don't have a child that people say you are neglecting by going to work," Marie said. She furrowed her brow and changed the subject. "It's very interesting that you visited Monsieur Thomas Edison's laboratory. Have you heard back from him about your scarf?" Loïe, who had mentioned the scarf in the letter she'd sent to Marie, admitted that she hadn't heard back from Edison yet and told the scientist that she'd started doing some chemistry on her own in her workshop.

Not long after her visit to Thomas Edison, Loïe met a politician by the name of M. François Deloncle. They'd been introduced at the home of Camille Flammarion, and Loïe had been delighted to learn that M. Deloncle was the man who had instigated construction of the gargantuan telescope at the 1900 Exhibition. It seemed that he had a keen interest in science, and he offered to help her set up a chemistry lab. As it turned out, like Loïe, Deloncle had far more enthusiasm than experience and things had taken an unfortunate turn. She paused, wondering whether to tell Marie the whole story.

"I have to admit that I'm embarrassed to tell you about my mistakes in the laboratory. As you can probably guess, I'm not formally educated in science."

"Ah, but you are interested in it and have tried your hand at chemistry, which is incredible. And without failure, there can be no progress," Marie exclaimed, assuring her that she'd made her own share of mistakes. "*S'il vous plaît! Continuez!*"

They were now on rue de la Glacière, walking past circus-striped awnings illuminated by streetlights. Loïe hoped they were walking toward the laboratory, but she didn't know the way.

"Very well," she agreed.

Loïe and Deloncle had gone to work with the luminescent salts, but besides being expensive, the chemicals proved difficult to work with. Again and again, they'd experimented with all kinds of adhesives as they tried to get the salts to stick to the textiles. They lost spoonfuls of the precious salts in gummy messes and before long, a fine dust coated everything in the lab. Finally, one day, they'd managed to cover a huge veil and dress by coating them with sulfur of calcium.

"We stood anxiously by as our assistant set fire to a calcium ribbon in order to illuminate the salts on the dress," Loïe explained. Phosphorescent materials, as they both knew, would glow only after being exposed to light.

"That sounds dangerous," Marie said.

"Maybe, but I was only focused on the results. It was an intense moment of anticipation." Loïe paused dramatically and they both stopped walking. Loïe turned to Marie, her eyes wide, making the most of the drama of the moment.

"*Oui?*" Marie hung on every word.

"*Boom!*" Loïe threw her hands up for dramatic effect.

Marie jumped back, startled by the unexpected outburst.

Loïe thought that perhaps she'd gone too far, but Marie looked amused. "Was anyone hurt? *Continuez!*"

"Suddenly, there was an enormous flash, and we knew no more. The place caught fire and we nearly lost our lives. My eyebrows, eyelashes, and all of the front part of my hair disappeared. So did my enthusiasm. But only for a time."

"*Mais non! C'est vrai?* It's true?" Marie looked at Loïe with an expression somewhere between pity and respect.

"*Oui.*" Loïe laughed. "Luckily, they all came back. Even my hair."

Marie looked a little more closely at her face, studying her eyebrows. "You were very lucky," she said.

Pierre caught up and the three of them walked together, passing in and out of the gleam of streetlamps. Loïe went on with her story, explaining that she'd quickly jumped back into her quest to create a glow-in-the-dark dress. By then, Deloncle had lost his appetite for her project, but she found a more experienced assistant when her friend Auguste Rodin had introduced her to an elderly chemistry professor called Janin.

"You know Monsieur Rodin?" Pierre sounded impressed.

Loïe nodded but quickly turned the subject back to chemistry. Normally, she'd be happy to go on and on about her famous friends, but she was walking through Paris with the Curies! She wanted to be in their world, completely enveloped by science for a few hours.

She explained that a conversation with the old chemist had led her back to experimenting with glowing salts, this time in Professor Janin's laboratory, since her own had been destroyed.

With a few grams of sulfur of calcium and sulfur of zinc, they'd been producing luminescent violet, green, yellow, and red, but once again they encountered enormous technical problems when applying the glowing salts to silk. Liquid gum, the adhesive they were using, melted the powder before it could stick.

Not only was the sulfur of zinc extremely expensive, Loïe told them, they estimated that she'd need six pounds of it for her dress. Marie chuckled. It was impossible to even guess at what six pounds of radium would cost. At the moment, less than a thousandth of an ounce of the almost-purified element currently existed on Earth. It was, in fact, priceless.

"That's almost three kilograms!" Pierre said.

Loïe went on with her story. "Needless to say, we were still failing miserably. When we finally accomplished the application of the sulfur salts to the silk, it was like a board!" Loïe exclaimed. "Nothing could be done with it. Even if I'd been able to make a dress, it would have been too stiff to get it on. It was, at the very least, discouraging! All that money and two years of work!"

Eventually, Loïe figured it out when she noticed that a scarf they were experimenting with, which had only patches of salt on it, became illuminated in the dark when it was in motion. It occurred to her to put the powder on silk in stripes, gumming the goods first and then sprinkling the powder on.

"This worked beautifully," she said, "and the stripes fell in pleats, giving treated fabric the suppleness I sought!"

"So you finally had your dress?" Marie asked, as they turned a corner.

"Well," Loïe said. "Sulfur of zinc is green and very beautiful, but it is far too expensive, so we took a dress of a hundred yards and permeated it with sulfur of calcium instead."

"The same chemical that blew up your laboratory before?" Marie asked.

Loïe nodded. "But this time, it worked."

The sulfur of calcium had glowed in the dark like the "light of the moon." Loïe's next act was to fabricate a dress and veil of black gauze and dot it with the same calcium. When the veil was thrown up in the air, she told Marie, it disappeared in the darkness, and only the falling luminous drops were seen, elongated in their descent, taking on the form of violet-blue tears.

"Someday I'll show you!" she promised.

She was still in the midst of describing the new laboratory behind her house when Marie stopped and they turned through a dark entrance that took them into a large courtyard, weakly illuminated by moonlight. Pierre took off in another direction and Loïe followed Marie across the courtyard to a low building lined by glass windows, where the scientist proceeded to pull a key from her pocket and open the door with a click.

Loïe was sure this must be the Curies' famous shed. She'd seen drawings of it in the newspaper.

"Since you are so interested in my work, I wanted to show you my laboratory," Marie said. "It isn't much to look at during the day, but I think it's quite beautiful at night. We have a small glassed-in workshop as well, but I spend most of my time here."

They walked into a pitch-black cavernous space and Loïe's heart sank. She couldn't see a thing. It was like walking into Aladdin's cave without a candle. If only she had a spotlight now, to flood every corner and illuminate every object. Loïe stood quietly, swallowing her disappointment.

"Wait here for a moment," Marie advised as she closed the door behind them. It was then Loïe caught the first glimpse of light. Soft shapes gleamed faintly on the perimeter of the black room.

"Is that...?" Loïe breathed the question.

Marie took her arm again and led her across the room, past barely visible tables. She pointed to the dark forms of two chairs and motioned for Loïe to sit.

"*Maintenant*, wait for your eyes to get used to the darkness," she said. "One must have patience to see true beauty."

As Loïe's eyes continued to adjust, her other senses were heightened. Strange sour odors wafted through the air, and the warehouse smelled of damp earth. The sounds of passing carriages, muffled conversation, and music were noticeable, but they seemed a world away as she sat silently in Marie's universe, watching dreamlike apparitions reveal themselves.

After a few minutes, she could make out the shapes of glowing containers sitting on shelves and tables, rather than suspended in the air as they'd first appeared. The revelation that the strange light was contained in earthly vessels didn't diminish their magic.

"Radium." Loïe breathed the word more than said it.

"*Oui.* It is not quite pure yet, but those are the compounds of radium," Marie whispered. "They look like jars of glowworms, no? I am sorry that I can't part with any of it for your dance of butterfly wings, but perhaps these petite glowworms will turn into butterflies someday, when radium is more plentiful? I hope to find a way to use our discovery for something that will make the world a better place."

"While I see only beauty, you are more practical," Loïe said.

"Yes, of course. I am a scientist, after all," Marie said. "But there is great beauty in practicality, if it betters the human condition."

They stared at the beakers, bowls, and vials of radium, which shined from within, radiating pale blue light. Some glowed slightly brighter than others, but Loïe didn't want to interrupt the magical moment to ask why.

"It *is* beautiful, though, isn't it?" Marie said.

Time dissolved as the dancer and the scientist sat side by side in worshipful silence, staring at the cool glow that transformed the curves of simple laboratory glassware into lovely ghosts, making the ordinary extraordinary.

Act III

The Radium is a soft-strange light.
It is like the moon
it throws no rays
it is not brilliant
and it must be seen in absolute darkness.

—Loïe Fuller

Scene I

The Thinker

1902

When the carriage pulled up in front of the gate that morning, Marie kissed Irène good-bye and hurried down the stairs. The yellow tulips she'd picked the day before sat cheerfully on the table between Pierre and Eugène. Her father-in-law was reading *Le Temps* while Pierre sat staring into space, his chin resting on his palm. The previous evening, Paul Langevin had stopped by, as he often did. After dinner they sat in the upstairs office, which overlooked the garden, discussing their own work and the latest scientific news.

Whenever Paul joined them, it was an intellectual free-for-all. They'd throw ideas out like fishhooks and eagerly grab onto the especially interesting ones. Marie insisted on clarity of explanation for each new hypothesis. She knew mathematics far better than Pierre did, and could untangle difficult problems quickly. As always, hours had flown by and they'd stayed up far too late. Luckily, it was Sunday, so they'd slept in until almost eight and stayed in bed until nine.

Marie put a hand on Pierre's shoulder. For the occasion, she'd abandoned her usual laboratory wear for a cheerful white blouse with a lace collar and a striped belt. Her hair was combed and pulled into a neat bun, but she could already feel wisps escaping and tickling her temples. She pulled a gray cloak over her shoulders as she announced that the carriage had arrived.

Pierre rose slowly and picked up the jacket he'd slung over the back of his chair. They said good-bye to Eugène and headed out the front door into the bright sunlight of a glorious April day. The damp smell of spring air reminded Marie of her childhood adventures in the Polish countryside. From the trees, robins and blackbirds whistled and trilled with voices that belied their rather ordinary appearances. She was thrilled to have a Sunday away from the shed so that she could come back fully energized to work on Monday. Even Pierre had been forced to admit that the invitation was far too interesting to refuse.

It was a cloudless day, but when Marie noticed Pierre was limping again, it felt like a shadow had blotted out the sun. She took his arm, asking him whether he'd rather go another day. As always, he straightened up, tried to disguise his limp, and insisted that he was fine. There was no use in arguing. Marie would go on with the day and pretend not to notice that he was grimacing at the phantom pain, which haunted him day and night. Sometimes he slept as soundly as a baby, but more and more often, he tossed and turned until dawn.

On the doctor's advice, she fed him chicken and vegetables and kept him away from red meat and red wine, but his limp continued to come and go with no rhyme or reason. Her experience with her own health had demonstrated that fresh air could cure the weariness brought on by working in the shed, and she'd been certain that he would recover when they fled Paris the previous summer for the seaside.

During those lovely weeks beside the ocean, she'd felt her energy return with each breath of salt air. Even as she dreamed about the radium awaiting her in Paris, she'd luxuriated in the days of leisure as warm weather helped clear her lungs. Her appetite returned and they'd rediscovered the joy of unhurried picnic lunches and long dinners under the stars. With saltwater hair and dreamy eyes, they'd searched for shells, picked bouquets of meadow flowers, swum in the sea, and she and Pierre had fallen asleep with sun-warmed skin pressed together until Irène climbed into their bed to wake them. When physics crept into the conversation, they explored it with leisure rather than urgency, drawing equations in damp sand.

It was almost heaven, but no matter how much fresh air Pierre breathed or how hard Marie wished for his pain to go away, she could not banish it. Rather than keeping him from the lab, the aches tethered him to their work. The constant reminder tugged on him like a leash, calling him back to Paris, and Marie had begun to worry that their mutual dream of scientific glory was killing him. While she could separate her life and work, he could not.

Now she pushed away sinister voices in her head that told her maybe he suffered from something less well known and more insidious than simple rheumatism. Was he so frantic to work because he worried that his time was running out? It was a question she would never pose to him. She didn't want to know the answer. She'd planned her scientific and family life around Pierre. To continue without him would be unthinkable.

"Let's go then." Marie pasted a smile on her face and took Pierre's arm.

She would make him better. If she could extract radium from tons of pitchblende, surely she could find out what was making him sick and fix it. Achieving the impossible was what she did best.

Together, they made their way down the walk and through the stone gate to the street. At the curb, a pair of chestnut mares were harnessed to a black carriage large enough for four passengers. Marie waved at the coachman, who opened the door to reveal the round face of Loïe Fuller smiling down at them.

Worry melted away as Loïe took both of Marie's hands and kissed her cheeks in the traditional French greeting.

Loïe beamed. "Bonjour, dear Marie! I'm so happy that you and Pierre accepted my invitation."

"But how could we refuse?" Marie said, only half joking.

She'd learned by now that when the dancer set her mind to something, there was no stopping her. Loïe's endless stream of stories was sure to distract her from Pierre's maladies, and to her relief, the dancer said nothing about his pained motions when he climbed in beside them. Instead, she greeted him so excitedly that he laughed out loud, reminding Loïe that she was the one who was a celebrity.

"To Meudon!" Loïe cried, thumping the roof. The carriage jerked and rolled forward. "And what a beautiful day it is!"

Men in hats and women with parasols strolled through the streets, and there were bicycles everywhere. As they rolled away from the city, Loïe asked Marie about her work.

Marie loved to see how the dancer's eyes came alive when she learned about science. She was extremely bright, asked insightful questions, and seemed to remember everything Marie told her, although she had a tendency to romanticize science.

"Surely you'll make enough money from your great discovery to build a new laboratory? You discovered how to extract the radium. Can't you patent the technique?"

Marie shook her head, explaining that she and Pierre were working for the expansion of scientific knowledge. They would publish their results in well-respected journals where scientists could document their discoveries, which in most cases would allow them to take intellectual credit for their discoveries and inventions. They would not, however, profit from their work.

"We do hope that one day our work will allow us to get funding from the Sorbonne to build a real laboratory," she said, looking at Pierre. "Now tell us about yourself. You just returned from Bucharest?"

Loïe told them about her tour, during which she'd performed some fluorescent dances in costumes illuminated by chemical salts.

"And please tell me that you didn't cause another explosion?" Marie joked.

"Not this time." Loïe smiled. "But I did have some trouble with a dancer named Isadora Duncan. Have you heard of her?"

Isadora was not just any dancer. She was the most interesting dancer Loïe had ever seen perform. Although Loïe had no idea that the young American would soon go on to be the most famous—and infamous—dancer in the world, she knew from the beginning that there was something special about her. They had been introduced in December of 1901 by their mutual friend Emma Nevada, a celebrated singer who had also left America to perform in Paris. Admiration mingled with envy as Loïe watched Isadora dance for the first time. She would later recall the experience in her memoir.

"She danced with remarkable grace, her body barely covered by the flimsiest of Greek costumes, and she bade fair to become somebody...In her I saw the ancient tragic dances revived. I saw the Egyptian, Greek and Hindoo rhythms recalled. I told the dancer to what height I believed that she could attain, with study and persistent work."

Isadora's determination and spirit reminded Loïe of herself. The twenty-two-year-old, whose dancing was so natural and sensual, had an air of innocence that made her even more compelling. Loïe, who loved playing the role of impresario, promptly invited Isadora to join her, Sada Yacco, and her newly formed group of young dancers on a tour of Vienna and Berlin. Isadora, who had been captivated by Loïe's and Sada Yacco's performances during the 1900 Exposition, immediately agreed.

Upon arriving in Berlin, Loïe had ordered a sumptuous, extravagant dinner for her troupe. Her spine had been killing her after the long voyage and she ate leaning back against bags of ice, which her entourage replaced frequently. Following dinner, she and her dancers had performed at the Wintergarten as Isadora looked on from a box seat, wondering how Loïe could perform with such an injury. Isadora would later write: "Before our very eyes she turned to many-coloured shining orchids, to a wavering, flowering sea-flower, and at length to a spiral-like lily, all the magic of Merlin, the sorcery of light, colour, flowing form. What an extraordinary genius!...I returned to the hotel dazzled and carried away by this marvellous artist."

Unfortunately, Isadora had fallen sick and was confined to her room the entire time they were in Berlin. The Germans, it turned out, were much less enthusiastic about Sada Yacco than the French, and Loïe found herself in financial trouble. As a result, the company left Berlin without their trunks, although Gab eventually resolved the situation. When they arrived in Vienna, Loïe began to work with Isadora. Enamored of the young woman's ideas and choreography, she decided to introduce the dancer to the city's most influential individuals and critics.

It was a fiasco. Isadora was absolutely impossible to work with. She showed up late to performances, sitting in her dressing room brushing her hair and soaking her feet. Besides that, she shocked audiences by dancing practically naked in short, transparent tunics that left little to the imagination. But she moved so beautifully and had the strong, lithe body that Loïe had always wanted. Loïe loved her, hated her, and wanted to be her.

Loïe wasn't the only one in her troupe who found Isadora irresistible and confounding. According to Isadora, a red-haired dancer whom they had nicknamed "Nursey" had assaulted her twice, once kissing her in the middle of the night and a few weeks later standing by her bed with a candle, saying that God had told her to strangle Isadora. Isadora had escaped, and the unstable young woman was taken away for medical treatment, but the experience left Isadora shocked.

Gab, who had been jealous of Loïe's devotion to Isadora since the beginning of the tour, didn't seem horribly upset when the young dancer, now in high demand, fled the company. Isadora would only return if Loïe wired her 10,000 francs. Loïe, whose contract to have Sada Yacco perform in Berlin had just been broken, had no money, so she walked away from the difficult young woman. The entire experience had been personally and professionally humiliating.

"Her dancing was the most beautiful thing in the world," Loïe said to Marie, "but she snuck out of her contract and ran off to perform on her own, leaving me with a good number of broken contracts."

A jolting bump stopped their conversation and Pierre took on a pained expression. Marie whispered to him as the carriage started a slow climb up a long hill. They were out of Paris proper now, and tree-covered hills greeted them.

"I think you will like Monsieur Rodin very much," Loïe said.

Loïe's friend Roger Marx had introduced her to the sculptor in 1899, the year before the Paris Exposition. His acquaintance was a challenge that Loïe felt she'd had to navigate carefully, as Rodin was constantly surrounded by a flock of women who guarded every moment of his time.

Obsessed with his beautiful work, she was determined that he would sculpt her likeness one day and was relentless in her pursuit of his friendship. When they met, he'd just broken off his affair with the sculptor Camille Claudel and was beginning a new one with a student. Loïe had invited him, in broken French, to several of her performances and visited his studios again and again until he finally accepted her into his circle.

"Has he sculpted you?" Pierre asked.

"Not yet, but I've sat for him several times," Loïe said.

During her numerous visits to Rodin's studio, Loïe had made friends with an artist named Emilia Cimino, who doubled as an art instructor and a go-between for Rodin and his lovers. Things got complicated when Emilia became infatuated with Loïe and jealous of Gab.

Despite Gab's complaints—she liked Rodin but disliked Emilia—Loïe loved the attention. Emilia wanted to draw her, and Camille Claudel and Rodin both wanted to sculpt her. In 1900, Rodin had his personal photographer, Eugène Druet, photograph her performing her Serpentine, Lily, and Butterfly dances outdoors.

Unfortunately, Loïe had been too busy building her theater for the exposition to sit for long periods of time, so although Rodin made several sketches and studies of her, the marble sculpture never completely materialized. Still, she had a marvelous time with him, and affectionately began to call him "Dear Master."

An observer passing through Rodin's studio one day wrote, "You might be inclined to smile on entering the statuary warehouse on rue de l'Université, where Rodin is making a sculpture of Miss Loïe Fuller, to see the two of them conversing, he in his large white smock, she in her black raincoat in the midst of the marbles and plasters. But you quickly become serious when you hear the warm and earnest discussion, in which the dancer holds her own with the sturdy and shrewd sculptor."

"Monsieur Rodin doesn't realize it, but he is completely controlled by the women in his life," Loïe confided to the Curies. "He can be very cruel, but they destroy each other to be near him. Naturally, I have to stay friendly with all of them. He lives here at Meudon with his companion Rose, who likes me and has put up with all of his nonsense since they were young."

The road leveled and the horses came to a stop. Marie, Pierre, and Loïe emerged into the sunlight and walked down a narrow avenue of gravel flanked by newly planted saplings. Arriving at a fence, Loïe drew up the latch and a bell sounded in the distance. They walked toward a red brick house, where a dog bounded up to them barking wildly and wagging its tail.

"Welcome to Villa des Brillants," Loïe said.

Marie reached her hand out to the dog and bent down to pet it. She'd had a dog of her own when she was young. When she looked up, a large man with heavy features was striding toward them slowly. The imposing, barrel-chested figure was as monumental as his sculpture of Balzac. Dramatic strokes of silver invaded his bushy black beard, but rather than aging him, they amplified his powerful aura. She wouldn't have been surprised to discover that he carried a thunderbolt in his hand.

Extending both hands to Loïe with a friendly smile, the man leaned forward and kissed her cheeks in greeting. Turning to Marie and Pierre, Loïe introduced them to Auguste Rodin.

The famous sculptor held his large hands out to Marie and enfolded her fingers in his enormous palms. His eyes seemed to look right through her, but Marie wasn't intimidated. She knew many "great" scientists who were just as flawed and human as she was, if you looked beneath the veneer of their fame.

Loïe Fuller as Little Jack Shepard, ca. 1886, photo by Napoleon Sarony *(Jerome Robbins Dance Division, The New York Public Library for the Performing Arts)*

Maria Skłodowska, 1888 *(Curie Museum and Archives, Paris, France)*

Loïe Fuller's Serpentine Dance in *Uncle Celestine*, 1892 (*Jerome Robbins Dance Division, The New York Public Library for the Performing Arts*)

Loïe Fuller in one of her costumes at the Folies Bergère, Paris, ca. 1892
(*Liz Heinecke personal collection*)

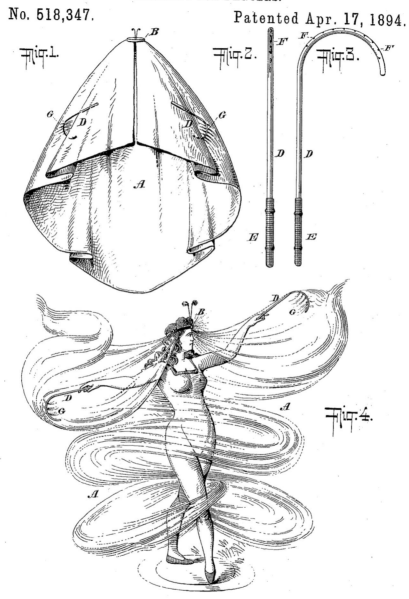

Loïe Fuller's patent for a "Garment for Dancers," 1894 (*U.S. Patent Office patent no. 518,347, April 17, 1894*)

Pierre and Marie Curie with their bicycles, Sceaux, France, 1895 *(Curie Museum and Archives, Paris, France)*

Illustration of "The Skirt Dance" from *Scientific American*, 1896 (Scientific American, June 20, 1896, *Vol. LXXIV-No. 25)*

Loïe Fuller performing "La Danse Blanche," photographed by Isaiah W. Taber, 1898 *(Jerome Robbins Dance Division, The New York Public Library for the Performing Arts)*

Loïe Fuller dancing outdoors, photo by Samuel Joshua Beckett, 1900 *(Joseph Rous Paget-Fredericks Dance Collection, Bancroft Library, UC-Berkeley)*

Loïe Fuller dancing outdoors, photo by Samuel Joshua Beckett, 1900 *(Joseph Rous Paget-Fredericks Dance Collection, Bancroft Library, UC-Berkeley)*

Loïe Fuller dancing outdoors, photo by Samuel Joshua Beckett, 1900 *(Metropolitan Museum of Art, Gilman Collection, Mrs. Walter Annenberg and The Annenberg Foundation Gift, 2005) (This file was donated to Wikimedia Commons as part of a project by the Metropolitan Museum of Art.)*

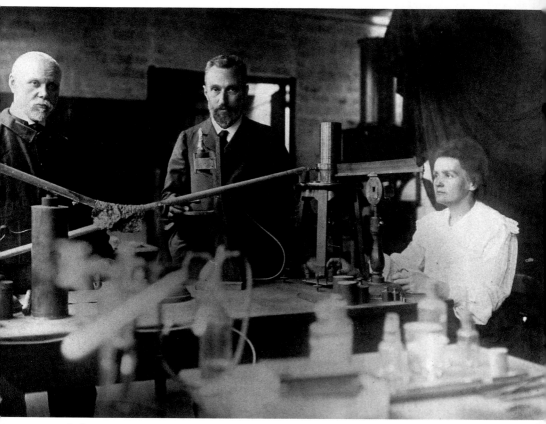

Laboratory assistant M. Petit with Pierre and Marie Curie in their laboratory at the School of Industrial Physics and Chemistry, Paris, 1898 *(Wellcome Collection)*

Loïe Fuller, 1901 *(Library of Congress, https://www.loc.gov /item/2004668223/)*

Loïe Fuller, 1901 *(Library of Congress, https://www.loc .gov/item/2004668224/)*

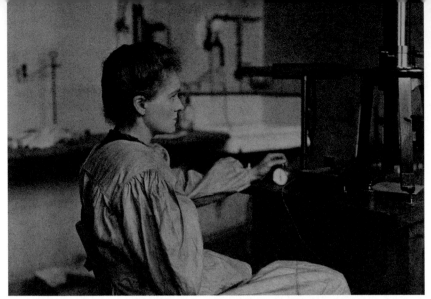

Marie Curie, stopwatch in hand, measuring radioactivity in the laboratory on rue Cuvier, 1904 *(Curie Museum and Archives, Paris, France)*

Loïe Fuller's phosphorescent costume for the Butterfly Dance, from her Radium Dances, ca. 1904 *(Collection of Maryhill Museum of Art)*

Photograph of Gab Bloch from Loïe Fuller's autobiography, *Fifteen Years of a Dancer's Life*, taken by Isaiah W. Taber around 1900 (Fifteen Years of a Dancer's Life *by Loïe Fuller*)

Loïe Fuller and her mother, Delilah Fuller, ca. 1907 (*Jerome Robbins Dance Division, The New York Public Library for the Performing Arts*)

Attendees of the first Solvay Conference, Brussels, Belgium, 1911
Left to right (standing): Robert Goldschmidt, Max Planck, Heinrich Rubens, Arnold Sommerfeld, Frederick Lindemann, Maurice de Broglie, Martin Knudsen, Fritz Hasenöhrl, Georges Hostelet, Edouard Herzen, James Hopwood Jeans, Ernest Rutherford, Heike Kamerlingh Onnes, Albert Einstein, Paul Langevin; (seated): Walther Nernst, Marcel Brillouin, Ernest Solvay, Hendrik Lorentz, Emil Warburg, Jean-Baptiste Perrin (reading), Wilhelm Wien (upright), Marie Curie, Henri Poincaré (*Curie Museum and Archives, Paris, France*)

Left to right (front row): Miss Manley, Ève Curie, Hans Albert Einstein; (back row): Albert Einstein, Marie Curie, and Irène Curie, on their trip to Engadine in the Swiss Alps, August 1913 *(Curie Museum and Archives, Paris, France)*

Loïe Fuller and her company on tour in Egypt, 1914 *(Jerome Robbins Dance Division, The New York Public Library for the Performing Arts)*

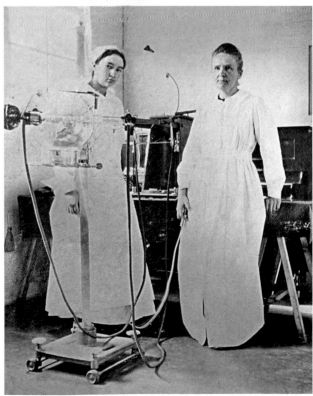

Irène and Marie Curie surrounded by X-ray equipment installed in a pavilion at Hoogstade hospital in Belgium, 1915 *(Curie Museum and Archives, Paris, France)*

Loïe Fuller and Rodin's sculpture *The Kiss*, 1916 *(Jerome Robbins Dance Division, The New York Public Library for the Performing Arts)*

Marie Meloney at left, with Irène, Marie, and Ève Curie, during the Curies' 1921 visit to the United States *(Photographer unknown, https://commons.wikimedia.org/wiki /File:Meloney-with-Irene-Marie-and -Eve_Curie-1921.jpg)*

Marie Curie on her balcony at the Radium Institute's Curie Laboratory, Paris, 1923 *(Curie Museum and Archives, Paris, France)*

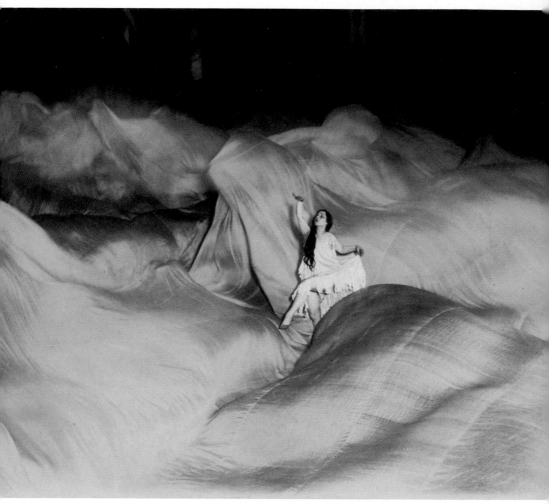

Sur La Mer Immense (On the Mighty Sea), Loïe Fuller Company, Paris, 1925 (*Joseph Rous Paget-Fredericks Dance Collection, Bancroft Library, UC-Berkeley*)

Opening his fingers, he studied her scarred fingertips before looking up at her with respect, smiling warmly. Releasing her hands, he took Pierre's in a similar fashion before gesturing for them to follow him along a small path. Rodin clasped his hands behind his back and, with Loïe at his side, led them to his temple of sculpture.

No one spoke a word. Loïe had warned Marie about the master's tendency to get carried away with the grandeur of silence. Once, Loïe said, she'd gone to a church with him and had to stand there for three hours while he contemplated every blessed thing in the place. When they finally left, he'd whispered to her that they hadn't had enough time, and she'd almost laughed out loud.

When they arrived at the top of the hill, they paused to take in the panorama that stretched out before them. A glass pavilion stood on their right, overlooking a stunning landscape. To the left stood a forest of ancient trees. Most people in Paris weren't acquainted with Rodin's studio in Meudon, which had been carried piece by piece from its original home near Loïe's theater at the 1900 Exposition.

Unusual for its time, the entire structure had been built with light in mind, and he'd consulted Loïe on its design. Large windows on each side allowed natural light to illuminate marble figures from every direction. A master of positive and negative space, Rodin loved how the shadows on his figures moved with the changing light, illuminating new angles and changing their appearance. Following the exposition, he'd tried to convince the city to leave the pavilion they'd built for his sculptures intact as a museum, rather than tearing it down. When they'd refused, he'd rebuilt it on his estate.

The sculptor opened the temple door and they followed him into his silent sanctuary. Sunbeams poured down through a glass-paned ceiling, and floor-to-ceiling windows with arched summits welcomed additional illumination from all sides. It was an aquarium of light.

Angels, devils, and everything in between posed boldly in the bright space among a menagerie of humanity cast in plaster and chiseled from marble.

While some stood captive behind a wall of glass doors on one side of the space, a host of twisted figures were scattered around the room, frozen in anguish and passion. Many were solitary, but others were eternally intertwined. Headless torsos, graceful hands, and beautiful faces lay on wooden pallets, as if expecting to be reunited soon.

They followed Rodin into the room. He put his hands behind his back and, without a word, took them from one sculpture to the next. On an elevated wooden platform that ran the length of the room, forms reminiscent of Loïe's dances stretched their wings beside twisting nudes. Blocks of marble waited half finished on spinning pedestals and wooden boxes. Joy, sorrow, lust, youth, and age were all represented in the army of figures. He rotated works in progress, pointing here and there to show them how he exposed the figures hidden in stone, and lingered at his masterpieces, caressing the marble. Marie and Pierre responded with gesture and expression, rather than words, and studied each piece of art at length.

Even Loïe, who was always full of questions and comments, had taken on the role of observer and kept her mouth shut. When Marie turned to look at her, she playfully mimicked tiptoeing behind them and then slowly and deliberately stepped on a dried leaf lying on the white tile floor, shattering the silence.

Marie smiled at her friend and turned her attention back to the art. She'd read in the newspapers that Rodin was simultaneously loved and despised, both as an artist and as a man. Former lovers clung to him as he moved from mistress to mistress, searching for truth in representation, capturing his emotional reactions to his subjects as he molded their likeness. A woman raising her hand to her hair might become a goddess, while a great man was as likely to look like a hulking shadow as an Adonis. The faces he carved were so realistic that it was easy to imagine them coming to life like Pygmalion's Galatea.

As they stood contemplating *The Thinker*, Marie glanced at Pierre. He was gazing, transfixed, at the famous sculpture with clear eyes. She was certain that he must see himself in the graceful figure, which echoed the dreamy, contemplative position he took so often, chin on hand, looking inward.

Marie recognized herself in the figures as well—woman, lover, worker—but felt that she had most in common with the sculptor himself. Minute shards of marble in his beard reminded her of the radium salts that always powdered her hair and skin. Covered by the dust of their labor, the two of them were stoneworkers, manipulating the elements into the forms they desired.

If only she could sculpt her radium into a cure for Pierre. It could kill cancer cells and melt ice. Surely it could save him from the mysterious illness. She would have to work harder and faster.

On the way back to Paris, Pierre gazed out the window. There was no pain in his eyes, and he wore a peaceful, happy expression. Loïe reached over to squeeze Marie's hand and they listened to the clip-clop of horses' hooves as Meudon receded into the distance.

Scene II

The Séance

1904

"Ça va, Marie? Are you feeling alright?"

Loïe studied the scientist's profile as they walked ahead of the men. There were dark circles under her eyes, and she seemed even more serious than usual, but Loïe was determined to pull her out of the somber mood. She was excited for the evening ahead.

They'd just left Loïe's new laboratory, which was housed in a shed she'd rented in the Latin Quarter. After the studio where she and Deloncle had been working with luminescent salts exploded, she'd been unceremoniously evicted from that workspace. Although she'd been grateful to borrow a table in Professor Janin's laboratory for a while, Loïe was thrilled to finally have her own space entirely devoted to microscopes, lighting gels, projectors, silk, and chemicals. Her lease on the rue Cortambert house had recently expired as well, so she and her mother had relocated to the Hôtel de la Cité du Retiro, a few blocks from the Place Vendôme. Only a large rehearsal studio in Passy, to which they were now headed for a performance and a séance, remained the same.

"I heard that you and Pierre are moving into a new laboratory," she said, hoping to perk Marie up a bit. "You must be so excited!"

Almost anything would be an improvement over their old situation. Marie's shed had proved to be much less romantic in the light of day. Visiting the scientist a few weeks after their first meeting, Loïe discovered that the shabby limestone buildings of the science campus were braced against collapse by roughly hewn logs, and old timbers supported the top section of the tall entrance into the main courtyard. Despite the run-down surroundings, as Loïe picked her way through the straw, dirt, and pebbles littering the paved courtyard that afternoon, she'd wondered what marvelous things were happening in the laboratories around her. She could almost feel inspiration in the air. Beside the famous shed, Loïe could see where Marie's boiling cauldrons of acid had left large, dark stains on the ground, but the windows were covered with a thick film of dust, making it impossible to see inside.

The Curie lab was a jungle of glassware. Borne aloft by her entrance, dust shimmered in the sunlight that poured through the transparent roof, and the large, open room smelled of chemicals. A simple wooden desk stood in the middle of the space, watched over by a funny little stove with a pipe that branched in two halfway to the ceiling, before rejoining into a single pipe, like a picture frame whose art had gone missing. The silent room was a ship without a captain, though. There wasn't a soul around. Feeling like an intruder, Loïe had stepped outside again to ask for directions to the Curies' other workroom.

She heard coughing as she entered the small laboratory, which was crowded with equipment.

"Marie?" Loïe called.

"*Je suis ici!*" Marie's voice responded from behind a heavy black curtain. To reach her, Loïe maneuvered carefully past a few tables of glassware and peeked around the curtain, which hung from the ceiling.

There she found the scientist, sitting in front of a complicated-looking apparatus that took up an entire table. Unsmiling, Marie had gestured for her to sit and flipped a switch that made a point of light appear on a clear bar resembling a glass ruler beside her. She picked up a stopwatch and placed a small white dish of powder onto a metal plate with a second plate hanging over it, before covering the entire thing with a metal cylinder.

After connecting a wire running to the second part of the device, she added a small weight to a scale. Without taking her eyes off the ruler, Marie plopped into her chair and clicked the stopwatch as the light on the ruler began to move. Adding small weights to a second device with her right hand, she kept an eye on the bright point of light the entire time. Eventually, Marie clicked the watch again and neatly penned some numbers in a notebook before opening the chamber to remove her sample, which she carefully covered and placed on a shelf behind her.

When she'd finished, Marie turned to Loïe and her serious face broke into a smile.

"I hope you don't think I'm rude. I am so pleased that you've come," she said, pulling a glass container filled with lumpy reddish-brown pitchblende off a nearby shelf. She knew how interested Loïe was in her work, and as Loïe held some of the dust in her palm, she patiently explained how radiation passing through air produced electrical charges they could detect and measure. With her electrometer, a timer, and a quartz scale, Marie told Loïe, she could indirectly measure the radioactivity of any sample. She proudly explained that Pierre had invented the piezoelectric quartz scale, which was so integral to her measurements, long before the two of them met. Loïe had been enthralled with every detail, and Marie had put a sample in the cylinder, turned the light on, and let her try the stopwatch, just for her amusement. On a more recent visit, Marie had even let her hold a vial of purified radium.

Now, the tables had turned and the Curies, along with a group of professors from the Sorbonne, had come to see Loïe's new workshop. That she would one day be lecturing to a group of renowned scientists was something Loïe had never imagined in her wildest dreams. It was nerve-wracking, to say the least. Without her robes and wands, she'd felt horribly exposed. But she was a good actor, with a strong voice at her disposal. Trying to ignore the feeling that the word "faker" was scrawled across her forehead in black ink, she'd told the professors about her work with luminescent salts and silk, showing them some of her chemically treated textiles.

Loïe's knack for storytelling came in handy, and the scientists leaned forward to catch every morsel that she dropped about her meeting with Thomas Edison. They'd delighted in her descriptions of his hands, his voice, and his love of pie, which she described to them as an American fruit tart. They'd been especially interested in his inventions, which she explained in great detail. When she told them of observing the bones of her hands under the fluoroscope, one of the professors asked whether she'd heard the news that Edison's resident X-ray expert, Clarence Dally, was dying of cancer, which had started in his fingers.

"I don't know anything about that," Loïe answered, studying her own hand, which seemed fine. "But I'm very sorry to hear it."

Professor Janin, who had been working with the luminescent salts along-side her, was there to help field chemistry questions that Loïe couldn't answer, but it was Marie's presence that bolstered her confidence most. Each time she faltered, or an explanation tangled her tongue, Loïe would look at her friend and the scientist would give her a small nod of encouragement, as if to say, "Go on, you're doing fine."

Marie had recently overtaken Loïe's star to become the most famous woman in Paris. A mere two months after their visit to Meudon to see Rodin, the scientist finally held in her hand the treasure she'd been seeking: a vial containing a minuscule but measurable amount of pure radium chloride. Extracted from approximately seven tons of pitchblende residue, the one-decigram sample was smaller than a grain of rice, but it was enough to allow Marie to determine radium's atomic mass. Radium, the magic substance that gave off radioactive emissions, burned skin, melted ice, changed the color of glass, and made luminescent chemicals glow, finally took its place on the periodic table. The world went mad for the element and fell in love with its unlikely discoverer. Soon, the legend of "Our Lady of Radium" was making its way around the globe.

Less than a year before, in November of 1903, the Nobel Prize committee had announced that Marie and Pierre, along with Henri Becquerel, had
won the prestigious physics award for their work with radioactivity. The
French, who were still licking open wounds from the anti-Semitic Dreyfus
affair, were happy to have a less divisive topic of conversation. The Curies'
story, which featured love, suffering, and a magic potion called radium, was
a balm for the nation.

At the time, few people were familiar with the Nobel Prize, which
had been established in 1895. Worth 70,000 gold francs to each winner,
the prizes for Chemistry, Literature, Peace, Physics, and Physiology or
Medicine were funded by the fortune contained in the will of Alfred
Nobel, the Swedish inventor of dynamite. They were to be presented in
recognition of scientific, academic, or cultural advances. Following Nobel's
death, the first prize was awarded in 1901, but it was the Curies who made
the prize famous.

Marie was almost excluded from winning the award, simply because she
was a woman. In 1902, a doctor on the Nobel committee named Charles
Bouchard had nominated Marie for her work on radioactivity, along with
Pierre and Henri Becquerel, but they were passed over that year. Then,
in 1903, four more prestigious men on the committee nominated Pierre
and Henri for their work with radioactive materials, omitting any mention
of Marie.

Three of these four men were familiar enough with the Curies' work to
know perfectly well that it was Marie who had discovered radioactivity in
pitchblende and single-handedly isolated radium. Despite this, they claimed
that Pierre and Henri Becquerel had "worked together and separately to
procure, with great difficulty, some decigrams of this precious material." It
was Marie's worst nightmare come true.

When Pierre learned what had transpired, with Bouchard's backing he
forced the committee to add Marie's name to the nomination and told them
that he would not accept the prize unless Marie were included. She was still

not treated as an equal, though, and when the prizes were awarded, Henri Becquerel was given 70,000 gold francs, while Marie and Pierre received a single sum of the same amount to share. Although she never complained, the experience made it crystal clear to Marie and everyone else that she was seen by many in her community as little more than a lab assistant, and that without Pierre as her advocate, she might have been a footnote in history.

Pierre, who had spent most of his career being ignored by the upper echelons of academia, found fame amusing at first, when French newspapers criticized the Sorbonne for their treatment of him and Marie. Journalists bemoaned the elitism of their most famous university, which was always eager to welcome wealthy and well-connected scientists but had completely ignored the Curies. When Pierre and Marie threatened to leave Paris in 1900, he'd been offered a slightly better job teaching medical students at the Sorbonne's P.C.N. (Physics, Chemistry, and Natural History) annex on rue Cuvier in a building across the street from the house where Henri Becquerel first discovered radioactivity. The position came with little influence and no lab space other than their tiny workroom, but the Curies needed money for their research, so he took the job and spent four years bicycling between the shed and the P.C.N.

Now, under public and government pressure, the Sorbonne had finally offered Pierre a physics chair, but once again no lab space came with the position, so he turned the offer down. All he and Marie really wanted was a better laboratory. The government tried offering him the medal of the Légion d'Honneur, but he declined the award, stating that he needed a laboratory, not a decoration.

At Marie's urging, he finally persuaded the Sorbonne to offer him better laboratory space at the P.C.N., along with a promise to secure funding for more. Marie was made laboratory chief there but was offered no place on the faculty. Before the Curies could move from their shed into the new laboratory, the money from the Nobel Prize made it possible for him to quit his teaching job at the P.C.N.

As the Curies' star rose, so did the popularity of radium. In addition to helping scientists unravel the mysteries of the universe, the beautiful element had healing properties and showed promise for curing cancer and other previously untreatable conditions. In the name of science and public interest, the Curies shared their method for chemically extracting radium from pitchblende with academia and industry, and the first radium factories were constructed. Without uranium ore, there was no radium, so the race was on to procure pitchblende mining waste. In France, a rumor had begun to circulate that Thomas Edison was buying up every bag of pitchblende that he could get his hands on.

Verbal battles raged as people argued about whether a woman could be a good wife and mother while working outside the home. When certain reporters arrived at the Curie residence to find Marie away at the lab, they called her a bad mother. It was difficult for traditionalists to imagine a husband and wife working side by side toward a common dream, although the creative consciousness was fascinated by the idea of science mingled with love. The strange circumstances of Marie and Pierre's relationship allowed writers to transform the shabby reality of their shed laboratory into a romantic radium-lit atmosphere, shrouded in mysterious vapors. Camille Flammarion wrote: "I see in my imagination, She and He, in the age of dreams, both impoverished but rich in hope and seeking I know not what magic talisman to cure the world of its worries…And one day, at the bottom of their crucible—joy intense and unforgettable—they find the treasure they were searching for."

Pierre Curie was celebrated for being a native son of France, and Marie was adopted by the French public as one of their own, her Polish heritage ignored or conveniently forgotten. Mountains of mail from admirers flooded their house. Everyone suddenly wanted a piece of their time, attention, or money. They were tirelessly pursued by journalists, who appeared at their front door day and night. At first, they patiently responded to the endless river of questions, but soon they were drained of answers. It was exhausting and distracting for the introverted couple, who just wanted to focus on their work.

Now Loïe and Marie stood on the street together to wait for a carriage to Loïe's studio in Passy, for the performance and séance. As Loïe had hoped, Marie perked up a little at the mention of the new laboratory.

"Yes, I'm very pleased that we have a new laboratory, but we haven't had a moment's peace since winning the Nobel Prize," she said. "I'm exhausted from worrying about Pierre. He pretends to be fine, but he is in so much pain most days that he cannot even take walks or play with Irène."

In fact, Pierre's health had been in steady decline. The doctors prescribed a small dose of strychnine, which only made him feel worse. His hands were so damaged by radium burns that Marie had to help him button his shirts, and he had no energy at all.

"Is it still his legs that bother him?" Loïe asked.

"And his back," Marie said. "He won't rest. The worse he feels, the more he is drawn to the laboratory." She blinked back tears. "He always wants me there with him in the lab, even when I want to spend time with Irène. Did I tell you that my little nephew in Poland died last year?"

She didn't elaborate, but Marie was dealing with much more than Pierre's illness. In the summer of 1902, her father had died. Then, in August of 1903, a few months after receiving her PhD in Physics at the Sorbonne, she'd miscarried a little girl after carrying the baby for five months. It happened while she was on a bicycling vacation that Pierre had insisted they take, but Marie would never blame him for the loss. Instead, she despised herself for ignoring her own health despite everyone's warnings.

The news about the death of her healthy five-year-old nephew in Poland, so soon after her own miscarriage, had been the final blow mentally and physically. Marie sank into a deep depression, and it had taken months for her to reemerge into normality. She and Pierre had postponed their trip to Stockholm to receive the Nobel Prize as she slowly recovered, but as she got better, Pierre's pain and weakness worsened. Now, she constantly felt as though she were standing on the edge of a cliff.

"I lie awake worrying about them," Marie confessed to Loïe. "What if something happens to Irène? What if I lose Pierre? How can I take care of both of them and do my work?"

"You won't be able to take care of either one of them if you don't take care of yourself," Loïe said sternly. "And if you make yourself so sick with worry, you won't be able to get any work done at all. Do your hands hurt?"

Marie realized that she'd been rubbing her thumbs along the cracked tips of her fingers as she spoke.

"They're fine. It's only a habit," she answered.

"Let me see," Loïe said, and Marie held out her hands obediently.

"Radium is so hard on your poor fingers," Loïe said. "Could it be making Pierre sick?"

Marie shook her head and explained that handling radium only damaged their skin. In fact, she said, research that Pierre was pursuing seemed to indicate that radioactive emanations from hot springs actually improved the health of visitors to the thermal waters. She didn't mention that some of his work also demonstrated that animals enclosed in small spaces with active radium emanations died within hours. In her mind, that particular study only showed that one must take plenty of fresh air when working with radioactivity.

"Well, then. You will go on," Loïe said, with great confidence. "There is nothing else to do. And maybe tonight will prove a distraction from your worries. You must try to enjoy yourself."

"You won't tell anyone about my troubles?"

"Of course not," Loïe said.

Marie dried her eyes. She had learned that Loïe was a reliable friend, but she didn't know her companion Gab very well yet. It was hard to imagine that the quiet dark-haired woman who guarded Loïe so fiercely and jealously would gossip to the newspapers, but Marie doled out trust sparingly.

Pierre joined them just as the carriage pulled up, and the three of them rode to Loïe's studio together, with the rest of their friends and colleagues not far behind. When they arrived, the dancer disappeared as the scientists filled neat rows of chairs that had been arranged at one end of the gallery. When everyone was seated, the lights were dimmed. Except for a soft green glow that escaped through a slit in the curtain, the entire room was enveloped in darkness.

Suddenly an apparition appeared before them. The vague form seemed to be covered with hundreds of tiny glowworms, galaxies of twinkling stars. It swept across the floor and lofted the glimmering lights into the air to form a luminous lily. Try as she might, Marie couldn't make out Loïe's face. Next, the robe of stars was replaced with an invisible woman: a spirit in a glowing blue dress with darkness where the head should be and a halo that appeared to be sitting on nothing. The figure moved in a solemn, ghostly dance before vanishing in a puddle of light on the floor.

Marie gasped with delight when next an enormous butterfly appeared. Red-spotted luminous wings of green and gold beat the air under shining blue antennae and glowing eyes. The ghostly insect fluttered round and round in the studio before momentarily disappearing, only to return with a smaller radiant butterfly, shining white. Worries forgotten, she clapped her hands together when the smaller apparition beat its wings over the head of the larger one. At the conclusion of the performance, the lamps were lit and she applauded until her hands hurt.

Loïe emerged from behind the curtain in the butterfly dress so that the scientists could examine her creation.

"You see," the dancer told the professors, fanning out her skirt, "this is silk impregnated with the salts I showed you in my workroom. In complete darkness, only the treated portions of the fabric are luminous, which gives the ghostly effect. I realize that I cannot use radium since it is so precious and might burn my skin, but as you know, these substances are similar and some have been extracted from the residue of pitchblende, which was introduced to me by our dear Madame Curie."

Marie had never seen Loïe look happier. When a reporter opened his notebook in the midst of the group, Marie instinctively shrank back, but Pierre surprised her by stepping up to the man to give him an interview. He told the delighted journalist that Loïe had made them look on their discovery in a new light, adding, "It's an application of the properties of radiant matter which I had not thought of."

Absolutely beaming, Loïe whispered "Thank you!" to Pierre. She left to go change out of her costume, and by the time she returned, Marie, Pierre, and the professors were seated around a large table that the dancer had rented for the occasion. They'd all agreed that the best way to follow up Loïe's new dance was a spiritual séance. Marie was somewhat skeptical of the practice of spiritualism, but many of her colleagues believed that it had some merit, and Pierre himself was intrigued by the practice.

Personally, she found it surprising that any scientist working to uncover facts and expose "supernatural" events as results of natural phenomena could believe in invisible spirits. Marie hoped that science would bring an end to superstition. Still, there was much to be learned about energy, and she couldn't fault Pierre and her friends for being curious.

Since the middle of the nineteenth century, séances had become extremely popular in Europe. As scientific discovery untangled the mysteries of the universe and upturned long-standing beliefs, many took comfort in the idea that the energy contained in each human soul took shelter in the atmosphere following death and could be detected by gifted humans and perhaps even scientific equipment. Obsessed with learning more about the "vibrations" of the universe, referred to as "radiations," some believed these vibrations could move through the aether from cell to cell, mind to mind, and could even allow communication with the dead. Even Marie had to admit that what one knew could only be gleaned from phenomena that affect the human senses directly, or indirectly through technology. The aether surrounding material things was still a mystery.

Pierre had been introduced to the idea of spiritualism by his brother Jacques. Disciples of magnetism and electricity, they'd continued to be fascinated by invisible forces, so the idea of spiritual phenomena did not seem so far-fetched. The existence of ghostly apparitions was yet to be demonstrated using scientific techniques, and Pierre was interested in studying séances in the laboratory, to see whether invisible forces called forth by mediums could discharge their electroscope.

They were not the only scientists interested in psychic phenomena. The chemist William Crookes had recently devised a spinthariscope for visualizing radioactive emanations on a phosphorescent screen, and he believed that psychic force could be harnessed by certain individuals. Loïe's friend the astronomer Camille Flammarion was also fascinated by the supernatural and would go on to write a book about it.

In *Mysterious Psychic Forces; An Account of the Author's Investigations in Psychical Research, Together with Those of Other European Savants*, Flammarion describes his first séance with the famous Italian medium Eusapia Paladino in 1897. After searching the room and the curtain behind the medium's chair for concealed mechanisms, wires, and batteries, Flammarion and a colleague had been seated at a spruce table on either side of Eusapia, holding her limbs in place. Flammarion writes, "At the end of three minutes the table begins to move, swinging to and fro, and rising ...A minute afterwards it is *lifted entirely from the floor*, to a height of about six inches, and remains there two seconds." He describes hearing raps on the table, a music box playing, and a bell being shaken. In low light, they are tapped, slapped, and pinched by invisible fingers, a hand seizes Flammarion's arm, objects move around the room, and the imprints of a hand and face mysteriously appear on a clay tablet, feeding the astronomer's curiosity. Near the end of the book he mentions Pierre Curie, regretting that the "lamented scientist" was never able to publish the studies he'd done with Eusapia at the General Institute of Psychology.

Despite Pierre's enthusiasm for the supernatural, Marie was skeptical and simply hoped that the experience would be entertaining, composed of rapping sounds and moving tables but not the ghostly figures that were said to appear at times. Certain psychic mediums claimed to read minds and communicate with the dead, at times having prophetic visions of dark shadows prophesying death and bad fortune. The scientists gathered around the table were obviously looking forward to the chance to examine these supernatural visions with their own eyes, and Marie was certain that many lively discussions would follow the evening's activity.

Loïe reappeared, followed by a young woman with her hair covered by a veil. After the dance performance, her electricians had rearranged the chairs and positioned them around the table, with one end directly in front of the curtain. Chatter died down as the mysterious figure sat at the head of the table and asked them to join her. She told them to rest their hands on the wooden surface and instructed them to touch their pinkie fingers to those of their neighbors in order to close the circle.

"Now close your eyes," she whispered.

When the lights went out, Marie prayed that she wouldn't open them to see a ghostly shadow crouched at Pierre's side. Beneath her fingers, the table began to rise. The séance lasted far into the night.

Scene III

The Accident

1906

Pierre is dead? Dead? Absolutely dead?"

As Marie said the words out loud, something inside her, closer to her belly than her heart, turned to ice. It couldn't be true. They'd argued a bit that morning, but the day had seemed so perfectly normal. How could her world implode without sending even the tiniest vibration down her spine?

Under a darkening sky still heavy with rain, she'd waited in the garden for his body to arrive, her head so heavy in her hands that she could barely support it. Someone handed her his things: a fountain pen, a wallet, and a set of keys that he'd never again jingle in his pocket. Pierre's pocket watch had somehow survived the accident and was still ticking. Shivering, she held his possessions in her palm, one at a time, before setting them down gently on her skirt to protect them from the wet surface of the bench.

The carriage carrying his body finally pulled up, and strangers carried Pierre into the house. Marie followed the procession numbly, and when they laid him down, she threw herself across him only to discover that he was still warm. With his eyes closed, she could almost imagine that Pierre was still alive. His fingers had not yet stiffened, and they bent when she grasped them.

But when Marie lifted her head from his chest to kiss his dear face, the illusion was shattered. She saw the wounds, which couldn't be entirely concealed by the dressings, revealing how badly he'd been hurt and how horribly he'd bled. He must have died instantly, but the fact offered her no comfort whatsoever.

As she stared at his body, she'd wanted to shout at him for being so careless. How many times had she gently reminded him to pay attention as they crossed the chaotic streets of Paris? Had he been lost in one of his daydreams or conjuring a new experiment? Did his legs give out when he stepped off the curb? Was he too weak to respond to the danger? Had he been frightened in those chaotic moments before the wheels struck him? Marie pictured his eyes open, his smile, his sweet face. Had he shouted out, in that grave, gentle voice she knew so well? She couldn't bear to think about it.

At some point, they pulled her off Pierre's body and carried him away in order to remove the scarlet-stained clothes. When at last they called to her, she ran up the stairs to find him lying on their bed with a new white bandage concealing his wounds.

She guarded him jealously after that, cursing herself for allowing anyone else to touch him. Beneath the crude wrapping, Marie could just make out his hair. Bone jutted from his beautiful, intelligent forehead, but his face was still sweet and serene, as if he were trapped in a dream.

It had been pouring rain that afternoon, and Pierre's umbrella was open when he stepped out into the busy intersection near the Pont Neuf and rue Dauphine. He'd collided with the flank of an enormous draft horse that was harnessed to a second horse and then to a heavy wagon thirty feet long. Perhaps if the wagon had been shorter, the wheels a different distance apart, or if Pierre's legs had been stronger, disaster would have been averted, but the laws of physics determined that Pierre would die that day.

He'd grasped at the horse feebly as he attempted to stay upright but lost his balance and fell to the street. The wagon's driver had tried to steer the horses away by pulling them hard to the left. For a heartbeat, it looked as though the prone man on the ground had escaped a horrible fate, but moments after the front wheels spared Pierre, the left rear wheel of the wagon crushed his skull. Onlookers rushed to the scene and were shocked when the victim was identified from the calling cards in his pocket as the famous scientist M. Curie. They carried him to a pharmacy and then to a nearby police station, where a physician proclaimed him dead.

Marie couldn't stop touching him. She put her hands on his beautiful head and kissed his cold lips, murmuring "Pierre, Pierre, Pierre, my Pierre," as if she could call him back to life. She kissed his eyelids as she had so many times before, willing them to open, but he did not wake up.

She lay beside his now cold body, grasping his hand. Would she forget the childlike sound of his laugh? Could she ever speak his name again once he was in the ground, or would it freeze on her lips? If only she'd asked M. Rodin to sculpt Pierre. She wanted his face carved in marble so she could trace the curves of his cheek forever.

Marie didn't sleep that night. Or maybe she did. Nothing seemed real. When she wandered downstairs the next morning, the first thing she saw was the vase of marsh marigolds that Pierre had carried back from their weekend in Saint-Rémy-lès-Chevreuse. She numbly wondered how it was possible that the flowers were still alive when he was not. How could they stand there, nodding cheerful and yellow, when Pierre was dead?

When he'd arrived that Saturday to join them in the country, Marie had let Irène, who was eight and very independent, ride her bicycle to meet him at the nearby train station. He'd given her a butterfly net, and they'd spent the day leisurely exploring ponds and meadows together. One-year-old Ève, with her dark hair and blue eyes, had made them laugh as she toddled around the countryside, crawling over rocks and ruts in the road. Marie had leaned against Pierre's warm frame as they watched the girls play, and she recalled the exact spot where he'd picked the flowers. Although he still wasn't healthy, for a few magical hours she'd had the most wonderful feeling that all was well.

As usual, the siren call of the lab had brought the magical weekend to an end, and Pierre insisted on returning to Paris on Monday morning. Unhappy with him, Marie had decided to stay on in the country with the girls until Wednesday, since it was a school vacation and she had to be with them anyway. Now she would have given anything to have those days back.

To make matters even worse, they'd fought on the morning he died. They'd just returned home, and as she was getting the girls ready, Pierre had shouted up at her to ask whether she would be joining him in the lab that day. It was more of an order than a question. She'd responded in a less-than-amicable voice that she'd love to go to the lab, but that it was still a school holiday and she would be taking Irène on an outing. Perhaps he would like to join them? Or maybe he would like to help get the girls ready?

As Pierre hurried out the door, the words she'd uttered were not the expressions of love and tranquility Marie would have spoken had she known they would be the last she'd ever say to him. Since he'd died, she'd played the scene over and over in her mind. Her harsh words would haunt her forever.

Fortunately, something strange and wonderful occurred on the day he was buried, which made her feel the tiniest bit better. As she waited alone in their room beside his flower-strewn coffin, Marie pressed her head to the cold wood of the casket, promising Pierre that she would always love him and never allow another to take his place. Suddenly, she felt what could only be described as a strange calm, an intuition that she would find the courage to live. She'd never experienced anything like it in her life.

Whether it was an illusion, or something more, Marie would never know. Had an energy accumulation, like the ones that Pierre believed in, somehow condensed in the cool interior of the closed coffin and flowed into her mind at that moment of contact? What happened wasn't measurable. Still, she couldn't help thinking of the spiritualism Pierre had become more and more obsessed with of late. Had his energy materialized to comfort her?

The year before, Pierre had persuaded Marie to attend the spiritual-ism sessions with Eusapia Paladino arranged by the General Institute of

Psychology. Although Pierre conceded that some of the spectacles they witnessed at the séances could have been accomplished by a magician, others seemed inexplicable. Marie still wasn't convinced that spiritualism merited scientific study, but Pierre and some other professors from the Sorbonne scheduled additional sessions to study the supernatural phenomena that Eusapia claimed to call forth. He kept detailed notes and measurements during the sessions, and the researchers always had "controllers" in the room, holding the medium's hands, feet, and knees during the séances.

"Eusapia strikes M. Curie on the shoulder and corresponding knocks are heard on the table," Pierre wrote in his observations. Another entry reads, "Eusapia scrapes M. Curie's hand and scratches are heard in the table." His notebook on the subject describes another research session in 1906, saying, "The table rises two, then four feet while one of Eusapia's hands is on the hand of M. Curie and the other is above the table…Eusapia's feet are attached to the feet of her chair."

Just before he died, Pierre had informed Marie that it was no longer possible for him to deny that these spiritual phenomena existed. He knew she was skeptical but told her he'd seen objects in a bright room displaced from a distance and watched their electroscope discharge, as if by radioactive matter. Very recently, he'd written a letter to a colleague claiming that spiritualism offered "a whole domain of entirely new facts and physical states in space, of which we have no comprehension."

Maybe Pierre was right, Marie thought, as the calming presence washed over her. Maybe he was still here with her. She couldn't bring him back, but if he wished her to go on, she would go on. That magical moment was the only thing that made it possible for her to put one foot in front of the other and to endure the small funeral in Sceaux, where she watched his casket disappear into the ground.

Visitors stopped by to offer their condolences, the days dragged on, and beautiful tributes to Pierre appeared in the newspapers, but Marie's grief didn't wane. On the Sunday following his burial, she snuck away to their new laboratory on rue Cuvier, only to discover that the space had acquired an unimaginable sadness. She'd hoped that work might dull her grief, but when she picked up a graph on which she and Pierre had each marked data points, her hands began to shake. Overcome by anguish, she failed miserably at making the next measurement.

Contemplating the impossibility of going on without him, she paced the lab, skimming her thumb across her rough fingertips. It wasn't his mind she needed. Marie could certainly think and work on her own. It was his physical presence she missed; his hand in her hair, his voice filling the air. Sitting at her desk, she pulled out a new journal and recorded the date: April 30, 1906. It had been exactly eleven days since the accident. Eleven days since her life had been destroyed.

"Dear Pierre, who I will never more see here," Marie wrote, "I want to speak to you in the silence of this laboratory, where I never thought I would have to live without you." The notebook became her constant companion. She wrote to him every day, recalling the days before he died and journaling her pain as she tried to go on.

Marie sensed his presence most of all in the vial of luminescent salts she kept beside their bed, the child of their shared scientific dreams. When she stared at radium's blue glow, she saw him: Pierre standing in the window when they met; Pierre writing equations on the chalkboard in the shed; Pierre brushing pitchblende dust from her cheek; Pierre speaking to the Nobel committee.

When they'd finally gone to Stockholm in the spring of 1905 to receive the Nobel Prize in Physics for their discoveries in the field of radioactivity, they'd fallen in love with the Scandinavian landscape. Pierre had given a wonderful speech, mentioning Marie's work twice as often as he referred to his own, and citing their combined work just as frequently. His words made it irrefutable that Marie was an equal if not superior partner in the work they'd done on radioactivity, crediting her with discovering radium and polonium, saying:

> Mme. Curie has studied the minerals containing uranium or
> thorium, and in accordance with the views just stated, these
> minerals are all radioactive. But in making the measurements, she
> found that certain of these were more active than they should
> have been according to the content of uranium or thorium. Mme.
> Curie then made the assumption that these substances contained
> radioactive chemical elements which were as yet unknown.

He spoke about the significance their discovery held for a number
of scientific and medical fields, and mentioned work he'd been doing to
study the energy that was constantly released from radium. In 1903, he'd
published a paper on radium, hypothesizing that if the enormous amount
of heat produced by a tiny amount of the element originated within the
radium, "this transformation must be due to a modification of the atom of
radium itself." Since then, Ernest Rutherford and Frederick Soddy had done
more work to demonstrate that atoms of radioactive elements did indeed
"disaggregate" to produce "projectile rays...emanations and the induced
radioactivities."

After noting that radium must be transported in a lead box, because
prolonged exposure would cause skin sores that wouldn't heal, and possibly
even paralysis and death, Pierre concluded his speech with a nod to Alfred
Nobel, who had invented dynamite, and a warning:

> It can even be thought that radium could become very dangerous
> in criminal hands, and here the question can be raised whether
> mankind benefits from knowing the secrets of Nature, whether it
> is ready to profit from it or whether this knowledge will not be
> harmful for it. The example of the discoveries of Nobel is charac-
> teristic, as powerful explosives have enabled man to do wonderful
> work. They are also a terrible means of destruction in the hands of
> great criminals who are leading the peoples towards war. I am one

of those who believe with Nobel that mankind will derive more good than harm from the new discoveries.

Marie had been so proud of him that day in Stockholm, but the memory was already fading. Bronya had helped her burn Pierre's bloody clothes, her family members went home, and the piles of condolence notes were thrown away, but nothing ever felt normal again. As the months dragged by, Marie confided to one of her former students that she still had a great deal of affection for her friends but had no desire to continue a social life. She stopped seeing almost everyone, except to discuss business, science, or the education of her children. Offending people who didn't find her sufficiently friendly became her new normal, and Marie discovered that she could no longer maintain a conversation that didn't have a fixed goal.

With her carefully constructed world in ruins, Marie often drifted off into the past, wondering what her life would have been like without Pierre. Some days, she wished that she'd never met him, so she wouldn't hurt so much now. Perhaps she would still be in Poland. She'd almost married someone else, a lifetime ago.

Now, she could barely remember that man's features, although she recalled that he was very handsome. Back then, she'd dreamed of studying in France but was focused on helping Bronya attend medical school, so she'd gone to work as a governess for wealthy estate owners north of Warsaw.

Eighteen years old at the time, she'd boarded the train for a three-hour ride and climbed onto a horse-drawn sled, which skated across a winter landscape. Arriving at an unfamiliar house, she was given a large upstairs bedroom and informed that she would be responsible for teaching the family's ten- and eighteen-year-old girls. At first, it had been strange teaching someone her own age, but she liked her students. The family's three boys, she learned, were being educated in Warsaw, with two at boarding schools and the oldest, Casimir, at the university.

Life had been hopelessly dreary there, surrounded by fields of sugar beets, factories spouting smoke, and people who were as dull as the landscape. At social gatherings, young men and women danced flawlessly, gossiped constantly, and veered away from the stimulating controversial conversation that Marie craved. She'd escaped the tedium by studying literature, sociology, and science upstairs in her large, peaceful room while the children played downstairs or slept.

Marie had also started teaching the children of the local peasants to read in Polish, which was illegal and put her at risk of being sent to Siberia, should she be found out. It was a struggle at first, but watching the young Poles write their own forbidden alphabet humbled her, and she bemoaned how many minds had been wasted by a lack of education. Days and then months had slipped by as her dream of Paris drifted farther and farther away.

Life on the estate became far more interesting when the family's oldest son, Casimir, returned home for the holidays and fell hard for Marie. Besides being pretty, she had undeniable wit and could dance, row, skate, and ride just as well as he could. Marie found him nearly as irresistible.

The age-old story replayed itself when the young man went to his parents to give them the news that he'd decided to marry the penniless governess. Casimir, who looked so strong on the surface, turned spineless under his parents' disapproval. He broke off the engagement and ran back to the university, leaving her heartbroken and embarrassed. Unable to let her father and Bronya down by leaving her position, she'd been forced to remain in the house, teaching the children of a family who she now knew considered her so far beneath them.

Her letters to Bronya during those years betrayed her disappointment and depression, going so far as to mention thoughts of suicide. She described falling into a black melancholy in the provincial intellectual vacuum, where it seemed that rain, mud, and wind had become her only companions. Marie wrote to Bronya that while Paris was a place where people move and think, her own existence reminded her of that of a river slug living in dirty water. She'd remained in the governess position for three more years, before Bronya finally saved her by insisting that Marie join her in Paris.

Pierre's death made the heartbreak she'd endured back then feel inconsequential, but she was back in that same dark place. Walking the streets alone on rainy days, Marie passively hoped she would be struck by a carriage. When she laughed at something funny that her girls did, she was choked by guilt. So tired that she often wished she would go to sleep and not wake up, she pulled herself out of bed day after day for the girls and Pierre's elderly father.

Existing rather than living, Marie found her only comfort in the vial of glowing radium beside her bed, and the memories it held in its soft light.

Scene IV

The Lecture

1906

In addition to having brown-tinged violet eyes and enviable eyebrows, Comtesse Greffulhe had the distinct advantage of sitting in the front row. She was wearing an enormous hat, but fortunately the seats in the lecture hall were tiered. Besides being a patron of artists, including Rodin, the socialite was a supporter of the sciences, and ran with the most fashionable crowd in Paris. When Pierre met her in 1903, he'd invited her to their home one evening to watch Loïe Fuller perform, in hopes of gaining a benefactor. Neither he nor Marie had any interest whatsoever in social climbing, but both hoped that she might make their dream of a radium institute come true, and Loïe had been happy to dance for the famed beauty.

Pierre was gone now, but their acquaintance had gotten the comtesse into the room on that November day in 1906, when the uncomfortable auditorium chairs were more sought-after than gold. The space was overflowing, the hallways were packed, and Marie Curie was about to give her inaugural lecture as the first woman professor in the history of the world-famous Sorbonne.

According to Ève Curie, newspapers claimed the hall contained "about a hundred and twenty places, the greatest number of which will be occupied by the students. The public and the press, which also have some rights, will be obliged to share at most twenty places between them."

Ève wrote, "For the first time a woman was about to speak at the

Sorbonne—a woman who was at the same time a genius and a despairing wife. Here was enough to draw the public of theatrical 'premières'—the audience for great occasions…Great and ignorant minds were mixed, and Marie's intimate friends were scattered among the indifferent. The worst off were the true students, who had come to listen and to take notes, but had to cling to their seats to keep from being dislodged."

Marie had been at the cemetery just an hour before, standing at Pierre's grave. It had been seven months since he died, but the pain was still fresh. Just weeks after his death in April, the Sorbonne had contacted her to request that she teach Pierre's physics course. She'd accepted the job because she knew it was what he would have wanted. He'd always hoped that she would teach a course at the Sorbonne one day, so she agreed that in November, she would become the university's first female professor. Although she should be happy about it, Marie wanted to scream at those who congratulated her. It felt as though she was being congratulated for Pierre's death.

She had arrived at the university's lecture hall dressed in black. Someone told her that she looked pale, but she ignored them and walked into the lecture hall at exactly one thirty, to find it packed with students, press, and the upper crust of society. When she took her place at the front of the room, the audience broke out in an ovation, but the applause sounded oddly hollow to her ears.

Marie somehow managed to control her emotion, and her gray eyes remained dry as she briefly bowed her head in tribute to Pierre. As the applause continued, she paused for a moment with her eyes closed, trying to picture his face and drawing strength from the fact that she was standing where he'd stood so often. The applause stopped abruptly when she looked up. There was an expectant pause, but she would not give the crowd the emotional performance they expected. Instead, she paid tribute to Pierre in the way she knew he would have wanted.

Ignoring the extra onlookers, Marie gripped the long table on which Pierre had performed so many demonstrations and began the lecture exactly where he'd left off. She directed her words to a group of young women sitting in the front row: her former students from the school at Sèvres. "When one considers the progress in physics in the last decade," she began, "one is surprised by the changes it has produced in our ideas about electricity and about matter."

Her voice came out as almost a whisper at first, but as she spoke, her tone strengthened and the blood returned to her face. Fortified by the familiar language of science, she fell into a rhythm as she discussed electricity, atomic disintegration, and radioactive substances. When the lecture was over, she left as quickly as she'd entered, almost running out of the room to escape the applause that assailed her.

Some journalists complained that the lecture had seemed somewhat boring, and others couldn't resist describing Marie's physical appearance. A month later, the *Sydney Morning Herald* would call Marie the Sorbonne's first "lady professor" and praise her discovery of radium, before spending more ink on her appearance than on her accomplishments:

> Madame Sklodowaka-Curie is 38 years of age. Her features, which are particularly Polish, are regular, although her forehead is higher than one is accustomed to find in women. Her lips are thin, which gives a touch of harshness to her mouth and suggests past privations. Appropriately her 'crowning glory' is her hair, which is like waves of spun gold. She is fairly tall, well-built and of good constitution—a necessary possession for one whose work is so mentally and physically exacting.

More astute writers, however, noted that, despite her modest dress and impassive countenance, the thin scientist in a black dress rocked the world that day. Newspapers across the globe wrote about her lecture under headlines like "Women Are Forging to the Front in Science" and "Most Important Professorship Held by a Woman." A columnist in the Paris paper *Le Journal* called her lecture "a great victory for feminism," going on to say, "For if a woman is allowed to teach upper-level courses to students of both sexes, what does that say about so-called male superiority? I tell you, the time is very near when women will become human beings."

In July of 1907, when Loïe saw Marie for the first time in over a year, her friend told her that giving the lecture had been a nightmare.

"Pierre would be so proud of you," Loïe said, grasping her friend's thin, cold hands. "I'm sorry that I wasn't there."

Loïe invited Marie to meet her at Rodin's Paris studio at three thirty that day. Marie declined Loïe's invitation at first, saying that she didn't have time for social visits anymore, but Loïe persisted.

Guessing that Marie didn't want to suffer through the awkward sadness of a string of condolences, when the scientist arrived Loïe hugged her and rushed her through the studio doors on rue de l'Université. Although she was frail and withdrawn, Marie seemed pleased to see Rodin again and managed a weak smile when he grasped her hands. As the sculptor led them through his workroom, Marie paused in front of a plaster figure of a woman twisted in anguish.

Hurrying to her side, Marie and Rodin reminisced about the beautiful spring day they'd spent with Pierre at Meudon. Marie recalled how happy he'd seemed there, surrounded by nature, light, and art. The happy memories appeared to bring her some comfort. She even smiled and told them how much *The Thinker* had reminded her of Pierre. Marie told them that besides working on her own book about radioactivity, she was busy completing some of Pierre's unfinished research in order to publish his results in papers and books, bringing to the world the work that had been so cruelly interrupted.

"He was always very kind to me, you know," Loïe told Marie. "Like you are. I still remember the last time I saw him."

Loïe had visited Pierre in the lab on rue Cuvier just before leaving for a tour of Germany. Although he'd looked tired and moved slowly, he was the same old Pierre, and enthusiasm masked the fatigue when he showed her his new "high frequency" electric machine.

What had excited Loïe the most, though, was the new ultraviolet light he'd demonstrated. Pierre had placed a glass of water in the path of the invisible light. At that point, the glass of water appeared to be filled with a dark blue light. Next, he'd sprinkled a tiny bit of white powder, which looked like sulfur, into the water, and the minuscule grains of powder were illuminated brilliantly as they fell through the liquid.

The powder looked white with a very faint blue tinge, not the violet Loïe had expected. In her experience, colored light always transformed objects into their own color or mixed with other colors in expected ways, so she'd expected the violet light to turn the white powder purple. Pierre explained that it was called ultraviolet light because it was made of invisible rays that lay beyond the violet end of the spectrum of visible light. He was interested in these invisible rays, he told her, because they produced unknown energy that could create chemical changes in matter and even kill microorganisms.

Loïe had been fascinated by his description of how ultraviolet light was discovered, and once she'd seen the ghostly illumination, she became obsessed with the idea of using ultraviolet light and the white powder to create a gown that would shine bright white in a dark room, illuminated by an invisible spotlight. The powdered substance hadn't dissolved or changed as it sank to the bottom of the glass of water, so it should be possible to transfer some of it onto a dress. All she needed to procure was one of the ultraviolet projectors. On that day, Pierre had been kind enough to give her some of the powder, and she remembered how he'd smiled warmly as he scooped it into a small bag for her to take home.

She'd been in Germany when he died, the news making a mostly miserable tour worse. Her only fond memory of the trip was sending funny postcards to Gab, who was staying at the same hotel but in a different room. She'd been penning one of them when news came of Pierre's accident, just a day after an earthquake had flattened San Francisco. Unable to return to Paris for the funeral, she'd written to Marie, knowing full well that the scientist would probably never see the note.

Loïe grieved in her own way. Gab had helped her make new programs for the last three performances of her tour, and she'd presented several of Pierre's favorite dances, concluding each evening with her "Radium Dance." Tears had come into her eyes when she opened her glowing butterfly wings, and she could almost feel her friend's sorrow stretching across the miles. In her dressing room one night, she'd written a poem, scribbling it on the back of a program.

The Radium is a soft-strange light.
It is like the moon
it throws no rays
it is not brilliant
and it must be seen in absolute darkness.
It is a new unknown light
and should not be looked upon
or judged by a bright light
and it should be seen very near.

Scene V

Salome

1907

Loïe peeked out through the curtain. Her career needed a boost. Most of the critics had hated her last production of *Salome*, but she hadn't been able to resist staging it for a second time. She was captivated by the exotic tale that intertwined dancing, temptation, and death.

The red velvet seats in the Théâtre des Arts reminded her of the Folies, but the auditorium was much more ornate and far more respectable. Six hundred thirty seats filled the orchestra section, and three balconies boasted pale blue and gold decorations. The venue seemed sufficiently large to keep her critics at a safe distance, but it was impossible to predict what they'd choose to focus on.

Tonight, at the opening of *The Tragedy of Salome*, Loïe was optimistic that her favorite reviewers would gush about her new inventions, special effects, costumes, and dancing. Unfortunately, newspapers always had in their employ a few artless men. These so-called critics couldn't seem to help but focus on her physical appearance rather than her art and loved nothing more than taking jabs at her.

"Now!" Loïe commanded. The stage darkened and she ran to her mark just behind the curtain, dragging the six-foot-long serpents behind her. When the low light came up again, she could just make out the purple-robed figure of King Herod through the ominous hue of the spotlight, meant to prime the spectators for her next trick.

A hypnotic oboe melody rose from the orchestra pit and Loïe shivered with delight. She adored the musical score, which had been written by an Alsatian composer named Florent Schmitt. The small orchestra pit at the foot of the stage, led by the young and extremely talented conductor Désiré-Émile Inghelbrecht, only held around twenty musicians, but they filled the auditorium with sound. Lifting her arms to raise the heads of the reptiles, which were extensions of her arms, Loïe brought the black figures constructed of wire and cotton into the light. She moved them back and forth in sinuous concert, closer and closer to the unsuspecting king.

When the serpents reared up to strike, hissing loudly, several women in the audience screamed. Loïe heard a collective gasp as the king jerked backward in terror. It was exactly the response she'd hoped for.

The shiny green scales of her dress made a swishing sound as she stepped onstage to join the serpents she controlled. Swaying her hips, Loïe became Salome. The choreography she'd invented was part dance, part snake charming, and part deathly struggle.

She played the part of rescuing the king and his bride from the giant snakes, while making the serpents writhe on the floor so realistically that people in the back of the theater were convinced they were real. After hypnotizing the serpents, she set them down on the stage, only to make them rear their heads at her again so that she could wrestle them back into submission. The dance was exhausting but thrilling, and she'd trained for hours to gain the strength and agility needed to bring the snakes fully to life.

Spectators who had arrived at the theater that night expecting the traditional version of *Salome* had been surprised. In the well-known biblical tale, a beautiful young woman named Salome seduces King Herod with a provocative dance, and he offers to give her anything her heart desires. Salome's mother, who has a grudge against John the Baptist, instructs her daughter to ask Herod for John's head. Herod doesn't really want to kill the Baptist but beheads him anyway, to keep his word, and the gory trophy is presented to Salome on a silver platter.

Back in 1895, Loïe had produced a version of the story where she portrayed Salome as an innocent, dressed all in white and tossed around by the whims of powerful men. At the time, it worked neatly into the ingenue image she was trying to convey. Unfortunately, the critics had hated it. They were disgusted to see La Loïe, the "Fairy of Light," sweating and revealing glimpses of her slightly plump body onstage. Following the debacle, she'd run back to her voluminous costumes.

Since then, the century had turned and she'd changed in more ways than she could count. Reprising the role of Salome took some amount of courage, since at forty-five she would much rather cover herself in veils than remove them, but Loïe was ready to take Salome on for a second time. Having some extra flesh on her bones kept Loïe's skin plump and smooth. She looked a good ten years younger than her actual age, and as far as the public knew, she was somewhere between thirty-eight and forty.

Loïe's modern Salome was no innocent, and she was nobody's puppet. She was a powerful woman, a seductive warrior. Loïe especially loved that in this particular interpretation of the story, John the Baptist was executed for trying to cover Salome's nakedness. She hoped it would send a message to any critics who told her to cover up this time around.

Her critic friend Jules Claretie had attended a rehearsal of the new production and was thrilled to see Loïe rehearsing in everyday modern clothes. Delighted, he watched her dance before Herod in a tailor-made dress with a jacket slung over her shoulders, stage lights blazing off the lenses of her glasses like flames.

He'd described the experience for *Le Temps*:

> The other evening I had, as it were, a vision of a theatre of the future, something of the nature of feministic theatre. Women are more and more taking men's places. They are steadily supplanting the so-called stronger sex. The court-house swarms with women lawyers. The literature of imagination and observation will soon

belong to women of letters. In spite of man's declaration that there shall be no woman doctor for him, the female physician continues to pass her examinations and brilliantly. Just watch and you will see women growing in influence and power; and if, as in Gladstone's phrase, the nineteenth century was the working-man's century, the twentieth will be the women's century.

He went on to describe watching Loïe at work.

I seemed to be watching a wonderful impresaria, manager of her troupe as well as mistress of the audience, giving her directions to the orchestra, to the mechanicians, with an exquisite politeness, smiling in face of the inevitable nerve-racking circumstances, always good-natured and making herself obeyed, as all real leaders do, by giving orders in a tone that sounds like asking a favor.

Claretie gushed about the sets and lighting, including a new projector Loïe had ordered for the occasion to transform the stage into Herod's palace, Mount Nebo, and a Dead Sea that could be filled with breaking waves or as smooth as mother-of-pearl. He wrote:

It is certain that new capacities are developing in theatrical art, and that Miss Loie Fuller will have been responsible for an important contribution…At the Théâtre des Arts, she has installed her footlights, her electric lamps, all this visual fairyland which she has invented and perfected, which has made of her a unique personality, an independent creator, a revolutionist in art.

As usual, Loïe had gone overboard with electric lights, positioning 650 lamps and 15 projectors around the auditorium. She'd forgone traditional physical props and modified an old magic-lantern technique to project scenery and create atmosphere. Magic lanterns, which had been invented by the prominent Dutch scientist Christiaan Huygens in the 1650s, shined light through images painted, printed or photographically reproduced on glass. One of these devices, paired with the right lens and a bright light, allowed an image to be enlarged and projected onto a flat surface.

Back in January, at the cavernous Hippodrome, Loïe had invented a technique that took advantage of the magic lantern, using two parallel screens hung from above the stage. She'd positioned a heavy white cloth behind the stage and a sheet of sheer white gauze near the front, just behind the footlights. Depending on where they were focused, certain images she projected from the magic lanterns moved through the sheer fabric and appeared on the white background, while others illuminated the filmy gauze with different special effects. One hundred twenty dancers had performed with her, between the two curtains, as she danced in six animated tableaux. The projected scenery depicted space, clouds, butterflies, spirits, and a dreamy undersea world. At the end, she'd set the entire stage on fire with red light, and hell's flames devoured the final tableau as she whirled like the devil.

For *Salome*, Loïe was using her new projected effect, but she'd also called on her gift for incorporating popular culture into her work, in the form of a well-known painting called *The Apparition*, by Gustave Moreau. On the famous canvas, Salome stands on a bloody rug in a palace, before Herod's throne. Half-naked, she points at the glowing vision of John the Baptist's gory severed head, which hangs suspended above her, staring down. The artist depicted the rays of light emanating from John's head in an explosive-looking halo shifting from gold to white to transparent, which Loïe thought was the loveliest thing she'd ever seen.

Loïe, it turned out, wasn't alone in her obsession with Salome. The veiled dancer held great fascination for Parisians of the era, who were generally passionate about all things exotic, erotic, and violent. Everyone was familiar with Moreau's lush painting, which was said to have been created under the influence of opium. And that spring, a scandalous version of *Salome*, based on a play written by the Irish playwright Oscar Wilde, had premiered in Paris, sparking a phenomenon known as "Salomania."

The balcony at that evening's performance of *The Tragedy of Salome* was filled with critics and celebrities. The drama, also loosely based on Oscar Wilde's version of the story, had started off with the Dance of Pearls, replete with ropes of luxurious white orbs, symbolizing Salome's chains. For the next dance, Loïe wore a dress consisting of no fewer than 4,500 emerald, teal, and azure peacock feathers. As the scene climaxed, she opened the dress to create an enormous feathered tail, which rose like a giant fan behind her. It took three assistants to help put the sumptuous dress on and take it off, but it was worth it.

Now, pleased with the reaction her serpent dance had just received, Loïe changed into her costume for the Dance of Steel, preparing herself for the pain that would soon shoot through her eyes. She'd become seriously worried lately that she might be going blind, but she was willing to sacrifice anything for a perfect special effect. She waited for the demonic music to begin and swirled onstage into the blinding metallic lights she'd designed specially so that it appeared she was being stabbed with a thousand knives.

When the dance was over, she ran offstage to change again and rubbed her eyes as her assistants helped her put on an elaborate robe covered in gold and silver sequins. They draped her with veils as projected clouds rolled in over the Dead Sea. Herod's palace was bathed in stormy hues by the time Loïe moved onto the stage to dance the Dance of Silver before the king. This dance was her favorite, since it allowed her to combine seductive moves she'd learned years before in burlesque halls with the tricks of lighting and fabric that had made her famous.

The changing light turned her veils to gold and silver, and when Herod stripped away her veil, John the Baptist cried out, throwing a robe over her exposed flesh. Of course, Loïe hadn't actually been naked, but her costume, paired with flashing lights and projections, let the imagination run wild. Afterward, no one could say exactly what they'd seen.

Loïe had attempted to convince M. Lou Van Tel, the actor playing John the Baptist, to have an electric arrangement placed in his hair so he'd have a halo like the one in the painting. She thought it would be incredibly dramatic to turn it on at particular moments, but when Lou saw the apparatus he refused in no uncertain terms to put it on. Angry at first, she'd eventually laughed and relented when he told her that while he would stand for being decapitated, he would not stand for being electrocuted.

A tempest of light and sound exploded in the theater and Loïe danced on, illuminated by flashes of lightning. John was carried off at the king's command to face his fate as Loïe panted with fatigue. The most dramatic part of the show was about to arrive. The Dead Sea churned, the sky turned black, and the orchestra brought the music to a feverish, discordant roar.

When John the Baptist's severed head was presented to her on a silver platter, Loïe picked it up, staring at it as though she didn't believe it was real. She studied her trophy and danced with it for a few eerie moments before slowing and standing still as the horror of what she held in her hands overtook her. Loïe put the head's mouth to her ear and feigned terror, as if it were whispering to her. She stretched her eyes as large and round as she could, despite the fact that they still ached from the flashing spotlights, and dramatically flung the gory trophy into the waters of the Dead Sea. At that instant, the lights bathed the water blood red and cymbals crashed.

It was glorious.

As the storm roared around her, Loïe looked up to where an image of the severed head had appeared, projected on a special screen above her. She reenacted Moreau's famous painting by pointing at the head accusingly. The script had at first suggested having the head reappear and disappear, but she'd wanted to embed the image from Moreau's painting in the minds of her audience. Finally, she looked away and spun into the violent, powerful Dance of Fear, throwing every last ounce of her energy into the performance.

When the ovations finally ended, Loïe stumbled back to her dressing room. Once they'd dimmed the lights and she had ice on her shoulders, she shooed her assistants away, hoping to rest for a few moments before her friends arrived. Gab, she knew, would be waiting for her at home. A crowded dressing room was her dear girl's least favorite place to be.

No matter what the critics said, Loïe was thrilled with the performance. The new effects she'd created for the show had done exactly what she'd hoped, making the audience scream in terror and gasp with delight.

A knock on the dressing room door made her jump. Water from the ice was dripping down her back. She dropped the ice in a basin on the floor, dried off, and adjusted her dress. Donning her most winning smile, she put on her spectacles, stood up from the couch, and moved to the door to receive her visitors.

Scene VI

Hiking with Einstein

1913

A lbert stopped suddenly and seized Marie's arm.

"You understand, what I need to know is exactly what happens to the passengers in an elevator when it falls into emptiness!"

Gales of laughter erupted from Irène and Ève, walking just in front of them. Marie's girls found his random outbursts hilarious. They also thought it was very funny that when the physicist was deep in thought or conversation, he'd walk along the edge of deep precipices without even noticing until Marie grabbed his arm and pulled him away.

She paused to consider the statement.

"I'm not sure what happens mathematically, but I know how it feels to fall into emptiness," she said.

Even after seven years, Marie couldn't speak Pierre's name without choking on the syllables. After moving to Sceaux with the girls and Pierre's father the summer after he died, Marie had pulled her girls from school and organized an educational cooperative with some of her friends, including the Perrins, the Langevins, and other academics. Much like her father, Irène learned more slowly than a traditional education allowed, and Marie knew that she'd thrive in a more relaxed environment. In the cooperative, one professor taught the children languages and another sculpture, while a professor from the Pasteur Institute led biology lessons, Paul Langevin taught mathematics, and Jean Perrin lectured on physics.

Marie had taken charge of chemistry lessons and hands-on experiments. During the two years her daughters had been in the cooperative, she'd enjoyed doing simple projects with the students, like making siphons and showing them how one could add salt to water in order to increase the density enough to float an egg. Physical education was emphasized as well, and every day they hiked, bicycled, swam, participated in gymnastics. Now they were back in traditional schools, but Marie still made sure that Irène and Ève got plenty of exercise.

Tucking her thumbs under the straps on her knapsack, she moved up the path behind them, pleased to see that they looked marvelously strong. As her own health had deteriorated over the last few years, she'd remained as fixated on theirs as she'd been when they were babies. At sixteen, Irène was now taller than Marie. Her sun-lightened hair was hidden under her hiking hat. Beneath the brim, her green eyes flashed with independence and insolence, making her look much more like Marie than Ève did. The dark-haired baby of the family, who had lost her father so young, sometimes felt like a stranger to Marie. Even at the tender age of eight, Ève's features hinted at the beauty she would become.

Edelweiss blanketed the slope beside them, so brilliant under the intense mountain sun that it made Marie squint. Albert followed a few steps behind, consumed by his efforts to work out a theory explaining how gravity, time, and space were related. He liked to talk about his ideas with Marie, who spoke the language of mathematics as well as he did. For her part, she enjoyed the long silences between their discussions almost as much as the conversations themselves. He was a good friend.

Marie met Albert Einstein at the Solvay Conference of 1911 in Brussels, which brought together what the organizers considered to be the greatest thinkers in physics to discuss their findings and theories. Among the twenty-one scientists were some of the most innovative minds of the early twentieth century, including Marie, Albert, Max Planck, Ernest Rutherford, and her close friends Jean Perrin and Paul Langevin.

Although Marie hadn't presented a paper, she'd been an integral part of the scientific discussions on blackbody radiation, quantum theory, the photoelectric effect, and general relativity. She and Rutherford argued about the radium standard she was making at her laboratory in Paris. During their free time, Albert joined the French scientists Marie, Paul, and Jean to socialize. The German-born Swiss scientist had been delighted with their company and later told his friends how impressed he'd been with Marie's intelligence and passion for physics.

Just as the conference was ending, Marie received a telegram containing the shocking news that she'd been awarded a second Nobel Prize. It was earth-shattering. Not only was she the first person to win two Nobel Prizes, she was the first to win them in two different categories. While the medal for her work on radioactivity had been in the discipline of physics, this prize would be for chemistry, specifically her work using chemical techniques to isolate and characterize radium and polonium.

She hadn't known whether to laugh or cry. Since Pierre died, professional jealousy followed her wherever she went. In recent years, the famous old scientist Lord Kelvin had claimed that radium was not an element at all, prompting her to produce even more precise measurements of its atomic mass. Leaving no more room for doubt, Marie had finally achieved her goal of isolating pure radium metal, which shined white for barely the blink of an eye before turning dark from exposure to air. She and Pierre had wondered about pure radium's hue for so long. She only wished he had been there to see it with his own eyes. Several scientists, including Rutherford, envied that she had been the one to publish a two-volume treatise on radioactivity, a monumental task, which Marie had completed in 1910 to establish her expertise on the subject.

Just ten months before the Solvay Conference, she'd been rejected by the French Academy on the sole basis of her sex. Women weren't even allowed to enter the building where the academy voted. The whole affair prompted an uproar in the press. Besides being embarrassing for her, the rejection had done more insidious damage, making it more difficult to publish at the academy and excluding her from the important discussions in the male-only sanctum.

Before Marie had a single quiet moment to let the good news about the Nobel sink in, disaster struck. A second telegram arrived, taking with it every ounce of joy from her body. Her hands shook as she read the small black typeface. It was a nightmare.

It seemed that an article titled "A Story of Love: Madame Curie and Professor Langevin" had just been published in *Le Journal* for all of France to read. Largely fabricated by Paul Langevin's wife Jeanne and his mother-in-law, it stated that the famous widow Marie Curie had run off to a love nest with Paul. Though the details were false, the premise was not. Marie's affair with Paul Langevin had just been made public.

In a panic, she immediately responded with a telegram to another paper, *Le Temps*, stating that the story was "pure folly," and colleagues confirmed that she was in Brussels for a scientific meeting. The next day, *Le Temps* contained an article concluding that *Le Journal*'s article was filled with falsehoods, but the fire had been lit, and the public was ravenous for more details, especially when they learned that Paul had been at the same meeting as Marie in Brussels.

The conservative, anti-Semitic paper *Le Petit Journal*, whose editor was Jeanne Langevin's ally and brother-in-law, ran a front-page story titled A ROMANCE IN A LABORATORY: THE AFFAIR OF MME. CURIE AND M. LANGEVIN. The article, besides noting Marie's "masculine" pursuits of books, laboratory, and glory, contained a wordy interview with Jeanne, which ended with the reporter's claim that, "While this poor and unhappy woman whose heart is ravaged by undeserved misfortune was thus expressing herself, her smallest little girl, an adorable baby, was pressing close against her and stammering, 'Don't cry, *maman*, *petit père* will come back.'"

By then, Marie was back in France and had consulted with her lawyer. She wrote a letter to *Le Temps*, which was printed on the same day as a retraction by the author of the original article in *Le Journal*. Her correspondence, while not explicitly denying the affair or apologizing for it, refuted *Le Petit Journal*'s version of events and threatened lawsuits against anyone publishing "writings attributed" to her or inflammatory allegations against her.

The letter began by saying, "I consider abominable the entire intrusion of the press and the public into private life. This intrusion is particularly criminal when it involves people who have manifestly consecrated their life to preoccupations of an elevated order and general utility."

Albert Einstein had been one of the first to offer his support to Marie, writing:

My very dear Madame Curie,

Do not laugh at me if I have nothing interesting to tell you, but I am so furious at the way the scoundrels dare to react against you in this way that I must give free rein to my feelings. I am nevertheless convinced that you despise these scoundrels, whether they show feigned reverence towards you or seek to satisfy their thirst for strong emotions. I need to tell you how I've come to admire you for your wit, your energy, your honesty. I consider myself lucky to have personally met you in Brussels. I will always be grateful to have among us people such as you—as well as Langevin—genuine human beings among us, with the company of whom we can rejoice. If the rabble continues to look down at you, no longer read these rags. Leave them to the vipers they were created for. I send you, as well as Langevin and Perrin, my warmest regards.

A. Einstein

The vipers, however, were hard for Marie to ignore. Over the next several months, the press speculated endlessly on Mme. Langevin's accusations.

Eventually, they published private letters from Marie, which Paul's wife had stolen to use as ammunition, and her life fell apart for a second time. Celebrity made Marie a perfect target. Everyone knew what she looked like, where she worked, and even where she lived, and the attacks were vicious. The same people who had once adored Marie and crowned her a "national glory" now called her a foreigner, a Russian, a German, or a Jew, pointing out gleefully that her middle name was "Salome." Those who correctly identified her as a Pole spat the word out with contempt, labeling her a Polish temptress.

The far right in France used the story as an excuse to stir up anti-Semitic, anti-immigrant, and anti-woman sentiment in the country. Since the Franco-Prussian war in 1870, the entire country cowered at the mere mention of invasion, and hateful rhetoric crushed logical argument. Although it was 1911 and that war was far behind them, nationalism had been gathering strength and reared its ugly head when the writer Gustave Téry published Marie's letters to Paul in his newspaper *L'Oeuvre*. He claimed that the Curie-Langevin story demonstrated that France was "in the grip of the bunch of dirty foreigners who pillage it, soil it and dishonor it."

It was hypocrisy at its worst. While the government had been using pro-family propaganda in an attempt to increase the birth rate, extramarital affairs among the French were as prevalent as ever. Although adultery was publicly discouraged, upper-class men were allowed to keep mistresses and still remain upstanding members of society. It was different for women, who risked social annihilation and possibly prison if they strayed outside society's norms.

Théodore Joran, an antifeminist, nationalist French writer, stated in 1905 that "Feminism, like Socialism, is an anti-French malady!" He went on to say, "I object to feminism because it allows women to envisage happiness as independent of love and external to love…In reality, if not in law…good households are those where the man considers the woman as an object made for his own personal pleasure and well-being and where the woman believes she ought to please her husband, to serve him, and applies herself exclusively to that end."

Unsurprisingly, the press quickly forgave Paul for straying from his marriage bed, but they continued to call Marie a homewrecker and accused her of leading him astray. Her very existence was perceived as a threat to wives everywhere. The scandal was also an excuse for social conservatives to reassert the claim that a woman's place was in the home and not in the "unnatural" habitat of a laboratory.

Marie's actions had very publicly shattered the Napoleonic Code, which held women so firmly under the feet of men. Besides being an immigrant and threatening the ability of Paul's French wife to bear more legitimate heirs for her husband, it was clear that Marie's occupation gave her as much satisfaction as any marriage ever could. Continuing to succeed in a job she loved, without her husband at her side, was perhaps Marie's most egregious sin.

The affair had begun in July of 1910, soon after Marie learned that Paul's wife had broken a bottle over his head during an argument. Friends and neighbors would testify to the fact that Jeanne Langevin had been physically and emotionally abusive to Paul since the beginning of their marriage. Looking through her husband's belongings was nothing new to Jeanne. Early on in their relationship, she'd rifled through Paul's pockets and stolen letters in which his mother voiced concern about the choice he'd made in a wife. She'd saved them as ammunition to use against Paul, should he ever try to divorce her. Fights between the couple were frequent and violent, and some days Paul would arrive at the laboratory covered in bruises.

While Paul and his wife were the worst of enemies, Paul and Marie had become the best of friends. For years, Langevin had been close to the Curies, but following the death of Pierre, who was so dear to both of them, their emotional bond strengthened. They taught together, homeschooled their children together, and worked together. In the summer of 1910, four years after Pierre died, they'd taken their relationship from the laboratory to the bedroom, and Marie fell in love again.

The Perrins had been shocked one evening when Marie showed up for a casual dinner party wearing a white dress with a pink rose pinned to the waist. No one could figure out what had inspired Marie to finally peel off her black mourning attire, and she could see them whispering to one another when they thought she wasn't looking. They weren't aware that she was daring to dream of a life shared with Paul.

She could once again imagine an existence where physical and intellectual desires mingled together. For a brief time, when their relationship began, she'd emerged from the darkness to become herself again. The light came back into her eyes and feeling returned to her limbs. Marie and Paul had rented an apartment together, where they could escape the world and dream about the future.

When everything came crashing down, her hopes for that future disappeared. To Marie, the loss of a future with Paul was far worse than the name-calling, the death threats from Jeanne, the stones hurled at her house, and the mobs of angry neighbors. The familiar physical and emotional numbness returned, and she resigned her body to exist solely as a vehicle for her mind.

Her friends tried to help when Jeanne Langevin used Marie's letters to Paul to blackmail the scientists. When excerpts from the letters were published in *L'Oeuvre*, a mob gathered outside her house in Sceaux, shouting "Down with the foreigner, the husband-stealer!" Marie's close friend Marguerite Borel and the chemist André Debierne rushed to rescue Marie and Ève, guiding them through the angry crowd. Marguerite and her husband Émile took Marie and Ève into their home, while Irène went to stay with the Perrins, who had a daughter close to her age. Call after call came to the Borel household, with friends and colleagues denouncing Marie, only to have Marguerite inform them that Marie was indeed staying with them and that they were supporting her.

This arrangement angered Marguerite's father, Paul Appell, who was the dean of the Faculty of Sciences at the Sorbonne and Marie's former professor. He had little sympathy for her plight. Gustave Téry, who had published Marie's letters in *L'Oeuvre*, was attempting to discredit the Sorbonne, calling it the "German-Jewish Sorbonne," and the university was under pressure from the nationalists to fire Marie. When Appell told Marguerite the Council of Ministers was planning to ask Marie to leave France, she stood up to her father, swearing that if he "yielded to that idiotic nationalist movement," he would never see her again. Appell, in response, threw a shoe across the room but agreed to hold off from taking such dramatic action against the scientist he'd once taught and respected. Thanks in large part to Marguerite Borel, Henriette Perrin, and other allies who defended Marie and brought people to their senses, she kept her position at the Sorbonne.

As much as Marie missed Pierre's father, Eugène, she was relieved that his death in 1910 had spared him the pain of watching this attack on their family. Pierre's brother Jacques defended her fiercely, and her own brother and sisters arrived to help, but Marie's depression deepened with each passing day. With a horrible pain in her abdomen that made it feel like her own body had turned against her, Marie took up residence with her girls in an apartment on the Ile St-Louis in Paris.

Even as the scandal raged and Marie was hunted like Frankenstein's monster, hundreds of letters of support arrived, some of them from male colleagues. Her friend Loïe Fuller had written, "I love you. I take your two hands in mine and I love you. Pay no attention to the lies. C'est la vie." Another friend, the scientist Hertha Ayrton, wrote letter after letter as well, praising her Nobel accomplishment, criticizing her detractors, and reminding her that she'd promised to bring her girls to the seaside for a visit that summer.

Despite her depression and failing health, there was one battle that Marie refused to lose. A group of male scientists were collectively trying to keep her away from Stockholm, but she was determined to collect her Nobel Prize. Paul Langevin made things worse by staging a pistol duel against Gustave Téry after the journalist published her letters in *L'Oeuvre* and wrote, "The truth is that, deliberately, methodically, scientifically, Mme. Curie has applied herself, through the most perfidious advice, through the most vile suggestion, to detach Paul Langevin from his wife and to separate his wife from her children." He called Marie "this foreign woman, who pushes a hesitant father of a family to destroy his home" and continued, "From above, she disposes of these poor people: of the husband, of the wife, of the children."

In the end, no shots were fired, but Marie's reputation was further damaged. The chemist Svante Arrhenius, who had been an advocate for giving her the Nobel and had initially reassured her that the ceremony would go on as planned, turned on her, writing, "A letter attributed to you has been published in a French newspaper and copies have circulated here," and the new situation had been "considerably aggravated by the ridiculous duel of M. Langevin." He went on to disinvite her from the Nobel ceremony, saying, "All my colleagues have told me that it is preferable you not come here on December 10," and begging her to stay in France and instead write them an official letter stating that she would only accept the prize once it had been proved that she and Paul didn't have an affair.

The sick feeling Marie got when she read Arrhenius's letter quickly galvanized into anger. She sent a telegram announcing that she'd be in Stockholm for the ceremonies and replied to Arrhenius by mail, writing, "The action which you advise would appear to be a grave error on my part. In fact, the prize has been awarded for the discovery of Radium and Polonium. I believe that there is no connection between my scientific work and the facts of my private life…I am convinced that this opinion is shared by many people. I am very saddened that you are not yourself of this opinion."

Her sister Bronya and Irène traveled to Stockholm with her and accompanied her to the awards ceremony. In her speech, Marie carefully cemented her discovery into the walls of history, reminding the attendees that "isolating radium as a pure salt was undertaken by me alone." She also noted the importance of her discovery of radioactivity, as it created a method in which new radioactive elements could be discovered. She spoke lovingly of her work that week, noting in one speech that "radioactivity is a young science. It is a child that I saw being born and I have contributed to raising with all my strength. The child has grown; it has become beautiful."

Marie returned to Paris and on December 29, nineteen days after collecting her Nobel medal and two months after the Solvay Conference in Brussels, she collapsed. At the hospital, she was diagnosed with a severe kidney infection exacerbated by old lesions on her ureter and kidneys. Tuberculosis was never mentioned in the report, but her doctors suspected that the disease she dreaded had been lurking in her body for years and was taking advantage of her weakened condition to attack her internal organs.

Severe depression was making her even sicker, and she swiftly lost twenty pounds. Her physician had hoped to avoid surgery, but in March they were forced to remove some of the lesions on her kidneys. Her pain and her depression were so intense that Marie longed for death. She made all of the proper arrangements, giving as much time and attention to the destiny of her radium samples as she did to the futures of her children, should she die.

After an unsuccessful stint in the Alps for her health, she decided to take Hertha Ayrton up on her invitation to visit her in England. Marie and Hertha had discovered how much they had in common when they first met in England in 1903. Both had been rejected by the academies of science, Marie for being a woman and Hertha for being a "married woman." Like Marie, Hertha was married to a man who was extremely supportive of her research. The British scientist studied ripple patterns in sand and water, and famously figured out that electric arc lamps hissed and flickered as the result of oxygen coming into contact with the electric rods. Unlike Marie, she was a political activist, fighting for the women's vote and for Irish independence.

Irène and Ève had been staying with a governess in France and were thrilled to join their mother in England at the old Chewton Mill House at Highcliffe-on-Sea in Dorset. Fortified by the crashing waves and changing tides, Marie allowed herself to be tended by Hertha, who had played nurse to many half-starved-to-death suffragettes in recent years.

The British scientist had two daughters who were slightly older than Marie's. One was a young suffragette who had spent time in jail for her cause. Ève and Irène loved hearing her stories. Marie didn't improve much physically but she was emotionally fortified by spending time with her friend, who urged her to get back to the lab as quickly as possible, reminding her that science would always be there, "grand and calm."

Although she'd accomplished almost nothing in the two years since she fell ill, Marie jumped right back into her work. By February of 1913, she was back in Paris and healthy enough to carry the radium standard she'd prepared, containing twenty-one milligrams of pure radium sealed in a glass ampoule, to the Bureau of Weights and Measures in Sèvres. Her radium now served as the world's standard, and the unit of radioactivity was called a "curie" after Pierre, per Marie's wishes.

"Albert! Which peak is that?" Marie stopped and pointed to a white-capped mountain on their right. The trail had been climbing up and up, and it felt like they were walking along the top of the world.

"Just because I'm Swiss doesn't mean that I know the name of every mountain in Switzerland," Einstein said.

They'd planned the trip that spring, when Albert and his wife, Mileva, were last in Paris. Mileva was a mathematician and physicist too, working with Albert on relativity, although Marie hadn't seen her name on any of his papers. The two of them had a wonderful time visiting Marie, and Albert had insisted that since she was feeling better, she must bring the girls to hike with him and his son Hans in the Alps.

Brilliant and very quiet, Mileva suffered from a limp and hadn't been able to join them on the trip. Instead, the British governess who had helped Marie with the girls in England came along. Albert's son Hans was the same age as Ève, and Marie thought he looked adorable in his hiking suspenders.

Rucksacks on their backs and walking sticks in hand, they'd set out to explore the beautiful alpine landscape of Engadine in the Swiss Alps. They hopped their way across a boulder field, and Marie and Albert rested on a warm slab of white granite. The alpine meadow where they sat was dotted with primroses, buttercups, and bellflowers. Irène, Ève, and Hans played nearby, dropping petals into a stream.

"I still can't believe that they tried to take your Nobel Prize away," Albert said, out of the blue.

"It was mostly Arrhenius," Marie said. "He told me that the academy wouldn't have given me the prize if they'd known about Paul."

"Svante Arrhenius is a good scientist, but he's a horse's ass," Albert replied.

"The amazing thing is that, before all of this, I considered him a friend," Marie said.

"Two things are infinite," he replied, "the universe and human stupidity; and I'm not sure about the universe."

Marie laughed, feeling like herself again. She was ready to climb the next mountain that came her way.

Act IV

Molded in the middle of ardent embers, Loïe Fuller
does not burn;
She filters and oozes light
She herself is the flame...
Erect in glowing coals, she smiles.

—Jean Lorrain on Loïe Fuller

Scene I

Sun Dance

1914

When the elevator jerked and the ground fell away, Loïe couldn't help but grab on to a handrail to steady herself. She was tired of worrying about the earth collapsing under her feet. In recent weeks, cavities in the rain-soaked streets of Paris had caved into ancient stone quarries that lay hidden underground. Paris, it seemed, was no longer steady ground.

Despite being reinforced with pillars, the catacombs and sewers beneath the city had been undermined by the great flood of 1910. Following a brief but heavy thunderstorm a few weeks earlier, twenty people had died when several busy streets developed large sinkholes. In one particularly horrifying incident, Parisians taking refuge from the deluge under a café awning fell screaming into a subterranean cavern as the sidewalk and street collapsed beneath them.

Luckily, the weather had cleared up just in time for the Sun Festival. For the past ten years, the French Astronomical Society had celebrated the longest day of the year by holding a fête at the top of the Eiffel Tower, and this year it fell on a perfect summer day. Loïe wished Gab was by her side, but when Flammarion told her there would be over two hundred people at the Sun Festival, she knew it was hopeless. After over ten years together, Loïe was well aware that her companion had no interest in trailing her while she chatted with every interesting person she encountered. Gab had, however, agreed to accompany Loïe's dance pupils—the "muses"—after dark to the Eiffel Tower, where they would dance with Loïe.

"I'll use the extra daylight to catch up on paying all of your bills," she'd joked, but Loïe knew that she'd probably spend the evening curled up like a cat, reading a book or writing letters until she brought Loïe's pupils to the performance.

When Loïe's mother had died of pneumonia in 1908, Loïe had been completely broken by the loss. In the weeks preceding her mother's passing, Loïe had nursed the elderly woman as well as she could, holding vigil at a table next to her bed while she penned the last few chapters of her memoir, which was already a month overdue. Aware of Loïe's weak lungs, doctors had warned her away from the sickbed, but she ignored them. An important chapter of Loïe's life ended when Delilah Fuller's frail body finally succumbed to the infection that cold February, just one day after Loïe completed her manuscript.

Loïe didn't know how she would have gotten through her grief without Gab. They'd briefly considered living together now that Loïe's mother was gone, and Gab had located a few possible apartments that she thought might work. One had two heated bathrooms, a bedroom and a sitting room with a divan, which Gab had offered to sleep on, should they take the place, so that Loïe could have the bedroom to herself. The other was a funny little apartment in Montmartre with a garden and electricity, but no steam heat. Loïe couldn't seem to commit to either of them, and the plan had fallen through. As usual, Gab, who was intimately familiar with Loïe's finances, had been practical about money while Loïe preferred to dream bigger.

They didn't speak for a week after the whole fiasco, but soon they were back together. Loïe promised that one day they'd find a situation they could both agree on. The idea of living together went back to that tour eight years before, when they'd been scribbling postcards to each other from different rooms in the same hotel. The notes had been mostly silly, but on one card that Gab had kept, Loïe had written "Souvenir of our visit here dear Gab, when we were wanderers in glory over the face of the earth and restless for quiet, peace and a home, with the time ours to stay in it, my life friend dear Gab," and signed it "Thy Loïe."

After their failed apartment search, Loïe had ended up moving into the luxurious new Plaza-Athénée hotel, while Gab rented a more modest flat across the river near Notre-Dame. Despite separate abodes, they remained tightly tethered. Loïe knew that she wasn't easy to live with. She traveled constantly, and when she *was* in Paris, Gab tired of listening to her go on about new ideas that far exceeded her budget. Loïe was, however, completely dependent on Gab. She couldn't risk losing the woman who so faithfully tended both her art and her soul, and she had given up arguing when Gab chose to stay home rather than joining her at social events.

She wasn't worried about being lonely at the solstice celebration. She knew several fellow members of the astronomical society, and Camille Flammarion would make sure she had someone interesting to talk to. Loïe had heard that the famous composer Camille Saint-Saëns would be there that night. A musical prodigy, he'd made his stage debut on the piano at the age of ten and was admitted to the Paris Conservatory when he was only thirteen. Saint-Saëns wrote songs, operas, and symphonies and by 1880 was considered the most famous composer in France. Loïe didn't often dance to his music, preferring the impressionist compositions of his rival Debussy, but she was determined to meet him and had worked one of his compositions into her performance that evening.

Through the metal bars of the elevator, she watched some of the astronomers taking the stairs, as was apparently tradition. Fortunately, M. Eiffel had an employee running the elevator for those who couldn't easily make the ascent on foot. Climbing 1,665 steps was a challenge for anyone, and doing it in a dress and heeled shoes was far more than Loïe wanted to take on. Following the initial jolt, the elevator rose smoothly to the second level, and Loïe recalled Sylvie Flammarion's description of how it felt to float upward in a hot air balloon. She closed her eyes for a few seconds to take in the sensation.

Loïe wasn't afraid of heights, but the ascent was dizzying. A lattice of steel girders dropped on every side as they rose. The buildings that had littered the landscape when she'd made the ascent at the Paris Exposition were mostly gone. Only the Grand Palais, the Petit Palais, and the Pont Alexandre III remained. She thought fondly of her little theater there and wished she could have somehow preserved it, as Rodin saved his pavilion. Maybe it was better, though. There was no need to dwell on the past when the future held so many new adventures.

Loïe stepped off the elevator and moved to the railing to look out over the city. There was a faint breeze on the platform and the air felt lovely. In the rich light of the late-day sun, Paris took on a magical veneer. Distance and altitude erased the grimy grays, and in the golden light the hill of Montmartre looked like an ancient ruin. She couldn't have asked for a more perfect setting for her new dance.

After dancing solo for so many years, Loïe had started incorporating other dancers into her productions. She'd included separate acts like Isadora Duncan in her tours before, but more recently she had dancers sharing her stage. Currently, she had a full-fledged dancing troupe consisting of girls and young women who ranged from age five to twenty-nine. Loïe referred to them as her muses, but they were, in fact, her students, and many Parisians called them "Little Loïes." Mostly British, the girls were all blondish, blue-eyed copies of her younger self. The muses wore filmy white gowns, danced barefoot, and provided her with endless inspiration, as well as fit bodies to perform dances that were becoming more and more difficult for her to undertake herself.

The dancing school, which Loïe had officially established around 1908, allowed her to preach a gospel of natural inspirational and spontaneous movement, teaching her disciples to listen to their instincts and respond physically to music. Whether they chose to leap like fawns, hop like frogs, pretend to chase butterflies, or dance using only their hands, she treasured the beauty of the spontaneous gestures and incorporated them into her dances.

Some critics accused her of imitating Isadora, who had started a school for dancers around the same time. Loïe only laughed, saying that while Isadora's dancers took their inspiration from the figures on old vases, her own girls were originals rather than imitators. Her students danced, Loïe said, with the movements that had originally inspired the art on ancient vases.

Gab managed the details for Loïe's school, and a large part of her job involved communicating with anxious parents as their young daughters traveled across the globe. Loïe and her troupe had recently returned from a tour to Greece and Egypt, where they'd visited the pyramids. It had been a spiritual experience. Wrapped in white, like an ancient queen come back to life, she had posed with her dancers before the noble stone sphinx for publicity photographs, hot sand burning their bare feet. Standing near the magnificent, sand-chewed creature, Loïe felt as though they'd traveled back in time. In one photo, her muses stood behind her in a circle with their hands clasped and raised toward the heavens. In another, she mirrored the silhouette of the sphinx, standing in front of the ancient stone creature with the girls bowed before her. The emotion she felt that day had inspired the new "Egyptian Sun Dance," which Loïe would perform that evening for the assembled astronomers and artists.

As they'd prepared for the tour in Egypt, Loïe and her troupe rehearsed by staging private performances for friends and financiers. They danced on the lawn at the Flammarions' château in Juvisy, in the moonlight at the Bois de Boulogne estate of a wealthy American named Mrs. T. Alexander Clarke, in Rodin's garden in Meudon, and at the country home of a Russian prince named Paul Troubetzkoy. Loïe adored Prince Troubetzkoy, who kept pet wolves and believed in sleeping outdoors in order to absorb the "radium-effluvia" of the earth. Over the last few years, Loïe and her students had experienced an equal number of successes and failures, but fate had smiled on them recently. They had tours lined up across Europe in 1914 and 1915, and the future looked bright.

Today, Loïe felt young again. Her lungs were clear, the sun was shining, and she was positively bursting with energy. Gab had commented that morning that the only time she saw Loïe so cheerful was on the days she spent time with her scientist friends, and Loïe agreed that she was probably right. But this evening was especially exciting. In addition to performing, Loïe was a member of the French Astronomical Society. She'd been part of the group for some time but had never been to one of their famous Sun Festivals.

In 1904, Camille Flammarion had presented the idea of a sun festival to M. Gustave Eiffel, who had designed and built the monument he named after himself. Flammarion envisioned inviting a group of scientists and artists and their wives to observe the longest day of the year, the summer solstice, from the heights of the Eiffel Tower. M. Eiffel, a new member of the Astronomical Society, loved the idea and offered to host a dinner for the founding astronomers, performers, and spouses, along with a buffet for the other attendees.

It had been an enormous success. After the dinner, nearly 250 people climbed to the highest platform of the tower to watch the sun set. Almost half of them stayed there until it rose again the next morning. Flammarion and Eiffel decided to hold the festival every year from then on.

Tonight would be the tenth anniversary of the Sun Festival and in March, Paris had celebrated the twenty-fifth anniversary of the Eiffel Tower. Astronomical Society members and performing artists would dine in a new space Eiffel had just opened. Loïe heard voices and noticed that a few individuals had already arrived via the stairs, looking exhausted. Below her, the golden dome of Les Invalides gleamed like a jewel, and the Champ de Mars stretched out like a carpet of verdant tennis courts.

"Bonsoir, Loïe! I am so happy that you can join us for this great event!"

Loïe turned to find Flammarion standing beside her. He wore a flamboyant summer jacket and his hair, magnificent as ever, had a thousand strands of silver running through it.

"Dear Camille!" she said, grasping his hands. "It's absolutely glorious up here!"

They moved around the railing together until he stopped and pointed up at the tower's highest platform.

"That is where you will dance," he said. "Your men have already set up your lights, and your gown has been placed in Monsieur Eiffel's office."

Camille excused himself to greet the next group who had arrived in the elevator, and Loïe moved into the crowd that had assembled to watch the sunset, hoping to run into M. Saint-Saëns. She didn't succeed in finding the composer but bumped into several friends. Everyone jumped when celebratory cannons went off at the official moment of sunset, and as dusk fell, everyone moved into the new banquet hall for supper, which was followed by several fascinating lectures.

The journal *Astronomy* later described the event. "The guests crowd. Flammarion talks to Eiffel...Camille Saint-Saëns seems to be inspired by a new melody, Haraucourt designs a new poem, Jean Finot celebrates optimism, and Séverine finds better humanity, while at the same time taking their places at the head table."

When they'd eaten, the astronomer Count Aymar de la Baume Pluvinel toasted M. Eiffel, and Camille Flammarion gave a speech titled "Le Soleil." The famous astronomer spoke about the sun's significance for world religions, new scientific discoveries, and his own research. Speaking about magnetism and the sun's powerful influence on the Earth, he reminded the crowd that in September of 1909 he'd correctly "accused the sun of being the author of the cessation of telephone and telegraph communications as the result of a solar storm" whose violent eruptions he'd photographed at his Juvisy observatory. He concluded the speech dramatically by stating that "The fiery surface of the celestial body of the day is a fantastic and unspeakable pandemonium...By coming here, once a year, on the day of the summer solstice, celebrating the sun, we pay homage to the powerful rector of all terrestrial life, to the marvelous star on whose rays all our existence is suspended and which holds in its glory the future destiny of our entire planet. He is the first saint of the natural calendar; he is the god sung by mythologies of all centuries; he is Phoebus-Apollo governing the symphonies of the worlds."

Following Flammarion's speech, the microbiologist and cinematographer Dr. Jean Comandon described how he'd attached a micrograph to a microscope to make movies of objects invisible to the human eye. He'd had the ingenious idea while trying to photograph a bacterium that caused syphilis, and everyone in the room was fascinated by the images he projected. To illustrate his lecture, he projected a remarkable film of red blood cells, microbes, and a roundworm egg, which doubled and multiplied into a cluster of cells before their eyes. Loïe barely heard Comandon's closing remarks. Caught up in her imagination, she envisioned how the strange, quivering objects would look projected on a screen behind one of her dances.

The crowd moved outside and Loïe was first in line for the elevator to the highest platform, where the artistic portion of the program would take place. At the top, Camille and Sylvie Flammarion joined her at the railing, along with the famous Gustave Eiffel.

Camille introduced her to the tower's illustrious architect, telling Loïe that Eiffel had done great studies in meteorology and other sciences from the top of his tower.

"Can you see the four lightning rods on the tower above us?" Eiffel asked Loïe and Sylvie. "And those antennae are for wireless telegraphy."

He pointed up at six parallel metal bars jutting out above them, explaining that in 1898, a wireless transmitter had been assembled on top of the tower. As scientists worked out the technology, the device could send telegrams across the channel to England, and then eventually much farther, to ships and even to America. By 1914, the wireless transmitter was sending out signals twice a day, broadcasting the exact time, which allowed ships to accurately calculate their longitudes, or east-west positions.

Upon its completion in 1889 for the Universal Exposition, the Eiffel Tower was the tallest monument in the world, and in 1890, Gustave Eiffel had signed a contract to operate it for twenty years. The tower was a popular attraction at the 1900 Exposition, but many Parisians considered it an eyesore and were anxious to see it go, so it was scheduled for demolition on December 31, 1909. Luckily for the tower, since the day it opened, scientists had been taking advantage of the enormous opportunity afforded by such a tall structure.

Eiffel pleaded with city officials and specified a new purpose for the tower, which was a perfect place to make meteorological and astronomical observations, conduct physics experiments, and locate optical telegraph and communications equipment, stating: "It will be for everyone an observatory and a laboratory, the likes of which has never before been available to science." The city granted the Eiffel Tower another seventy years of existence.

"There is more meteorological equipment above the lights, at the top, which we can't see very well from here," Eiffel told Loïe.

He'd built a weather station on the third platform when the tower first opened. Since that day, scientists had performed innumerable experiments from the tower. Physicists raced objects down cables running from the top floors to the ground below in order to measure air resistance, and hung an enormous Foucault pendulum from the tower. A mercury-filled U-shaped tube called a manometer, which was an enormous pressure gauge, stretched from the top of the tower to the ground. In 1909, the French army established a permanent radio station on the tower, and Eiffel had set up wind tunnels at the base of the tower to allow the testing of airflow over airplane wings and propellers.

"A few years ago," Flammarion added, "a German physicist named Theodor Wulf used an electrometer to measure levels of radiation at the top of the tower versus levels at the base and discovered that there may be a source of radiation other than the earth."

"Madame Curie would find that so interesting!" Loïe exclaimed.

She hadn't seen Marie in some time. Lately, the scientist always seemed to be out of town when Loïe was in Paris, and the other way around. She often thought of her, though. Radium was still all the rage in Paris and around the world, and tiny amounts of it had become available to the public, for a price.

Loïe had a grain of her own radium salt now, embedded in one end of a small brass spinthariscope. The other end of the tube held a viewing lens, and between the lens and the radium was a screen coated with zinc sulfide, which produced tiny flashes of light whenever it was struck by a radioactive particle. One could even dial the radium closer to the screen to make the flashes more frequent, and when Loïe had recently carried one of the viewing tubes to New York, it felt as if she'd tucked a little piece of Marie into her bag.

"I recently took a spinthariscope to America, you know," Loïe blurted out, launching into a story about how she'd shown it off to the American reporters the moment her ship arrived. Although she hadn't gotten the science exactly right, they'd been impressed. One newspaper article went so far as to claim that Loïe was a "scientist of ability."

Flammarion nodded. "Ah yes. Very interesting device. Are you sure that it's altogether safe to carry in your bag?"

"It's only a very tiny speck of radium salt," Loïe said, "much too small to cause a burn. Besides, I've been working with pitchblende and other radioactive substances in my workroom for years, and I'm perfectly fine. For goodness' sake, people are brushing their teeth with radium now and drinking radium water. How dangerous can it really be, when it's so highly diluted?"

She turned to see Gab and the girls stepping out of the elevator and excused herself to go prepare for her dance. As Loïe crossed the deck to greet her troupe, the lovely lilting voice of a soprano from the Paris Opéra floated through the air. Loïe happily squeezed Gab's hands and kissed her cheeks, hushing her pupils so their excited voices wouldn't interfere with Miss Mati's rendition of "Hymn to the Sun." When the singer launched into the famous air from the opera *Sigurd*, Loïe made her way into M. Eiffel's office, which was located in the middle of the platform, while Gab assembled the muses, who had scattered to take in the view.

Loïe expertly pulled her robe over her head and smoothed her hair. Using a kohl pencil, she lined her eyes dramatically and rouged her lips. Winding the long sleeves of her dress around the wands and lifting her skirt up, she went back outside to listen to the final notes of the aria with Gab and the girls.

The sight of so many scientists, poets, writers, and musicians enjoying the ancient celebration together against the backdrop of Paris almost brought Loïe to tears. They were next on the program, so she removed her glasses and handed them to Gab. Camille Flammarion introduced Loïe as a member of the astronomical society and a dear friend who would be performing a new Egyptian Sun Dance with the pupils from her school.

"Please try not to dance right off the edge," he joked before the crowd. "All of Paris will hate me if I turn you into a falling star."

"If I fall," she said with a wink at him, "I'll simply use my robe as a parachute. Monsieur Eiffel can add it to his list of experiments."

The crowd laughed and Loïe beamed. Taking her place on the platform in front of the railing, she waited for her muses to gather in a semicircle, bowed before her on the cool steel. When they were ready, she nodded to the man who was operating a phonograph and then to her electricians. She gripped her wands and dropped her head, waiting for the musical cue. Loïe was a little dizzy but elated and wondered whether the altitude was affecting her mind. She felt twenty years old again.

A faint breeze ruffled her gown and the silk caressed her bare legs. Loïe imagined she could feel the audience's eyes on her as the oboe began to play the notes Saint-Saëns had written. Light flooded her eyes. She lifted her head and raised her arms, and the music of *Samson and Delilah*'s "Bacchanale" rose to a frenzy. With Paris at her feet, Loïe was Salome once again. She spun and swooped on the platform among her muses, dancing for the sun, the Earth, the stars, and the ancient gods. The only sacrifice she demanded was adoration.

No one knew that all hell was about to break loose.

Scene II
Little Curies
1915

The lead apron was heavy. Marie pulled it over her head and secured it snugly behind her back before handing one to Irène. She didn't always wear an apron, but she didn't want Irène to get radiation burns and was trying to set a good example. Perhaps some people would consider her a bad mother for bringing her seventeen-year-old daughter to the war front, but Irène, who was every bit as stubborn as Marie, had been determined to come.

Irène was taking nurse training and had made up her mind to help her mother set up X-ray stations closer to the fighting. It was their second trip to Belgium together in a portable radiology unit, and in that time, Marie had grown to trust her daughter more than she did almost anyone else on earth.

Back in August, when alarm bells sounded across the country to announce French troop mobilization, Irène and Ève had been at the rugged seaside town of L'Arcouest along with a Polish governess and housekeeper. The small town on the Brittany coast had become a colony for scientists, and several of Marie's friends, including the Borels and the Perrins, were staying nearby. Marie had sent the girls on ahead in order to get some work done. She'd been looking forward to joining them for some quiet weeks by the sea when the news of war arrived.

It had been a shock to realize that life as she had known it was coming to a dead stop. For her, it wasn't the change that she found so frightening, but the uncertainty. She knew they were safe for the moment. The Germans were advancing on Paris, but no one knew when, or even if, they would arrive. Perhaps they could be stopped, but nobody knew for sure. If the Germans came to Paris, what would happen to her institute, to her radium? How long would a war go on? She could endure hardship, but unpredictability was much harder to bear.

Her girls were about as far away from Germany as they could be within France's borders. Although her initial panicked instinct was to bring her daughters back to Paris to be with her, Marie knew they'd be safer in Brittany. She wrote telling them to stay where they were for the time being, and to do whatever the Perrins and Borels thought was best. It was one of the hardest decisions she'd ever had to make.

Perhaps Pierre's death had prepared her for the absence of normality, but Marie discovered that she wasn't afraid. She remained in Paris with her precious radium as the city emptied. Wealthy and middle-class Parisians fled to the countryside, and government offices relocated to Bordeaux as the Germans advanced on Paris. It was eerie to walk past the silent monuments, which felt old and sad in the absence of crowds. The birds still sang as though nothing had changed, and Marie imagined how the city would look if no one ever returned and grass grew wild through the cobblestones while twisting vines climbed the Eiffel Tower.

She was used to extended separations from her girls, but Marie found herself missing them as she never had before, writing that she longed to hold Irène and Ève close. As much as she wanted to join them, even her strongest maternal instincts couldn't overpower her will to stay with the almost-completed new Radium Institute and the treasure inside. That summer before the war, she'd planted flowers in the garden just outside her new laboratory, imagining how happy Pierre would have been to see their dream finally coming to life.

When the institute opened, Marie would run the laboratories for the

Physics and Chemistry department, while the physician Claudius Regaud treated patients and researched radium therapy in the building designated for medicine and biology. It was unbearable to have construction of the Radium Institute abandoned for a senseless war, but Marie reminded herself that she was luckier than many. Like everyone else, she would have to wait for the war to end to resume a normal life. In the meantime, she would help her country and prove her loyalty to France.

Under government orders, she'd packed her vials of radium salts in a lead-lined case only a month after the war began. The case was almost too heavy to lift. Surrounded by French soldiers, Marie carried her radium to Bordeaux and deposited the precious cargo for safekeeping at the university.

It was an enormous relief to know that her treasure was safe, at least for the moment. Returning to Paris by train, she sent her girls more missives, telling them how desperately she missed them. Irène, who was sixteen at the time, begged to join Marie to help with the war effort, but Marie told her to wait a little longer. She had a new project to focus on.

When the broken bodies of soldiers had begun arriving in Paris, Marie learned that they were dying in droves because surgeons at the front lines couldn't locate the bullets and shrapnel that had entered their bodies. Without X-ray equipment and technicians who knew how to use it correctly, finding metal fragments buried in flesh was the equivalent of looking for a needle in a haystack. Foreign objects lodged in tissue under the skin hid from medics, only presenting themselves days after surgery as pus-filled abscesses. All too frequently, deadly gangrene would set in. To avoid this risk of infection, surgeons would often take the prophylactic step of amputating injured limbs immediately.

Determined to help these young men, who should have been at the university or in the cafés of Paris, she knew that her familiarity with radiation and technology offered her a unique way to help. Marie decided to set up X-ray units for injured soldiers in Paris. A friend trained her in radiological techniques, and in no time, she was able to run the equipment, do radiography, and take clear images on photographic plates. Aware that deserted laboratories and consultation rooms around Paris contained a treasure trove of X-ray and photographic darkroom equipment, Marie got permission from physicians and scientists to borrow the equipment for wartime radiology units.

Unfortunately, it could take days to transport injured soldiers back to Paris for X-rays. By then it was often too late. Imagining that lives and limbs could be saved by immediately locating and extracting foreign objects from wounds, Marie decided to bring X-ray equipment and trained technicians directly to the injured soldiers and medics. There were a few X-ray units along the front lines, but she'd heard rumors that they weren't very well operated.

She hit her first set of obstacles as she attempted to cut through the red tape preventing her from bringing her X-ray equipment closer to the battle. Not only wasn't she military, she was also a woman, and the army didn't want her anywhere near the front. While she worked on getting access to the front lines, Marie installed X-ray equipment, along with a lightweight table, inside an automobile donated by the Red Cross and dubbed it a "radiologic car."

Since her "on the spot" X-ray consulting room would have to carry its own power supply, and X-ray tubes required large amounts of electricity, Marie figured out how to combine two types of technology to solve the problem. In the past, military X-ray units had been fitted with large, extremely heavy generators. Marie wanted to be able to transform any vehicle into a mobile X-ray unit, so she fitted hers with a smaller, lighter dynamo, which could be attached to the running board of the car and easily hooked up to the motor.

The dynamo allowed the mechanical energy supplied by an automobile's motor, which ran on gasoline, to be converted into enough electrical current to power an X-ray tube. Marie was extremely proud of her radiologic car, and soon it was traveling all over Paris, carrying a doctor and an X-ray technician. Marie was often that technician, finding it immensely rewarding to spend her days assisting surgeons as they saved lives.

As her automobile raced from hospital to hospital, it became obvious that one mobile X-ray unit wasn't nearly enough to serve all the injured. Moreover, they needed to get closer to the battle to save more lives. To raise the money needed for more cars and equipment, Marie turned to the women of Paris, specifically a private organization called the Patronage des Blessés, whose aim was to reform health care for wounded soldiers. They promised Marie financial assistance, and soon a wealthy Parisian donated a second car. Marie's fleet of mobile X-ray machines began to grow until she had equipped eighteen passenger cars and vans with radiological equipment.

In the meantime, she kept up the fundraising for her mobile radiology units. In October of 1914, she met Loïe Fuller and one of her prosperous acquaintances for lunch. It had been nice to see the dancer, who had recently returned from the United States. She always seemed to reappear in Marie's life to offer light in difficult times, and Loïe's sparkling blue eyes brought back good memories of the hardscrabble days with Pierre.

Loïe's rich friend donated generously to Marie's mobile X-ray unit fund, but Loïe, as usual, was in uncertain financial straits. It seemed that besides running her dancing school, whose European tour had been derailed by the war, she was on a mission to introduce French art to the United States. She'd met a wealthy woman from San Francisco who loved art and planned to help Loïe build a museum. After meeting up with Rodin in Rome, Loïe planned to head back to America by way of England.

Like Marie, she was supporting the war effort, raising money to help the wounded in France and Belgium by selling books and art signed by her famous friends. Marie promised to send her a few signed copies of her *Treatise on Radioactivity*, in addition to the personal copy she'd promised her.

As full of ideas as ever, Loïe told Marie that she would write a letter about the need for more X-ray units to the readers of the *Queen*, a periodical written for middle- and upper-class British women, and would contact everyone else she knew who had the means to offer financial support for Marie's radio field service.

Loïe asked Marie to explain again in detail exactly what medical problem the cars would solve and took notes in a small book she carried. Later, when Marie saw a copy of the letter Loïe had sent to England, which included the address of Marie's apartment, she was somewhat relieved that an entire car hadn't arrived on her doorstep.

"Be safe, and please tell Gab and Monsieur Rodin hello from me," Marie told Loïe, kissing each of her cheeks. "I hope that next time we meet, this senseless fighting will be finished."

"You too. Please be careful in your automobiles," Loïe had answered, grasping her hands. "After all, who will teach me about science if something happens to you?"

By late October, more friends had jumped in to raise money for Marie's ambulances, which had been nicknamed "Little Curies." Feeling that Paris was safe for the time being, Marie finally sent for her girls. While Ève went back to school, Irène was eager to help, so Marie let her train as a nurse. By November, Marie had finally secured permission to take the Little Curies to the war zone. She and Irène began accompanying radiologists to posts near the front lines where, under Marie's tutelage, Irène became an expert X-ray technician like her mother.

~

"What's your name?" Marie asked the young man, whose face was drawn tight with pain.

Pulling out her notebook, Marie wrote down his name and infantry number, noting that he was complaining of pain in his left leg. She put a hand on his forehead, introducing herself as Marie. As hideous as war was, it offered the anonymity she craved.

"He reminds me of Maurice," she whispered to Irène, who nodded.

Her nephew, Maurice, was hunkered down with his unit along the war front and wrote to her frequently, relating tales from the trenches. In one letter, he'd make light of the situation, telling her that they'd served a breakfast of mortar fire to the Germans, but in the next he'd complain about the cold, the filth, and body lice that plagued them.

Besides the constant volleys of gunfire and artillery that flew back and forth between the German trenches and their own, there were innumerable ways to die. Infection was a constant threat, and in the mud and dirt, even a simple cut could prove deadly. Once gangrene had blackened an appendage until the skin crackled and it emitted a putrefying smell, only amputation offered hope.

Gas was a new, invisible adversary, and in April the Germans had used poison gas to attack French and Algerian troops in Belgium. Unfortunately, gas masks were painful to wear for long periods and gave soldiers migraines. Only the imminent threat of suffocating, blistering gas induced men to put them on.

By now, all of Marie's friends were involved in the war effort. Out of necessity, the yokes holding women bound to their homes and their children were temporarily broken. Hertha Ayrton's research on water and air currents prompted her to invent a canvas-covered fan to blow deadly gas out of the trenches before it killed soldiers or forced them out into the open. Marie's close friend Marguerite Borel went to work running a hospital. Paul Langevin, who was no longer Marie's lover but remained a good friend, enlisted as an army sergeant. Most of the men at the university labs left their research to join the fight against the Germans. Now Irène had joined her effort, and Marie couldn't have been more proud.

When they'd arrived at the hospital that afternoon, a doctor she'd never met before silently helped them remove the equipment from her car and carry it inside. Marie was learning to drive, after an automobile accident on the way to the front convinced her that she'd prefer to take charge of her own safety, but she still needed a chauffeur to make her runs. She was even learning to repair automobiles as the need arose.

Their Little Curie was parked close enough to the small hospital building that it was simple to run a cable from the X-ray tube in the operating room to the generator attached to the car's engine. Marie and Irène had the equipment set up in less than an hour. Then, they blanketed the windows with black cloth and calibrated the X-ray tube.

When the soldier was laid out on the examination table they'd carried in, they positioned a large viewing screen over his legs, parallel to the table. He looked nervous, but Marie assured him that the X-rays wouldn't hurt a bit. She positioned the spherical tube under the table so that the young man's legs were sandwiched between the chemically coated viewing screen and the X-ray tube.

"Ready," she told Irène.

Irène flipped a switch and with a buzz, electrical current flowed through the vacuum tube. Beams of invisible radiation shot up through the wooden table and the flesh of the soldier's leg as if they weren't there. Only bone and metal blocked the rays.

When the image of his femur appeared clearly on the fluorescent screen, Marie pointed out to Irène what was almost certainly a piece of shrapnel. She reached under the viewing screen and placed a piece of metal shaped like a cross on the target.

"Now turn it off and move the X-ray tube," she said. Marie wanted Irène to learn by doing rather than watching. Irène confidently slid the tube to a second position under the table.

"One more," she told the soldier, flipping the tube on for a second time. "We're almost finished."

They marked the changes they observed, turned the tube off, and switched on an electric light. Marie moved the screen to one side so they could measure the distance between the markers and triangulate the position of the metal. Irène was exceptionally good at math and had no trouble with the equations.

The doctor came in just as they were completing their calculations. Military surgeons were often in the room observing the radiology process, but this one had been called away to tend to a gravely injured soldier and he'd returned with his apron splattered with blood.

"There's one piece of shrapnel in this soldier's leg," Marie said. She looked over at Irène, who was double-checking her numbers.

"Approximately where do you pinpoint the location of the shrapnel, Irène?" she asked.

"Here? Maybe ten centimeters deep?" Irène said confidently, pointing at the same spot where Marie had calculated the metal to be lodged.

"Very good." Marie nodded.

"That can't be right," the surgeon said, pointing. "The entry wound is here. It can't possibly have traveled that far."

He gave Irène a sideways glance. "She's very young."

"Are you determined to butcher this young man's entire leg with a scalpel when I can show you exactly where the metal is?" Marie asked, making little effort to control her impatience. "I'll show you."

Apologizing to the soldier, she turned the light off and the X-ray tube on one last time and explained to the doctor how they'd located the metal.

Many surgeons wore Edison-like fluoroscopes attached to their heads by straps as they operated, so they could visualize bones and foreign objects as they cut and probed. The fluoroscopes looked like trapezoidal goggles with flat, chemically coated viewing screens, which could be pointed at patients to give the doctor X-ray vision or flipped up and out of the way. Unfortunately, in order to use the fluoroscopes, X-ray tubes had to be left running until an object was extracted.

Marie hoped to train surgeons on the front line to use the larger viewing screens for triangulating the position of objects, so they could simply mark a patient's skin, estimate the depth of a foreign object, and then turn the X-ray tubes off. She wasn't as afraid of X-rays as many people seemed to be, but leaving an X-ray tube running during a lengthy surgery would almost certainly expose doctors, nurses, technicians, and the patients themselves to an enormous amount of radiation.

When the surgery was finished, the surgeon stitched up the wound and turned to Marie and Irène.

"You were correct," he said, picking up his forceps and showing them a piece of metal the size of a postage stamp. "The object was exactly where you said it would be. I apologize for doubting you, Madame..."

"Curie," she said, oddly satisfied with the surprised look on the man's face.

He closed the wound and they brought the next soldier in. Marie lost track of time as she stood side by side with Irène, passing invisible rays through flesh to decipher the damage wrought by war.

Scene III

San Francisco

1915

Loïe handed her leopard stole to a pretty young servant and strode through the vestibule into the most talked-about social event of the season. Her friend Alma was nowhere to be seen, so she made her way to the rotunda to look out of one of the tall windows. The view from the hill-top Pacific Heights mansion, which was spectacular during the day, had transformed into a dreamy nocturnal panorama.

To make up for the cancellation of her Austrian and German tours because of the war, Loïe had signed a contract to have her muses dance at the Panama-Pacific Exposition. It was a spectacular affair celebrating the completion of the Panama Canal and San Francisco's recovery from the earthquake that had destroyed the city nine years earlier, in 1906. Modernity and progress were overarching themes of the fair. Located along the north shore between the Presidio and Fort Mason, its attractions included the Palace of Fine Arts, a monumental statue of a pioneer woman, and a sculpture of an Indigenous warrior slumped over on his horse, which had been titled *The End of the Trail.*

The lights of the exhibition spread out at Loïe's feet, clinging to the edge of the San Francisco Bay like an incandescent blanket. In the midst of those lights, an architectural showpiece dubbed the Tower of Jewels rose up like a glittering starlet, a hundred thousand cut-glass crystals sparkling in a pyramid of spotlights. Fog had rolled in over the bay, and a barge nicknamed the "Scintillator" painted the misty droplets from sea to sky with forty-eight dazzling pastel beams radiating from a single point. Loïe stood before the glass, transfixed by the juxtaposition of the crowd's reflection on the spectacular view outside.

Waiters with silver trays of fresh oysters and Champagne moved between handsome men in long-tailed black formal jackets and women who seemed to have come straight from the pages of a magazine. Loïe couldn't help thinking that they looked like exotic birds in their brilliantly dyed evening gowns sewn from silk and velvet and trimmed with feathers, pearls, beads, and crystals. The bright, plinking sound of jazz piano floated through the air, rising and falling over the sound of voices, giving the scene a warm, golden aura. Jazz certainly wasn't Loïe's favorite kind of music, but she had to admit that it lent the perfect tone to the party.

The gathering was rumored to be the greatest-ever celebration of art and literature in the West, but it seemed fairly tame to Loïe. She would have loved to see how these partygoers would react to an artists' party in Paris, populated by women dressed in French designer Paul Poiret's long, baggy trouser skirts. They'd probably find it shocking. While Parisians were constantly pushing the boundaries of fashion, Americans were still a rather uptight group when it came to anything that challenged their puritan beliefs and Victorian sensibilities.

After trying unsuccessfully to get an engagement for her troupe at New York's Metropolitan Opera House earlier that year, Loïe was convinced that the organization considered her barefoot dancers too controversial for their hallowed halls. They were quite prudish, in her opinion. In 1907, they'd closed Strauss's opera *Salome* after only four days, the sensual performance far too scandalous for local church leaders and American audiences.

Turning to face the room, she noticed a few women wearing the pleated gowns that were so popular in Paris, but most of the distinguished guests seemed to have a style all their own, a sort of Wild West of fashion. The younger women had rouged their cheeks and were casually applying lipstick from bullet-shaped cases that appeared to be all the rage. Though the lip-stick cases were clever, the ammunition-like cosmetics felt somehow wrong to Loïe, considering the war raging across the sea.

She'd been onboard the *Laurentic*, en route to deliver the first batch of Rodin's drawings and plasters to San Francisco, when she learned that Germany had declared war on France. The announcement came on August 3, only a month or so after she'd spun fearlessly atop the Eiffel Tower, feeling immortal. Her first thought was that her company's European tour would be canceled. Then she thought about her friends. Panicking, she'd cabled Gab, who was safe in London with the muses. Fearing for the Rodins and the Flammarions, she'd cabled them as well, begging them to come to America. She was strangely comforted knowing that she was bringing some of the master's work here to safety, and became even more convinced that her mission to bring French art to the United States was an important one.

"Loïe Fuller?"

A fine-boned brunette in a refined blue-velvet gown introduced herself as Constance Paget-Fredericks. She explained that she had been following Loïe's career with great interest and that she and her twelve-year-old son, Joseph, were very much looking forward to seeing Loïe and her muses perform at the exposition in June.

As it turned out, they were well acquainted with Loïe's former protégée Isadora Duncan, who had been born in San Francisco and grew up in Oakland. Although Loïe's relationship with Isadora had ended badly, she felt sorry for the dancer. Fame and alcohol had not been kind to the talented artist, and in 1913, Isadora had been upstairs in her Paris apartment when her chauffeur made a mistake that cost the lives of her two children. Accidentally leaving the automobile in gear, the man went to crank the engine, and when the motor engaged and roared to life, the car bucked forward and plunged into the Seine, carrying Isadora's six-year-old daughter Deirdre and two-year-old Patrick into the river, along with their governess. None of them survived.

As if the tragedy itself weren't enough to bear, in October of the next year, American newspapers, including the *San Francisco Examiner* and the *Minneapolis Sunday Tribune*, published a full-page article titled "The Fate of the House Built on Sin." Nestled in the illustration of a fanged snake, the article began, "It is as though the structure is built upon the coils of a serpent, that symbol of sin. Sooner or later, it uncoils and then—destruction!" It went on to detail several tragedies that it blamed on the moral lapses of women who had strayed from society's norms. After a sensational description of Mamah Bouton Borthwick's affair with the architect Frank Lloyd Wright and the horrific murders at their love nest, Taliesin, in which she, her children and four other people were killed, the writer implied that Isadora's children's deaths were the result of her "immoral" behavior and the fact that she'd had the children out of wedlock.

"It is terrible to publish something like that," Loïe said to Constance. "Hasn't the poor girl suffered enough?"

Constance nodded. "Tragic."

"Another of my friends was viciously attacked by the press in Paris," Loïe said. "They're even worse there than they are here. I think it almost killed her."

She didn't say any more. Normally, Loïe loved to drop the names of her famous friends, but it was different with Marie. She respected the scientist's privacy and intuitively knew that their friendship depended on her discretion.

When Constance asked Loïe where her muses were staying, Loïe told her that they were en route to San Francisco, which was a half-truth. Following the recent death of their main financier, Loïe's troupe of sixteen girls and one boy, ranging between eleven and sixteen years old, were stranded in Philadelphia until she could persuade someone to pay for their transportation to San Francisco.

Loïe was almost completely broke, but she wasn't particularly concerned. She'd secured a few engagements in the next couple months and planned to recruit local California girls and train them to dance for these performances. Gab had written to her, forbidding her to speak to anyone about how much money their deceased benefactor had already given them for their tour, in case a greedy heir tried to make them pay it back. Despite the setback, Loïe was certain that they'd find a way to get her dancers to San Francisco.

"And is your school similar to Isadora's?" Constance asked. "I've heard so much about it."

"Oh no," Loïe said. She may have felt sorry for Isadora, but she still hated to be compared to her. "I've freed my muses from the structure of formal dance education. They move naturally, barefoot, with their hair unbound. I encourage them only to be inspired by their imaginations and music, like Beethoven, Grieg, and Polignac," Loïe gushed. "I never teach them. They learn by instinct, by intuition."

"You must bring your son Joseph to my dressing room when you come see us dance in June," Loïe said, changing the subject. She'd heard quite enough about Isadora Duncan. "Only warn him that he will be greeted by a rather short, regular person in glasses, rather than a fairy of light."

"That would be wonderful!" Constance appeared to be thrilled at the prospect. "Joseph knows that great performers are remarkable because they transcend the ordinary," she bragged. "He is a gifted artist with a sensitive soul, and I'm sure that he will find you as lovely as I do."

"I look forward to meeting him," Loïe said.

Constance drifted away through the crowd just as a six-foot-tall woman in a beautifully draped ivory silk gown strode across the parquet floor toward Loïe. With dark hair, classical features, and a simple string of pearls around her neck, she was monumental, a statue of antiquity, and the crowd before her parted like the Red Sea.

"Dear Loïe," Alma Spreckels greeted her warmly.

Loïe took Alma's hands. "You look as beautiful as ever, like Juno come to life."

Alma laughed. "Are you ready for your lecture?"

"I was just thinking of telling everyone that looking at French art will make them a little less boring," Loïe joked.

"How amusing, especially coming from a former temperance lecturer," Alma quipped back.

"How's this?" Loïe clasped her hands together and recited, in the manner of a great orator, "When our day shall belong to the past, when generations have come and generations have gone, the immortal works left by Rodin will remain, and his genius will stand like a giant in the storm, unshaken, unmoved."

"Perfect," Alma said. "I've been talking to my friends about having you and your muses perform a pageant at the Palace of Fine Art, to raise funds to preserve the building when the exposition ends. It's so beautiful."

Loïe could easily picture her muses dancing barefoot in white tunics before the pillars and dome of the beautiful structure. The arts palace had been designed to look like an ancient Greek or Roman ruin and sat on the edge of a lushly planted reflecting lagoon. She loved the idea.

"Could we possibly drape the steps with fabric, or have my muses make a dramatic appearance by boat?"

"I don't see why not," Alma said.

Alma and Loïe had met in the spring of 1914 at a luncheon. The wealthy American had been in Paris for the first time to buy art, and was happy to meet a fellow English speaker. Alma remembered Loïe from her early years and recalled the old gossip about Loïe's first marriage, so over their foie gras and toast, Loïe had related her lurid tale to break the ice.

"We first met when I was about twenty," Loïe said.

She'd actually been twenty-seven when she met Colonel William B. Hayes, but Loïe was in the habit of always subtracting at least five years from her age. At the time, she'd been working on a play called *Caprice* with the well-known actor William Morris. Morris had been in love with Loïe. She'd heard that he wanted to marry her but had never summoned the courage to ask. Together, they'd created a company of actors, hoping to take the play to Jamaica and other islands in the West Indies, where they could profit from the growing tourism industry.

To stage the production, pay the actors, buy costumes, and cross the ocean, Loïe and Morris needed investors. Colonel Hayes, a portly stockbroker, railroad lawyer, and Florida real estate dealer, was introduced to Loïe as someone with the resources to fund their theatrical venture. The fiftysomething businessman oozed confidence and almost smelled like money. Loïe and Morris asked him for a small loan, which he gave them, before pressing him for a larger one.

"I was much more attracted to his money than I was to him," Loïe confessed. "I was determined to make our play succeed."

She didn't tell Alma that when Hayes had declared that their written promises to return his investment weren't convincing enough, Loïe gave him some compromising photographs as security. "Should Morris and I default on the loan," she'd told him, "you can ruin my reputation with these pictures." Loïe was clothed in the photos, but the placement of the shadows let the imagination run wild. In return, William gave her a large check for their theater company, along with his undivided attention. Hayes was well practiced in flirtation, and Loïe found the way he talked about throwing thousands of dollars around irresistible.

"Within a week of our meeting, he asked to kiss me," Loïe said, "and within three weeks he'd proposed, but I'd heard that he was already married."

About to set sail with her acting company, she said no, despite his assurances that his divorce was imminent. After a stormy voyage, Loïe, Morris, and their acting company arrived on the island paradise of Jamaica, where they performed *Caprice* three times a week. Hayes sent Loïe telegraph after telegraph, but she told her married suitor to stay away.

At the end of three months, they met up again in New Orleans. The plan was to form a theater company together, along with Morris. Hayes and Morris hated each other, but the deal was struck. With business concluded,

Hayes joined Loïe on a trip to Florida, where her parents now lived. Her father, Reuben, as restless as ever, had invested in an orange grove and some other property in Tampa, which he hoped to develop.

Hayes and Loïe persuaded a banker in Jacksonville to give Reuben an $8,000 loan, with the orange grove and his "sandlots" as collateral. Loïe's father then invested a portion of this money in her play. At the same time, Hayes continued to pressure Loïe to marry him, conveniently producing a decree of divorce. Worried that holding him off anymore would endanger his financial backing, Loïe finally agreed to marry him. At the time, she thought they would make a good team, with his money and her ideas.

Hayes, who was trying to start a new bank in New York, persuaded her to forgo a traditional ceremony, claiming that he didn't want to be associated with a burlesque actress until the business was established. Loïe, Hayes, and her mother, Delilah, took the train to New York, where Loïe entered into a secret common-law marriage. In a little room on Broadway, with her mother as their witness, Loïe and Hayes signed a piece of paper stating that they were taking each other as lawful husband and wife. Loïe, however, refused to live with him until their relationship had been made public, and she continued to share a room with her mother.

Soon after, Loïe and Hayes leased the Royal Globe Theatre in London in hopes that *Caprice* would perform better there than it had in Jamaica. Loïe boarded a transatlantic ship to meet up with her theater company, while Hayes and her parents followed a few weeks later. At some point during their voyage, Hayes had apparently insisted that Reuben shave off his beard and buy a more respectable suit for London.

"That," Loïe said to Alma, "is when he cheated my father out of nearly four thousand dollars."

"How scandalous," Alma gasped, although four thousand dollars was pocket change for her.

Loïe went on with the story.

Hayes stayed in London long enough to convince Loïe's hotel that he would be paying all of her expenses. He then wrote some bad checks and boarded a boat bound for the United States. In the meantime, *Caprice* was a flop.

The English critics loved Loïe but hated everything else about the production. As the play floundered, Hayes sent Loïe letter after letter signed "Your loving husband," but he stopped paying her bills when he realized that *Caprice* wasn't making any money. Eventually, he desisted from writing altogether, and Loïe learned that all the checks he'd written, including the one to the Globe Theatre, had bounced. She begged him to come back to London, but he refused. He was busy with his new bank, which, it turned out, was financed with more bad checks.

"To make matters worse," Loïe told Alma, "I received a letter from a woman claiming to be William's wife, and my father went to New York to confront the scoundrel."

Instead of finding Hayes with his wife, Reuben discovered that the colonel was seeing yet another woman. Hayes wrote to Loïe, denying that he was involved with "Miss Earl," worried that Loïe would take revenge by going with another man. He said he would choke the life out of Loïe if he ever thought someone else was touching her, and in the same letter asked whether he should sell the Fullers' family land in Florida.

"That's how I learned that he was a violent man," Loïe said. "A few days later we received news that my father was dead."

Loïe's brother Burt traveled to New York to retrieve the body, which had been embalmed and placed in a very expensive casket by Hayes, who hadn't paid the mortician. Burt found himself responsible for all of the expenses. With no money left, and no one to help him, he'd been forced to wheel the casket through the streets of New York to put it on the slow train to Chicago. Tired and broke, he went hungry.

News later reached Loïe and her mother that her father and Hayes had dined together at a hotel in Fort Lee, New Jersey, the night he died. According to the reports, Reuben had dropped dead immediately after dinner, and Hayes had rushed to have the body embalmed. They had no evidence to prove it was murder, but Loïe knew that Hayes wanted the money from her father's orange grove. On top of that, her father may have uncovered more evidence that Hayes was a bigamist.

When a reporter asked Hayes about Loïe's claim that he'd had her father's body embalmed with suspicious haste, he'd laughed and said that he hadn't been anywhere near Reuben the night he died. Instead, he claimed to have gone to Fort Lee to attend to the removal of the body, only to discover that it had already been embalmed.

"No!" Alma said. "I'm so sorry!"

"My father's death certificate stated that he'd died of typhoid fever," Loïe snorted. "Can you imagine? Then William started gossiping about me, calling me immoral and saying that I was his cast-off mistress. When I got back to New York, I had him arrested."

Although Loïe's charges of bigamy fell through as a result of the flimsy marriage document she produced for the judge, another woman came forward to sue Hayes, and he went to prison for perjury. In addition to his financial crimes, William had taken up with a seventeen-year-old girl named Anna years earlier, lied about being married, given her a ring, and impregnated her.

He and his childless wife attempted to trick Anna into giving up the child so they could raise it as their own. Anna had two more children by Hayes, including one four months after he married Loïe. As the scandal erupted, Loïe mustered up the courage to return to the courthouse with a signed document that proved he'd lied to her about his marriage and cheated her financially as well.

Newspapers around the country had a field day writing about the whole torrid affair. The *New York Sun* published a full-page story on the legal battle. The January 20, 1892, issue was headlined: "BIGAMY, SAYS LOIE FULLER. The Nautch Dancer Has Lawyer W. B. Hayes Arrested, And Produces a Marriage Agreement Which the Lawyer Says Is a Forgery—His Wife

Stands by Him—Hayes Says the Girl Got a Good Deal of Money Out of Him—Photographs as Collateral."

Loïe had denied Hayes's accusations, and was quoted as saying, "As to the statement that his signature to the marriage agreement is a forgery, that is a point for the courts to decide. I can only deny it."

Besides her side of the story, the article included several paragraphs detailing Loïe's career. The public applauded when the philandering cheat was sent to Sing Sing. Hayes settled with Loïe as well, by writing a public statement declaring that she was a woman of good character, free from immorality and misconduct, and denying the existence of any indecent photographs. Newspapers declared it a double success, and Loïe reclaimed her honor just as the critics were lauding her skirt-swirling performance in *Uncle Celestin*.

"It was a miserable affair, but happily the press took my side, for the most part," Loïe told Alma, who was now quite taken with her new acquaintance.

Before long, Loïe had convinced Alma that she must spend her money on contemporary art in Paris, rather than dusty old antiques. She took her to Meudon and introduced her to Rodin. Eventually, Alma and Loïe were dreaming up a museum of French art in San Francisco.

Loïe, they both decided, would act as Alma's agent in Europe and acquire art from Rodin and other artists. Alma funded the purchases. After delivering the first shipment of Rodin's work and being briefly delayed in the States at the beginning of the war, Loïe had returned to Europe to obtain more paintings and sculptures. While she continued to collect art for Alma, Loïe turned a great deal of her energy toward raising money for French and Belgian war victims. She called on her celebrity friends and collected a number of books, postcards, and pieces of art signed by French artists, scientists, and politicians.

Once more Loïe braved the sea crossing and arrived in San Francisco in March 1915 to prepare for the exposition, carrying more of Rodin's art with her. They'd agreed that his work would be exhibited in the French Pavilion, and when the exposition closed, Alma would buy it. With Loïe's encouragement, she was using the fortune her husband's family had amassed from sugar to build the first great French art collection on the West Coast.

The books and signed art that Loïe had amassed were also displayed in the French Pavilion. In December, when the exposition closed, some of the items would be sent back, but most would be sold in America and the money sent back to France for the war effort. Gab had been making a gallant effort to keep track of all Loïe's acquisitions, but it was proving to be rather complicated. Loïe freely admitted that she was no good at keeping the books, no matter how often Gab reminded her, and she often lost track of the inventory.

Although Gab was still running Loïe's business from France, since the war began she'd felt the call to help. She'd turned the care of Loïe's dancers over to others, in order to devote her time to driving an ambulance to the war front. Loïe had promised Gab that while she was in San Francisco, she would raise money to support the ambulance service as she'd done in the fall of 1914 to help Marie Curie set up portable X-ray units.

Despite the distraction of the war, it was obvious that Gab was getting fed up with all the projects Loïe was dreaming up with Alma. The wealthy socialite had already decided to have a copy of the French Pavilion at the Panama-Pacific Exposition, just down the hill from her mansion, reconstructed as a museum for her French art collection. When Loïe mentioned to Gab that she and Alma were thinking of doing a lecture tour together in the United States, Gab was furious. She had just written Loïe a letter begging her to focus on her performances and be responsible with her money so that she could bank a sufficient amount to pay her debts, come home, and settle down. "Before it's too late. For the sake of you, for the sake of me," she'd written.

"I think Gab wants me to quit touring and come home for good," Loïe told Alma. "She wants to take a flat together so that we can be quiet, like other people," Loïe said. "But she knows that I'm not quiet like other people, and I still worry about what the papers would say."

"Can you really blame her for wanting you home?" Alma asked. "You're constantly rushing back and forth between Europe and America. I can't imagine how exhausting it must be for her. The poor woman has to manage your school, the muses, your contracts, and all of your finances. It can't be easy."

Loïe shot her a sideways glance. Why did Alma feel so sorry for Gab? After all, Loïe was the one who had worked so hard to collect the French masterpieces for Alma's collection.

"If I weren't running back and forth, you wouldn't have your sculptures at all. Sometimes sacrifices must be made in the name of art. Besides, I think Gab is altogether too jealous. She was jealous of Isadora, she's jealous of Master Rodin, she's jealous of Queen Marie, and now she thinks I'm too devoted to you."

Loïe had met the beautiful Romanian princess Marie when she'd danced for her royal family several years before. And Loïe was taken with Marie's beauty. Now Marie was queen, they'd recently rekindled their friendship.

"You can hardly blame her for being jealous of Marie," Alma said. "I've read the gossip."

"It's only gossip," Loïe said, not admitting that she wished the rumors were true. "Gab and I will be fine. But perhaps I should write to her soon and apologize."

The two of them weren't so starry-eyed anymore. Although Loïe always meant well, Gab was the one who had to deal with the stress of her overdue bills, broken contracts, and broken promises. Only Gab could make heads or tails of Loïe's business dealings, often steering her away from total disaster. A few days before, when Loïe had seen a poster announcing that the French composer Saint-Saëns would be conducting a new composition at the fair, she'd cabled Gab immediately to have Flammarion send her a letter of introduction. Buffalo Bill would make an appearance at the exposition as well. Loïe was looking forward to seeing her old employer and taking her muses to his Wild West show when they finally arrived.

"The lights are lovely from up here," Loïe said, taking Alma by the arm. "I promise to give your guests a wonderful lecture on Master Rodin, but first I want you to introduce me to the most interesting person at the party."

"That will be quite impossible," Alma said, smiling. "You are by far the most interesting person here."

Scene IV

The Girl with Radium Eyes

1921

Perched on the edge of the Grand Canyon, the El Tovar Hotel offered stunning panoramas of the savage beauty of the famous park. Marie was completely exhausted, but the view from her third-floor balcony was magnificent and she was perfectly content for once to sit still and enjoy the scenery, rather than hiking through it. She couldn't help wondering how much radium one could find in the monumental gash carved by water and wind over millions of years.

Studying the exposed layers in the red-and-yellow cliffs, she traced the passage of time. If she had the energy, she would have gone searching for interesting rocks, but she was happy to have purchased a turquoise-and-silver necklace made by a local artist the day before, as a souvenir of her trip to the American West. Marie didn't own much jewelry, but she'd been enchanted by the opaque, blue-green mineral, which was a hydrated phosphate of copper and aluminum.

Paul Langevin had given her a locket once, but she'd never worn it and hid it away after the scandal. He had a new mistress now, sanctioned by his wife as a more appropriate choice. Their intense need for each other had faded into a distant memory, leaving her with affection rather than fire. In the end, the experience had demolished her dream of physical love, destroying her passion with physical and emotional pain.

"*Ma douce Me! Ma chérie.*" Irène poked her head out the door. "Is it very nice outside?"

"It's perfect!" Marie replied.

Irène smiled. "You look better today. I'm glad." She turned to the door and shouted, "Ève! Hurry up! I'm always waiting for you," and went back inside.

Marie leaned back in her chair. Their tour of the West had been cut short due to her poor health. The girls, young women now, had been disappointed at first, but the change allowed them to stay at the luxurious lodge for several days, and they were having a marvelous time. That morning, they'd had breakfast together, but Irène and Ève were leaving to ride mules down the canyon.

Although she was looking forward to a day of rest and solitude, Marie had grown to enjoy her girls more and more as they'd gotten older. They could not have been more different. Ève was not especially interested in science, but she was proving to be a talented musician and quite a good writer. Marie was happy to see her working so hard to master the piano, but got tired of the endless sound of sonatas echoing through the house on rainy days when they were all stuck inside. Ève was friendly, fashionable, and if Marie hadn't given birth to her, she would have wondered how it was possible that they were related.

Irène followed a path more familiar to Marie and came to work at the Radium Institute with her mother. After those early days with the two of them riding across the front, Marie opened a school for X-ray technicians, called *manipulatrices*, at the new Edith Cavell Hospital. Together, she and Irène trained over a hundred women in the science of X-rays and how to set up, operate, and take down mobile X-ray units. Teams of manipulatrices traveled where they were needed along the war front and could usually set up a working radiology unit in under an hour. They were also skilled at repairing the equipment and filling in at other jobs as they were needed. Marie's manipulatrices proved to be extraordinarily adept at their work, and since the program began in 1916, they'd helped surgeons save thousands of lives, often working with no radiologist present.

Eighteen at the time, Irène had been stationed at various radiological posts along the front, often sleeping in tents. Independent and resourceful, she'd written to Marie about retraining technicians who couldn't do the math to locate bullets and repairing broken machinery. All the while she'd been studying. Like her mother, she excelled at school. As the war raged on, she was awarded degrees in math, physics, and chemistry from the Sorbonne in the space of three years. The government had even awarded her a medal for her service to France during the war. Marie couldn't have been more proud.

It had been Ève, however, who shined more brightly when the girls joined their mother on the trip to America. The voyage had been planned by Marie's American friend Missy Maloney. Marie and Missy had become acquainted when the petite journalist interviewed Marie in France. During the interview, Marie told Missy that she was using her own radium to create radioactive sources for radiation therapy for cancer, leaving little for her own research. Missy learned that Mme. Curie, who had worked her fingers to the bone and invented the process for extracting radium, had only one gram of the stuff in her possession, while America had fifty. On the heels of World War I, France had little, if any, extra money to devote to the Radium Institute.

Missy had been appalled by Marie's lack of resources. When she returned to the United States, she launched a massive fundraising effort to collect enough money to buy the "gentle woman in a black cotton dress" a gram of radium for her laboratory. Maloney, who had promised to muzzle the press about the Langevin affair, cultivated Marie's legend with a specific slant. Although she was a prolific journalist, Missy was not a feminist, and rather than touting Marie as a brilliant scientist, she billed her as a self-sacrificing mother who had almost worked herself to death in her quest to help humankind, discovering a cure for cancer in the process. It turned out to be a brilliant marketing ploy.

Pleading to the American public to help Marie, she painted a picture of the scientist as a great but humble woman, whose war-ravaged country could not afford to give her the money or resources needed to run her Radium Institute. The women of America responded in droves, sending in small amounts of cash that grew into a pile as big as the mountain of pitchblende Marie had mined for her radium. Before long, she'd managed to raise $150,000 to purchase a gram of American radium, for which the going rate was $100,000, and equipment for Marie's Radium Institute.

The radium industry was exploding in America. Besides its use in radium therapy, America's capitalists had discovered that radium held enormous financial potential. A wealth of radium-containing ore called carnotite lay underground in Colorado, and entrepreneurs started digging it up and chemically treating it in order to extract the precious element. The radioactive salts they retrieved were then combined with other compounds, and an unimaginably varied line of "radium" products was spit out of the industrial machine. Some inventions had proved to be extremely useful, like the glowing green paint that could illuminate watch dials. Others made impossible health claims and used the Curie name without permission.

In 1914, the American Medical Association's Council on Pharmacy and Chemistry had approved the use of radium salts for "new and nonofficial remedies," including solutions for subcutaneous injection, drinking, and bathing, and had approved radon gas dissolved in water for ingestion, for inhalation, and in sealed sources. People stored drinking water in "Radium Ore Revigators," ceramic crocks lined with radioactive materials, which promised to add radioactivity to water, transforming it into an elixir that would cure everything from arthritis to flatulence. There was radium hair tonic, face cream, toothpaste, and suppositories, and the words "glowing" and "radiant" made it simple to sell them to everyone looking for youth or a cure.

While most scientists understood that the element had to be handled carefully to avoid burns, few contemplated the long-term effects of being exposed to tiny amounts of radioactive matter. Technology, availability, and greed had far outpaced understanding. The public generally saw radium as a great hope for the cure of cancer, and assumed that what was good for one malady must be good for all. The craze for radium only fueled the excitement about the famous Mme. Curie.

At first, Marie had been resistant to Missy's plea to come to the United States, asking if they could just send the radium to her instead. Her health was still uncertain, and she hated crowds. In the end, however, Missy persuaded her to come collect her treasure at its source.

Marie agreed to travel to the United States for a seven-week tour, at the end of which she would receive the radium from President Harding himself. She, Irène, and Ève left France to an enormous send-off by the public, who had forgiven Marie's affair and decided to once again adopt her. At a ceremony before they boarded the ship to America, French dignitaries had assembled at the Paris Opéra's Palais Garnier to celebrate Marie. There the actress Sarah Bernhardt read an ode to her that named her as the sister of Prometheus, who stole fire from the gods and gave it to humankind.

Despite a luxury suite on the *Olympic* and having her every need attended to, the cold gray waves had been violent, and Marie had suffered horribly. Seasick and tired, she wrote to Henriette Perrin from her shipboard cabin that she longed for their summer place in L'Arcouest and its sweet blue sea. Besides her gram of radium, the only thing that excited her about the upcoming tour of America was the prospect of seeing Niagara Falls, the Grand Canyon, and the Standard Chemical Company in Pennsylvania.

When they finally arrived in New York Harbor on May 11, Marie discovered that Missy had made her a celebrity. They were greeted with cheering crowds of people as hordes of journalists poured onto the ship to shout questions. Americans, it seemed, adored her as much as the French loved her friend Loïe. She most enjoyed seeing all the young people—

groups of students, Girl Scouts, and Polish delegates—who welcomed her with cheers and flowers.

As Marie sat in an armchair on the ship's deck, people grabbed at her hands, shaking them so hard that it hurt her shoulders. Her girls stood behind her, looking amused by the attention paid to their mother, and the reporters didn't fail to notice how pretty and personable Ève was. Ignoring her more serious sister, they promptly nicknamed her "The Girl with Radium Eyes."

After spending the night in a peaceful apartment in the city, they'd attended a luncheon thrown in their honor by Mrs. Andrew Carnegie to kick off the American tour, and on May 13, Marie, Irène, Ève, Missy, and a New York physician named Edward H. Rogers set off on their adventure. The schedule would have been exhausting for even a young woman, so Missy had hired Dr. Rogers to monitor and protect Marie's rather fragile health. The itinerary called for thirty stops across the United States in just forty-six days. Besides getting her gram of radium from the president, Marie would visit academic institutions, hospitals, government institutions, and radium processing plants.

Marie's first three stops were at women's colleges: Smith, Mount Holyoke, and Vassar. Later, she would also visit the Woman's Medical College of Pennsylvania and Bryn Mawr, as well as Wellesley and Hunter. She'd given what was considered an especially memorable speech at Vassar College, which she concluded by saying, "It is my earnest desire that some of you should carry on this scientific work and keep for your ambition the determination to make a permanent contribution to science."

Her health was already beginning to fail, but on May 23, she presented a piezo electrometer made by Pierre Curie, which they'd used to discover polonium and radium, to the College of Physicians of Philadelphia, and the next day she stopped at the Woman's Medical College of Pennsylvania to thank them for the honorary degree they'd bestowed on her.

As a result of Missy's articles, Americans, and men in particular, found it easier to place her in the role of a healer rather than a brilliant scientist. With a few exceptions, she was treated rather poorly by the male scientists she encountered. While she received a number of honorary degrees, Harvard's Physics department voted not to award her one, with one representative telling Missy that they didn't think credit for the discovery of radium should have gone entirely to Marie, especially since she hadn't done anything really important following Pierre's death.

Marie bore the entire ordeal patiently, knowing that a gram of radium lay glowing at the end of the road. Her schedule was a whirlwind of banquets and excursions. She endured being horribly misquoted by newspapers and made corrections when possible. Wherever she went, Marie was showered with awards, honorary degrees, and the adoration of American women, who had just won the right to vote.

Although she was generally exhausted, she found joy in some places and moments and spoke for pure science, reminding the crowds who came to hear her that radium's cancer-killing potential would never have been discovered had she considered science only from the point of view of the direct usefulness of it. On May 27, Marie rallied her body and spirit for a tour of the Standard Chemical Company in Canonsburg, Pennsylvania, which lay eighteen miles southwest of Pittsburgh. The radium-refining mill, established in 1911, had produced the radium she would carry back to France.

The company had been started by James and Joseph Flannery in order to procure radium to cure their sister, who had cancer. They'd processed five hundred tons of Colorado ore to produce their first gram of radium. Following a short lunch, company president James C. Gray and plant manager Louis F. Vogt took her on a tour. Mr. Gray, Marie learned, was a cancer survivor who owed his life to radium therapy.

Marie was back in familiar territory. She especially enjoyed seeing the fractional crystallization laboratory. Rows of porcelain bowls containing radium-barium salt solutions sat in the circular cutouts of heatproof asbestos sheets, positioned over burners. She was particularly interested in the fume hoods they used to vent the steam and acid vapors. Her discovery had given birth to an entire industry in America. In 1917, Standard Chemical had started a division called the Radium Dial Company, which employed young women to paint glowing watch dials.

Marie didn't get to meet the esteemed Flannery brothers, however. It seemed that they had passed away within a month of each other during the previous year.

The *Pittsburgh Sun* newspaper reported on her visit the next day:

Between vast tanks, containing 27 tank-carloads of muriatic acid, past steaming press filtration rooms, where fumes rising from the liquid almost gag one, in the carbonating department where the raw ore is treated in a soda ash wash; even in the smelter room where a cupola of vanadium by-product was tapped into ladles, Mme. Curie seemed strangely in place.

Bareheaded, with wisps of gray hair blowing about her anxiously wrinkled forehead, dressed simply in black, Mme. Curie seemed entirely in her own element, as she has not appeared since coming to America...

No pair of steps was too arduous, no tank of acid too malodorous, nor was the distance through the many buildings of the plant too long for this scientist, who came to the plant obviously a travel and reception-worn woman, seemingly too tired to walk even a short distance. After delving into every phase of the process, which would have tired a strong man were he not interested, Mme. Curie asked for a few moments with Mr. Vogt, who has been connected with the Standard Chemical Company since the start of the plant and knows more about radium extraction. At the end of 15 minutes, during which time the visiting scientist asked a multitude of questions and did a vast amount of figuring, she emerged fresh and radiant. It was a remarkable exhibition of the ascendency of the technical and scientific mind over the frail and weary body.

Another paper, the *Pittsburgh Post*, noted President Gray's worry that Vogt wouldn't know when to stop talking to Marie, quoting him as saying, "Vogt's a radium nut too." However, they'd peeked into the office to discover Marie "taking voluminous notes" and "plying the manager with questions, much as a lawyer cross-examines a witness."

Although Marie still refused to admit that radium posed a threat to those who worked with it, she was beginning to worry that exposure to X-rays and radon gas had taken a toll on her own health. Her eyes were cloudy, and she was anemic. For the medical "emanation service" she'd established during the war, she'd spent days on end collecting the radioactive gas produced by her radium salts in tiny glass ampoules and then sending them off to the hospitals. Besides implanting the glass tubes into tumors to kill malignant cells, many doctors believed that the radioactive element aided in the healing of scars and the stimulation of nerves. At the time, she hadn't worried about the radon gas she inhaled during those long days in the lab, but perhaps she should have. She was so sick and tired now, almost all the time.

On May 29, American newspapers announced that she was cutting her tour short and would not be able to visit all the scheduled West Coast stops. She'd been especially disappointed to miss seeing the carnotite mines in Colorado, where the ore for her radium had been collected. They'd spent some time in New York before leaving for the Grand Canyon, and she'd had enough energy one day to visit the radium laboratories in Memorial Hospital. When reporters asked Dr. Rogers if Marie's health had been injured by radium, he'd replied:

There is not a word of truth in it. There is nothing the matter with Mme. Curie at all except that she has been trying to do too much. She has been confined most of her life to work in the laboratory.

She is a woman of 53 years. With a delicate physique and un-accustomed to outdoor life, she has been attempting to go through with a strenuous program in this country and it has tired her...

There is no case on record of anyone being injured in health by radium. It causes slight burns, of course—that was the way it was discovered—but these have never had any after effects.

Mme. Curie has now been working with radium 20 years. Many others have handled it constantly for about the same period. If it had any deleterious effects they would have been noted long ago. Even those who have in the past opposed its use have not asserted that it was injurious.

Mme. Curie is anemic. But she is not seriously ill. She will in all probability go as far west as the Grand Canyon.

Besides being exhausted, Marie had one arm in a sling. Her hand had been shaken too many times, too enthusiastically. Luckily, Ève and Irène had stepped in to take over when she couldn't go on. They both spoke English, French, and Polish fluently. At sixteen, Ève was intelligent, beautiful, and very social, dazzling guests at formal functions and speaking easily with reporters. Twenty-year-old Irène was shy, serious, brilliant, and fluent in the language of science. When called on, she could talk confidently about physics, chemistry, and her mother's work. As Marie's daughters traversed the states with her, they took advantage of all the delights that America had to offer, picking violets, swimming in the icy-cold clear waters of Lake Michigan, and seizing every opportunity for adventure.

They'd loved the three days they'd spent on the Santa Fe train line, speeding across the sands of Texas to arrive at the Grand Canyon hotel, which Ève later called "an islet of comfort on the edge of that extraordinary fault in Earth's crust—a precipice sixty-five miles long and ten miles wide, of which the first sight, grandiose and almost terrifying, leaves the spectator voiceless." She and Irène had spent the first day there riding ponies along the crest of the canyon, and Ève had given Marie a vivid description of the violet, red, orange, and pale ocher rocks they'd seen lining the walls of the canyon.

Marie couldn't help imagining how different the trip would have been if she were ten years younger and had Pierre at her side. Watching the sun set over the Grand Canyon brought the grief back in waves. Dulled after years in France, it felt fresh and sharp in the new landscape. He would have loved to see the American wilderness.

She wished most of all that Pierre had been with her in Washington, DC, on May 15. The simple ceremony had taken place in the East Room of the White House, and Marie found the experience deeply moving. In the presence of a number of dignitaries, President Harding handed her a gold key to the lead-lined box, along with a deed to the radium that gave her complete control over the substance. In his speech, the president praised her for being a devoted wife and loving mother, who "aside from her crushing toil, had fulfilled all the duties of womanhood."

Marie had listened to the words quietly, wondering whether she had indeed fulfilled those responsibilities and thinking that nobody ever spoke about men fulfilling the "duties of fatherhood." Ève would probably say that she wasn't an ideal mother at all, but she'd done her best. When the speech ended, she thanked the president for honoring her, took his arm, and they stepped outside into the brilliant May sunshine.

Marie had been beaming. It was a radiant day and the radium was finally in her possession. Sealed in twelve glass vials inside a lead-lined mahogany casket weighing 130 pounds was one gram of the precious element, which would accompany her back across the ocean to her Radium Institute, "a remembrance never to be forgotten," she later wrote, "in which the chief representative of a great nation offered me homage of infinite value, the testimonial of the recognition of his country's citizens."

Staring out at the Grand Canyon now, Marie imagined that she could see the layers of her own life in the striated rock: her childhood, her life in Poland, the Sorbonne, Pierre, radium, the girls, the war. One day, Irène would take her place at the helm of the Curie Institute's laboratory. It was a relief to know that her own flesh and blood would continue her work and keep her precious element safe at the institute. France might remain a patriarchy, but she would pass her legacy on to her eldest daughter. The radium would outlive them all in the end. As their fragile lights went out, it would shine on, diminished by half only every 1,600 years.

Act V

When Loie Fuller's Chinese dancers enwound
A shining web, a floating ribbon of cloth,
It seemed that a dragon of air
Had fallen among dancers, had whirled them round
Or hurried them off on its own furious path.
                                        —William Butler Yeats

Scene I

Dragon of the Air

1922

Loïe squirmed on the wooden bench, staring at the harlequin pattern of the black-and-white floor tiles. Had Marie picked them out? The scientist seemed to have little interest in such trivial things, but Loïe knew that her friend had seen to every detail of the Radium Institute. The waiting room was neat, clean, and felt very modern.

Sadly, this was not a social visit. Loïe would rather have been almost anywhere else, but this was one argument that Gab refused to lose. After driving an ambulance in the war and watching so many men die of infections, she didn't want Loïe to go under the knife. Surgery was, she'd said, a last resort, and she'd written to Marie Curie to inquire about radium needle treatment.

"Surgery isn't a death sentence," Loïe reminded her. "People do it all the time now."

But Gab's smooth, calm face had crumpled as she said in a choked voice that she couldn't bear to lose Loïe. Loïe had wanted to get the whole ordeal over with and have the damned thing cut out, but as she sat there watching the tears spill over her dearest companion's thick black eyelashes, she had finally given in. What else could she do? She'd agreed to go to the Radium Institute for a consultation with Dr. Regaud, the foremost radiation therapy doctor in Paris.

It felt strange to be sitting there now, in the waiting room of a building that owed its very existence to her friend. If it hadn't been for her acquaintance with Marie and Dr. Regaud's wife, Gab almost certainly wouldn't have been able to make an appointment at the famous medical institution so quickly. There were scores of desperate people waiting to get in.

Gab had wanted to come along, but Loïe insisted on going to the appointment alone. She wouldn't have any treatment that day, after all. Whatever happened, whatever the doctor said, she wanted to let the news trickle through her body and fully soak in, so that she could decide for herself what to do. It was her body, after all, and not Gab's.

It seemed so odd that radium, the very object that had first pulled her to Marie, might now be the thing that saved her life. Loïe's beliefs had always wavered in the undefined space between God and nature, but the intersection of Marie, radium, and her own destiny now felt like the work of some higher power. She'd never know whether it was fate or divine intervention that brought them together, but it was certain that Marie had changed her life in more ways than she could count.

When the nurse called Loïe's name, she stood slowly and followed her into the small, white examination room with leaden feet. She changed into the light blue gown as quickly as she could, so that she wouldn't catch a chill, but it was far cooler in the room than she would have liked. Another round of bronchitis or pneumonia would only make things worse.

Being sick was an enormous waste of time. She'd always liked her body, no matter how imperfect other people said it was, but lately health problems had begun to make her think of it as a traitor. When she was young, she hadn't appreciated how useful it was to be healthy. Throwing around huge swaths of fabric under intense spotlights had left her with shoulder problems and damaged eyes, but these maladies seemed trivial now, like nothing at all.

The thought of growing old terrified Loïe, so she surrounded herself with youth. Gab was much younger than she, and her muses had become her artistic doppelgangers, performing the dances she no longer could. They depended on her to book engagements and come up with new special effects and choreography, but she no longer performed and traveled with them.

In June, they'd performed *Ballets Fantastiques* at the Théâtre des Champs-Élysées, astonishing the audiences with the special effects Loïe had created for the show. To the music of Mozart, Grieg, Wagner, Ravel, Debussy, and Saint-Saëns, she'd utilized footlights to project fantastical images on a brilliantly lit screen. In one dance, called "Les Sorcières Gigantesques," the audience watched the tiny shadows of her muses dwarfed by enormous fingers as they fled giant silhouettes of witches with monstrous, grasping hands. One thrilled spectator wrote that Loïe had taken hold of shadow, which had previously been only an annoyance to theatrical illusion, tamed it, and made it an essential element.

Loïe's ailing lungs sometimes kept her from rehearsals, but she made every effort to be there for her troupe. Sometimes that meant calling out instructions to the girls while she lay on a couch near the stage, but she did her best. During long stretches when she was healthy, she spent hours in her workshop and often brought the girls in to assist her in dyeing fabric and costumes for new productions.

The lung ailments that had plagued her since she was young had amplified as she aged, coming on stronger and lasting longer. Over the last few years, she'd spent weeks in bed with bronchitis. A few recent brushes with pneumonia, including one especially frightening episode in January of 1919, had very nearly killed her. As terrifying as the feeling of drowning in her own lung fluid was, though, it was an enemy that she knew well. This was the first time she'd faced the possibility of her very cells having gone rogue.

Sliding one hand under the tunic, she felt for the lump under the skin of her left breast. Her heart lurched every time she touched it, but she couldn't quite leave it alone. Each time she ran her fingers over the flesh, Loïe hoped desperately that it would have somehow dissolved and gone away, but it was always there, like a stain that wouldn't come out.

She'd been horrified to discover the lump one morning while getting dressed. Was it cancer? The timing couldn't have been worse. She was about to depart for Romania, to visit Queen Marie and finish some business, and she knew that if anyone learned about the lump, they would prevent her from taking the trip. Swearing her doctor to secrecy, she'd asked him to examine the lump.

To her enormous relief, her physician declared that the tumor probably wasn't dangerous. It was, he said, egg-shaped, not attached closely to her body and most likely not cancerous. However, he recommended that she have it removed as soon as possible. Determined to finish her work first, Loïe decided to go on with her trip anyway and get a second opinion when she returned home.

The visit to Bucharest had been planned rather last-minute in order to discuss financial problems with a film she and Gab had made, *The Lily of Life*, based on a story written by Queen Marie. Loïe hoped the queen would help her deal with a man named Paul Turner whom she and Gab had initially partnered with to stage the play their film would be based on. They'd fallen out, Loïe had won a lawsuit against him, and now he was demanding that Loïe and the queen pay back funds he claimed to have advanced for the film.

The moving picture cost much more than Loïe expected, with the bills adding up to around 400,000 francs. When it was finally released in the fall of 1921, *The Lily of Life* was universally praised by critics but turned out to be something of a flop when it came to ticket sales. Although initially she, Gab, and the queen had hoped to raise enough to cover expenses and make a large contribution to Romanian war relief, the moving picture's revenue didn't come close to its cost.

Loïe was the first to admit that she didn't know much about making movies when they'd embarked on the project. She hadn't seen many, because they hurt her eyes, but that didn't stop her from making a groundbreaking film. Inexperience, for her, was fertile ground for creativity. The cast of the film consisted of her muses, along with a young actor named René Chomette who played a prince, and a singer and actress called Damia whom they'd double-cast as the queen and the witch. René Chomette, who adopted the stage name René Clair around that time, would go on to become one of France's greatest movie directors. They shot the footage in late 1920 and early 1921 in Nice and Cannes and filmed interior scenes in Paris, where they edited and processed the film.

While making *The Lily of Life*, Loïe had managed to create some cutting-edge movie techniques, including playing with the crank speed of the camera to create slow motion and incorporating negative images. Loïe had loved how strange the negatives looked and spliced them in with the positive film to create special effects, like fantastical images and dream scenes. In 1922, she patented her negative image technique in France. Loïe also designed the lighting for *The Lily of Life*, bringing in her own lights and concentrating them on her subjects to illuminate scenes. Soon, everyone in the film industry was imitating her techniques, which was flattering but it didn't pay the bills.

Loïe was happy to see Queen Marie again. Despite the trouble it caused her, the *Lily of Life* project had kept Loïe tightly connected to the queen. Loïe was infatuated with Marie but they shared nothing more than a frequent correspondence. An irritated Gab knew perfectly well that Loïe always addressed the queen as "My Beloved One" and signed letters to the Romanian monarch "Thy Loïe." Loïe was fairly certain that Gab tolerated her flirtation in order to pursue filmmaking, which she seemed to enjoy immensely.

As it turned out, Queen Marie was friends with the enormously powerful American lawyer William Nelson Cromwell. Together, Loïe and the queen composed letters to Cromwell about the whole affair. Paul Turner eventually gave up on collecting any money from Loïe or the queen. Normally, Loïe treasured every moment she and Marie spent together, but on that particular trip to Bucharest, worry gnawed at Loïe. She couldn't stop thinking about the tumor.

When she returned to Paris, things got worse. The lump started to hurt more. She tried to ignore it, but jostling carriages and sudden bumps shot sharp pains through her breast. Loïe tossed and turned at night to find a position that kept it from aching. Occasionally, while walking, she had to hold her bust up as unobtrusively as she could in order to relieve the discomfort. Her doctor insisted that she tell Gab about the situation and have the lump removed.

Physicians of the time recommended radium therapy, X-ray therapy, and electrotherapy as alternatives to surgery, while Loïe just wanted to get the painful lump cut out. When Gab wrote to Marie Curie about radium needle treatment, they learned that the treatment for breast cancer involved inserting needles containing 10 milligrams of radium salts into tumors, adjacent flesh, and sometimes lymph nodes to kill the rogue cells. Radium, Marie told them, was very good at killing cells, and ideally the tumor would shrink away to nothing. If surgery were still required, Gab told Loïe, it seemed that this therapy was an effective way to shrink the tumor and prevent potentially deadly cancer cells from spreading.

Loïe shivered, wondering how much it hurt to have radium needles poked into your flesh. Her immense capacity for imagination, which was so helpful when inventing, was a nightmare when it came to worrying. She could easily imagine thousands of horrible scenarios. Had her doctor been wrong about the lump? If it was cancer, how long did she have to live? Her mother had never had cancer. Her father was healthy until the day he was poisoned, and all her siblings were fine.

Then again, after cancer had killed his assistant, Thomas Edison had given up work on the fluoroscope and abandoned his research with luminescent chemicals. Loïe didn't work with X-rays, but she had been tinkering with luminescent salts for years. Recently, Gab and her muses had been helping her to apply a variety of them to fabrics in the lab. She didn't think the chemicals were the cause of her tumor, but how could she be sure? The lump wasn't in her fingers or her arms, which had been exposed to the salts, but in her breast. It didn't make any sense, but she still wondered.

If luminescent salts like radium caused cancer, Marie Curie would have been dead long ago. The scientist's fingers were scarred, but not cancerous, and she'd probably been covered in radioactive compounds for years. She even ate and drank in the same lab where she isolated the salts. Marie had also told her that she kept glowing radium salts in a vial beside her bed, to remind her of Pierre. The salts Loïe worked with in her lab might have been mildly radioactive, but they were nothing like pure radium. Therefore, working with the salts couldn't possibly be responsible for the lump in her breast. Could they?

Maybe it wasn't cancer at all. Or maybe it wasn't an especially dangerous type of cancer. Loïe didn't have time to be terminally ill. She still had far too much to do. What would happen to Gab if she died? Would her ideas all die with her if she didn't survive this? Sometimes she wondered whether anyone had even noticed that she was no longer physically present at the center of the swirling vortexes of silk in her productions.

The public had a short memory, especially where women were concerned. Loïe feared that her achievements would yellow and crumble away with time, and that her inventions would live on without the mention of her name. Would anyone remember what she'd created, or would she just be a colorful figure on old posters? The symbolist Irish poet William Butler Yeats had recently used her as a symbol of a fading era in his poem "Nineteen Hundred and Nineteen," in which he penned the words:

> *Many ingenious lovely things are gone*
> *That seemed sheer miracle to the multitude,*
> *Protected from the circle of the moon*
> *That pitches common things about...*

When Loie Fuller's Chinese dancers enwound
A shining web, a floating ribbon of cloth,
It seemed that a dragon of the air
Had fallen among dancers, had whirled them round
Or hurried them off on its own furious path

Gab could carry on with some of the work, Loïe supposed. Surely her dear companion would be fine without her. Perhaps she'd even be better off, Loïe thought miserably, free of all the debts and crazy ideas. Still, the thought of Gab alone made her want to weep.

There was a short, courteous knock on the door and Dr. Regaud stepped into the examination room. He was a thin, serious-looking man whose baldness, high cheekbones, and triangular white beard gave his head the shape of an upside-down pear. Black eyebrows punctuated his hooded eyes and contrasted sharply with his pale skin and white facial hair. Loïe couldn't help thinking that he looked more like an undertaker than a healer.

"I hear that you're a friend of Madame Curie," he said. His voice was far less intimidating than his appearance. "I've seen you dance many times and I'm sorry to hear that you've been suffering."

"Thank you," Loïe said. She didn't really know what else to say.

"You are familiar with radium therapy?" he asked.

"I'm familiar with radium," she replied. Loïe didn't mention that next to her bed were books filled with notes for a lecture on radium that she'd presented in London back in 1911. Her interest in the element had never waned. It still stoked her creative fires. As Jules Claretie told the *Los Angeles Times* in 1907, "The idea of radium haunts her. She would like to catch and imprison its light."

"Then you are aware that there are risks involved with the use of radium?"

"Madame Curie has told me that it can cause burns of the flesh," Loïe said. "I've seen what it's done to her fingers."

"Yes, that's how bioradiology works," he said. "When it is applied to a tumor, the radioactivity kills all the nearby cells. It is especially harmful to cells which grow very quickly, like cancer cells, but it can damage normal cells too. There are side effects, and in some cases, it can cause other health problems."

"If that's true," Loïe asked, "then why add it to everything? Hair tonic, medicines—a friend of mine even sleeps outside to take in the radium emanations from the earth."

Dr. Regaud shook his head, disgusted.

"I'm beginning to see more and more patients arriving with cancers which appear to have been caused by these 'miraculous' radium products. Just the other day, a man came in whose jaw was disintegrating from cancer. He told me that he'd been perfectly healthy until very recently, and when I pressed him further, I learned that he'd been brushing his teeth with radium toothpaste."

"So the radium itself can cause cancer? Then radium therapy must be very dangerous too?" Loïe was genuinely confused.

"In most cases that I treat," Regaud said, "the benefits of the therapy far outweigh the risks. I will examine you, but if I agree with your physician that your tumor does not seem dangerous, I would not recommend taking that risk. Have it removed and then we will see. If it is malignant, or your lymph nodes are cancerous, then come back to see me. We have had good results treating breast tumors."

Loïe nodded.

"There's hope then? No matter what you find?"

"Thanks to your friend Marie, there is hope," he said.

Scene II

Blind Faith

1923

È ve Curie was a breath of fresh air. Her cropped hair shone like raven's feathers, and her intelligent dark eyes flashed like bright jewels. Years had passed since Loïe last saw the girl, and it was hard to believe that she was eighteen. When Marie mentioned Ève's skill on the piano in a note, Loïe had invited them over for lunch and specially requested that Ève play for her. She had an idea. Irène, it turned out, was busy in the lab that week, but Marie replied that she and Ève would be delighted to come.

When Marie stepped into the room behind her daughter, it was as if one of the Fates had followed Persephone through the doorway. Loïe was so shocked by her friend's appearance that she almost took a step backward. Marie looked so old.

Of course, Loïe knew that she'd changed too. She was sixty now, but had continued to lie about her age, and people still mostly believed she was fifty. Despite having a large chunk of flesh cut out during her surgery and losing some weight while she recovered, she'd continued to struggle against plumpness, and her clothes had become quite tight.

The scientist, on the other hand, appeared to have shrunk. Marie was thinner than the last time Loïe had seen her and seemed to have faded. Her hair was pulled back in its usual bun, but it was white now, except for a silver streak that still clung to the crown of her head. Milky cataracts clouded her beautiful eyes, and the rosy glow that had once suffused her

266

cheeks with color was gone. Gravity had collapsed her dimples into flat lines, and the parentheses between her cheeks and her lips had deepened into creases. Marie's beauty was still evident in the architecture of her noble forehead and her proud, intelligent expression, but the heaviness of the years had come crashing down on her all at once.

A chill ran through Loïe. Was she sick? Although they didn't see each other all that often, the scientist had become a constant in her life. Marie was one of the people whose friendship she valued most. It seemed that these days, she was surrounded by reminders of how quickly the years had passed. In recent years, many of her treasured friends and acquaintances had died.

Auguste Rodin had passed away in November of 1917, not long after Loïe returned to France from one of her trips to San Francisco during the war. Near the end of his life, he'd finally married his lifelong companion, Rose. Tragically, she'd died of pneumonia sixteen days after the ceremony. Although the sculptor's memory had faded during the last year of his life, Loïe had continued to visit him at Meudon from time to time when she was in France. Now, she preferred to remember him as the strong, passionate figure he'd been when they first met.

Their friendship had been tumultuous, often because of a jealous mistress or her overzealous attempts to purchase his art and donate it to museums, without necessarily having the funds to do so. She'd been enamored of him from the beginning, though, moved by his art and the fact that he took her seriously as an artist. "*You are a strange man / As deep as the sea / Mind of genius / A cauldron of fury,*" she'd penned in a poem amid one of their fights. "*Proud as Lucifer / Sensitive as a plant / Fine as burnished steel / Hard as iron / Cold as ice / Hot as Hades.*" She went on to conclude, "*Cruel as Fire / Pitiless as the Ocean / And yet / An angel of mercy.*"

About a year before his death, Rodin signed an agreement putting all his works, both originals and reproductions, under the control of France. His Parisian residence and studio, the Biron mansion, would become a museum for his work. Loïe, who had just secured an agreement with Rodin to buy more sculptures and have his famous sculpture of Balzac cast in bronze for the Palace of the Legion of Honor in San Francisco, found herself out in the cold.

The curator of the planned Rodin museum canceled Loïe's order for the Balzac and eight other pieces. He wrote to Alma Spreckels that if she wanted to buy any more of the master's art, the deals would go through him, and from that moment on, anyone who wanted to purchase Rodin's work would pay the prices he decided on. Loïe was angry and hurt, but was comforted by the fact that her earlier acquisitions were now centerpieces for new museums in America.

She still wished that Rodin had sculpted Marie, though she probably would have refused to sit still long enough to have her likeness made. She'd rather be in her lab, working with the earth's elements, than having her image rendered in them. Now, Marie squinted at Loïe and smiled. When her eyes crinkled in the way they always had, the years fell away and Loïe saw the woman she knew so well. She exhaled, unaware that she'd been holding her breath, and gently grasped Marie's hands.

"It's so nice to see you," she said, kissing her friend's papery cheeks, wondering how well Marie could see her face.

One afternoon, years before, Marie had given Loïe a tube of purified radium to hold. It was enclosed inside another thick protective tube, and Marie told her to shut her eyes and bring the tube close to her eyelid for a few seconds to see what happened. They'd done the experiment in a dark room, and although there had been no visible light coming from the tube, when Loïe moved it to her eye, it felt as though she was staring into the sun.

Her closed eye had been filled with a light so powerful that the intense white circle remained in her vision long after she moved the tube away. She'd always understood that the eye was like a photographic plate, which needs light to make images, but radium, even with its visible glow blocked, created a burning image. Marie had told her not to try it more than once, but the experience left an indelible impression on Loïe. Radium's rays had somehow penetrated her skin and entered her body, leaving their signature in the center of her vision.

Scientists had been studying radioactivity and were using it to disintegrate the atom, but there was still so much to understand. Marie had been exposed to those invisible rays for years. What had they done to her friend's eyes? Had they penetrated even further? Could radium burn you inside as well as out?

As a woman whose own vision had been permanently damaged by electric light, Loïe understood how it felt to be the victim of your own vocation. At one point, she'd been sure that she would go blind, but a physician had ordered her to rest and her sight had mostly returned. Since then, she'd worn eyeglasses when she wasn't onstage. Recently, she'd bought some tortoiseshell frames that she liked very much.

She dropped Marie's hands and turned to Ève.

"I've heard that you're very talented at the piano," she said. "I hope that you'll play for us after lunch. Gab wants to hear you as well."

Ève said she'd play but protested that she wasn't as good as her mother had led them to believe. Ève was said to be one of the most beautiful young women in Paris. She obviously loved fashion. Besides her cropped hair, she had the slightest bit of kohl around her eyes, and her lipstick hinted at a smart Cupid's bow.

Marie had always favored dark, practical clothes, wearing them until they were ragged, and hated frivolities like makeup, which she and Irène never wore. Although Marie would never admit to having a favorite daughter, it was obvious to everyone who knew them that she and Irène were much closer to each other than Ève would ever be to either of them. Marie's extended depressions had taken their toll, and although Ève loved her mother, she would always resent the emotional abandonment she'd endured in the years following Pierre's death.

Ève, therefore, often found herself the odd person out. She clung to her individuality fiercely, wearing lipstick and practicing piano sonatas while Marie and Irène were away at the laboratory. Still, it was clear to Loïe how much Ève loved her mother, as she watched her help Marie with her coat and hat. When the valet had whisked their vestments away, Loïe showed them into the mansion she was currently renting. Perhaps "château" would have been a better description, since the eight-bedroom house was the most extravagant place she'd ever lived.

Owned by the Grand Duke Alexander of Russia, the residence, which came fully furnished, was run by a cook, a valet, and two maids. Loïe's favorite feature, though, was the steam heat. She was always cold, and the warm damp air felt wonderful in her lungs. Large windows overlooked the mansion's spectacular garden, and sun poured into the house all day long.

Gab had told Loïe that she couldn't afford the place, but her dancers had been working steadily, so she ignored the advice and signed the lease. Loïe knew perfectly well that she should be saving, but it was lovely to live so well, even if it was for an indeterminate amount of time. Recent health scares had reminded her that life is short, and she was determined to enjoy it.

"These are beautiful," Ève said.

She was studying the enormous pieces of silk Loïe had hand-painted and hung on the walls of the living room. Drenched in lush colors of her own design, the fabric was tinted with undulating, random swaths of homemade dye. She conceived the idea of coloring the draperies at random, so they might give the effect of shifting colored lights at night or be made even more brilliant by sunshine. Loïe had hung them up in the house for inspiration. Ultimately, she planned to create acres and acres of silk that could be used in outdoor performances featuring her muses. She was certain that her textiles would be absolutely spectacular under spotlights or bathed in sunlight for varying effects.

"The designs are random, spurred only by my imagination and instinct," she told Ève. "I believe that this technique unconsciously produces a real expression of one's self."

"You sound like a surrealist," Ève teased.

Loïe laughed. "I don't know what I am. I might try to patent this technique, but I'm not sure that it's worth it anymore. No matter what I do, people copy my ideas while I scrape by to pay my debts in order to create something else for them to steal."

"You must take credit for your work, even if you don't profit," Marie said, speaking up from behind them.

"It's not so easy for artists," Loïe replied. "There are no such things as scientific papers in theater. I suppose I'll keep trying, though. Otherwise, when I'm gone, no one will remember me at all. I'm not rich like Alma or beautiful like Isadora, and there's no Nobel Prize for dancing. At least some of my textiles will be hung at the Louvre for a little while. Can you imagine? I only wish that Monsieur Rodin were still alive to see it."

The Decorative Art department at the Louvre had decided to recognize Loïe's influence on art, architecture, and interior design. Her work, which had been such an enormous influence on the symbolists and Art Nouveau, was now setting the stage for the soft tints of the sleek new Art Deco style. They'd asked Loïe to exhibit her painted silk in the museum in the spring of 1924, and she'd happily agreed.

The show would be titled "Retrospective on Studies in Form, Line and Color for Light Effects, 1892–1924." In addition to her new textiles, the museum was planning to exhibit some of her earlier dance costumes, which she'd dyed and painted herself. Several of her friends, as well as other collectors, were contributing pieces to the exhibit. Alma Spreckels, Queen Marie of Romania, and the famous American movie actor Rudolph Valentino were among the collectors who were going to loan the museum Loïe's painted fabrics for the exhibit.

When Ève had finished examining the silk, they moved into the dining room for lunch. Ève ate with the appetite of a teenager, while Marie only pecked at her food. Loïe, as usual, tried not to eat too much and nibbled on cucumbers as she told them about the Maryhill Museum, which she had convinced the American millionaire Sam Hill to build.

Sam's father-in-law was the railroad builder James J. Hill, who had completed the Great Northern Railway from Saint Paul to Seattle in 1893. A friend of Alma Spreckels, he had done very well financially and thoroughly enjoyed spending his money, which made him an ideal friend for Loïe. The gray-haired millionaire, who had separated from his wife, was in the process of building a French-styled château nicknamed "Maryhill" in Washington State. Standing beside the poured-concrete walls, Loïe declared to Sam that the site was absolutely perfect for a museum, and by the trip's end, Sam had agreed to put the new Maryhill Museum in Loïe's hands. They'd planned to open it in autumn of the following year, but construction had been slower than expected and Loïe had to keep pushing to keep the project on track.

"The museum overlooks the Columbia River gorge," she gushed, "and the day I visited, wildflowers were blooming and Mount Hood was visible in the distance."

"I wish we had made it to the Pacific," Ève said, "but Mother's health prevented it. We did see the Grand Canyon, though!"

"You must tell me all about your trip to America," Loïe insisted. Like everyone else, she'd read about it in the papers, but it was nice to get the firsthand version.

"And now you have an entire gram of radium for yourself?" Loïe asked. "Surely, there's no one more deserving. If it weren't for you, it wouldn't even exist!"

"It would exist," Marie protested. "But perhaps we wouldn't yet have discovered it."

Upon returning home from the United States, her work had continued to focus on the production and measurement of pure radioactive elements, as well as the discovery of new ones. The Radium Institute had become famous for having the best, strongest radioactive sources in the world. Besides doing fractionations and crystallizations to prepare high-activity radium, actinium, and polonium, her lab prepared radon seeds for Dr. Regaud to use for radium therapy in his clinic.

Following her trip, Marie had also begun collecting previously used radon seeds from France and America. She collected radioactive products from the glass ampoules, taking advantage of the fact that radon has a half-life of just under four days, after which it decays into polonium, which has a much longer half-life. Now, researchers around the world were using the Curie lab's radioactive sources to make groundbreaking discoveries about the structure of the atom.

Marie was thrilled that radium therapy was proving to be so successful, and Loïe still loved hearing Marie talk about her work. When the scientist spoke about her lab, her eyes sparkled and the heavy cloak of weariness seemed to fall away.

"My American friend Missy Malone discovered that she had a malignancy near the end of our trip," Marie said. "At the time, she didn't tell anyone, but she recently wrote to me that she has undergone radium therapy, which has saved her life."

Loïe smiled.

"Your radium might have saved my life too, if surgery hadn't been successful," Loïe said.

"What was it like?" Ève asked. "The surgery?"

"That's a rude question," Marie chided her.

Loïe didn't mind talking about it now. She'd found the entire experience rather fascinating.

"It was rather dreadful," she said. "But I think you would have found it terribly interesting, Marie. There were three surgeons, with their faces all covered with veils, and my personal physician was there as well. I was terrified, but the nurse had forgotten to ask me whether I had any false teeth. It seems that they were all afraid to broach the topic, and when the doctor finally blurted out the question, he was so embarrassed that I almost laughed out loud.

"They put a circle of needles around the tumor to numb it, which was very unpleasant, and then covered my face when they began the surgery so that I wouldn't breathe any microbes towards my breast. I couldn't see anything, but I could hear and feel, and it seemed as if they were cutting my very heart away. Then the surgeon called for anesthesia, and when I woke up, it was finished. I was missing a great piece of flesh, and the recovery was very unpleasant, but I won't talk about that."

"And now you're fine?" Ève asked.

"Yes. As fine as can be. And if I weren't, your mother's radium would have surely saved me. Isn't it strange to think that you discovered a cure for cancer when you weren't even looking for it, Marie?"

"I'm very pleased that radium has given hope to so many," Marie said. "I only wish Pierre were here to see you talking so happily about radium therapy."

"So do I," Loïe said, wondering if she should ask the next question that popped into her mind. A small voice inside told her to keep quiet, but her curiosity got the better of her.

"Do you ever wonder whether radium is perfectly safe? They're starting to put it in everything now, and Dr. Regaud suggested to me that it might actually be giving some people cancer."

Marie looked uncomfortable.

"It's ridiculous to drink it," she said, "or use it to brush one's teeth, but it's perfectly safe when used correctly. There are emanations of radiation in the air we breathe every day."

Ève looked like she wanted to say something, but she remained silent.

"The French Academy of Medicine recently put out a report calling the fears of radioactivity unjustified," she continued. "They went so far as to state that small doses of radioactivity might be beneficial to one's health."

"But are you not exposed to very large doses in your laboratory?" Loïe asked.

"Yes, but we've had no major accidents or illnesses, and we work with some of the strongest samples in the world," Marie said.

Ève spoke up. "You do test the blood of your workers."

In July of 1921, two months after Marie had collected her gram of radium from the United States, the X-ray and Radium Protection Committee, a British committee of experts, published a report stating that the danger of overexposure to X-rays and radium could be avoided "by the provision of efficient protection and suitable working conditions." The report judged that "The known effects on the operator to be guarded against are: (1) Visible injuries to the superficial tissues which may result in permanent damage. (2) Derangements of the internal organs and changes in the blood." They recommended the following precautions for those who worked with radiation:

1. Not more than seven working hours a day.
2. Sundays and two half-days off duty each week, to be spent as much as possible out of doors.
3. An annual holiday of one month, or two separate fortnights.

The committee also recommended using forceps rather than fingers to handle radium and radon sources, as well as carrying and storing the element in lead-shielded containers. Recognizing the health hazards of breathing radon gas, they also suggested ventilating laboratories with exhaust fans.

The Curie Institute had been ahead of its time in safety standards and was already taking similar precautions. The labs contained fume hoods to whisk radon gas out of the lab and into the atmosphere outside. Forceps were used to pick up highly radioactive material, and workers were encouraged to spend some time in the garden each day, to take the fresh air. However, convenience and habit often trumped safety, and many workers still used their mouths to suck radioactive liquid up into straw-like glass pipettes in order to measure it accurately.

"Of course we do," Marie admitted, "and if anyone is anemic, I send them on a vacation. Radiation can overstimulate the blood. Fresh air and a few weeks in the countryside always seem to bring things back to normal, and my workers are back in the lab, just like new."

"And your own health?" Loïe ventured. "Has it been affected by the radioactive materials?"

Marie gave her a sideways glance.

Ève picked at her dessert.

"My health has almost certainly been damaged by working with X-rays during the war," Marie said, glancing at Ève, "and perhaps a little from the work I did before we started using lead shields and venting equipment. I have other more serious internal issues, which are completely unrelated to radioactivity."

No one asked the obvious question. Scientists were viewed in a romantic light at the time, as martyrs for their work who made great personal sacrifices. It was well known in Paris that a large number of radiologists and nurses were sick or dead from their work with X-rays. Had Marie unknowingly endangered her own daughter? Irène had been working with the dangerous X-rays for almost as long as her mother.

Marie put her napkin on her plate and stood up, ending the conversation.

"Radium may have cracked my fingers," she said, "but it has not harmed me badly. Ève, it is time for you to play. Where is the piano?"

With impeccable timing, Gab walked into the room and broke the tension. She greeted Marie and Ève with genuine happiness. She'd been so excited when Loïe told her that they'd get to hear Ève play.

"You're just in time," Loïe said. The four of them walked into the parlor, and Marie, Gab, and Loïe took their seats in beautiful velvet chairs facing the baby grand. Ève sat down at the piano, adjusted the bench, and sat silently with her head bent forward on her long neck before beginning to play.

As strains of the first movement of Saint-Saëns's Piano Concerto no. 2 floated through the air, Loïe looked over at Gab and gave her an almost imperceptible nod. It wasn't perfect, but Ève played with skill and passion. Perhaps Loïe's friend Gabriel Pierné, who was a rather famous composer, would give Ève some lessons and take her to the next level. The wheels were turning in Loïe's head. Americans would come in droves to see the Girl with Radium Eyes on a piano tour. She could already see the headline: "Child of Radium Gives Up World-Wide Opportunities in Science For Life of Artiste in Music."

When Marie and her daughter had left, Loïe picked up a pen and wrote to her friend, "I love you very much, and your little girl has walked and played herself right into my heart." She meant every word.

Scene III

Bone Killer

1925

Marie set her sample down beside the desiccator and put the small glass bottle inside a glass-fronted oak cabinet. Her back was tired, and she knew better than to keep standing at the lab bench. All she needed was some fresh air to revive her energy.

It seemed like long ago when she'd been able to work from morning until night without stopping. Now, she sometimes didn't even come into the lab until dusk. Still, she couldn't stay away. Double-checking that the gas valves were off, she washed her hands and opened the doors of her laboratory, whose long glass panes overlooked the garden and led to a small balcony. She stepped outside, leaving the white tile and gleaming glassware behind.

From where she stood, Marie could see Jean Perrin and one of his assistants sitting in the speckled shade of the courtyard, deep in conversation. He'd moved into the lab next door a few years earlier, and it was always nice to hear his familiar voice echoing through the halls. She clasped her hands together, leaned her forearms on the railing to relieve the aching in her back, and stared up at the trees. A soft breeze brushed her face and she reached up to push a stray tendril of hair out of her eyes. Everyone called her "La Patronne" now. She'd become a fixture in this spot, leaning on the iron balustrade.

The plane and lime trees she'd planted, long before the foundations had even been laid for the physics-chemistry and biology laboratories, were thriving. Even the trees she'd put in after the war seemed to be getting taller by the day. Their spreading branches now provided some shade for the scientists who took breaks here. The courtyard she'd envisioned so long ago had become an invaluable meeting place for researchers.

The roses in the courtyard were in full late-summer bloom, surrounded by a riot of green that ranged from lime to deep emerald. In the midst of the shrubs, a single bloom the color of apricot sorbet dwarfed pale pink single flowers with yellow centers. Vines twisted up the railing of the balcony she leaned against, and she pinched off an unruly branch that was growing too high. Marie never tired of roses and loved to put her nose to the dewy blossoms and breathe in their bittersweet perfume. Her sense of smell was slightly dampened by all the years of breathing chemical fumes, but the scent still gave her pleasure.

Bright blue sky floated high over her garden, framed by the bricks of her institute. It was a perfect day, but try as she might, Marie couldn't get the image of the dead pigeon out of her mind. The poor thing had been lying on the cobblestones just outside the gate of the Radium Institute that morning, and she'd almost stepped on it. Fat, gray pigeons roamed the streets of Paris like they owned it, and Marie had seen her share of dead ones, but for some reason, this particular corpse felt like a bad omen. It had looked normal at first, but a closer glance revealed that it had been hollowed out by a rat or some other creature, and she could count its ribs.

Bones had been on Marie's mind since late June, when she'd received Missy's letter from America about the rotting jaws of the watch dial painters. Her friend wrote that her husband's physician was involved in treating two of the young women painters who appeared to have radium poisoning. One of them had already died, and the autopsy revealed that her body was riddled with radium. Missy had written to inquire whether Marie knew anything about how factory conditions could have affected these young women, and whether there was any treatment at all.

The more Marie learned about the dial painters, the more upset she'd become. It seemed that young women, some not even twenty, had fallen desperately ill from using a radium solution to paint watch dials so they would glow in the dark. Now, not only were they dying, they were dying horrible, painful deaths. It was obvious that corporate greed and stupidity, which she'd always despised, had been the cause of their illness. Marie was furious.

She barely remembered Dr. Sabin von Sochocky, the man who had started the first dial-painting company in America. He'd come through their lab in the years when Marie was working to isolate radium, but he spent far more time with Pierre than with her. The young physician had taken the knowledge he'd gleaned about radium in their lab to the United States and proceeded to use the Curies' techniques to found a radium company.

He'd named his business the Radium Luminous Materials Corporation, but later changed the name to the US Radium Corporation. Von Sochocky's factories extracted radium from American ore and then dumped the industrial waste or sold it to schools as playground sand. In order to fund the medical research he was interested in, he'd invented an extremely popular luminous paint, which he called "Undark." Von Sochocky had been so enchanted by the stuff that he predicted that someday people would live in houses illuminated by the soft glow of radium paint.

As it turned out, his paint, which could be made by mixing fine zinc sulfide dust containing a minuscule amount of radium together with water and an adhesive, was more useful for painting dials than houses. His liquid sunshine could be applied to everything from watch dials to airplane instruments, and the enormous demand for it had only been fueled by the war.

The Curies had always warned their coworkers of the danger of overexposure to highly active radium, and Von Sochocky should have known well enough to do the same, but he wasn't always careful and had been forced to amputate the end of one of his own fingers after an accident with the element. At his new factory facility, he provided lead aprons and forceps for the men, but he set a horrible example himself. Everyone at the factory knew that Von Sochocky handled tubes of radioactive matter barehanded and could often be found up to his elbows in radioactive substances. Unsurprisingly, many of his employees followed suit.

The Radium Corporation had hired a slew of young women to brush the delicate lines onto watch dials and other equipment. In order to make the fine, perfect strokes, they used a technique called lip pointing. The job paid very well. They sat at tables in sunny, pleasant workrooms, mixing up the paint. Each young woman had her own supply of radium dust and would dab a tiny bit of the luminous powder into a small dish, add water and mix it.

As they stirred, traces of the fine powder rose into the air and floated on invisible currents to coat every surface in the room. The girls used their tongues and lips to form ultrafine paintbrushes into sharp points before painting each stroke, dipping again and repointing their brush with their mouth as they went along. Water in small dishes beside them was rarely used for rinsing the brushes. Lip, dip, paint, lip, dip, paint, for hour after hour, day after day.

Marie shuddered to think of it. She'd probably consumed some radium in her time, but not on purpose. Back in the old shed laboratory, she and Pierre ate their lunches and drank tea regularly in the midst of radioactive dust, but what Missy described seemed more like a fiendish experiment on unsuspecting test subjects to see what would happen if one regularly consumed radium.

From what Missy said, the girls at the dial painting factories had essentially been eating radium since 1917, and some were still doing it. Workers in Europe always applied radioactive paint using needles or sticks with cotton wadding. What kind of insanity had taken over in America? The almighty dollar?

281

There was far more to the story than Marie knew. Concern and questions voiced by the dial painters had been brushed aside from the beginning. Before they started getting really sick, some of the workers hadn't liked the taste and feel of the gritty paint. A few had broken out in rashes and pimples soon after they started painting dials, but the US Radium Corporation had assured them that the paint was perfectly safe.

The radium was highly diluted, the management said, insisting that if the girls did ingest it, the radioactive element would pass right through them. Besides, radium was the latest health fad, sold at a high price in lipsticks, medicines, and health drinks. The company went so far as to suggest that dial painting might actually make the girls healthier. And some of the girls loved the sheen the radium gave their skin. They'd apply leftover paint like makeup and walk home shining in the dark.

Unlike the men in the factory, the radium painters had no protection at all, and they took no precautions. Why would they? The young women worked with a minuscule amount of the precious element, and they'd been reassured that it was safe. Hard candy often sat beside the dishes in their work area, accumulating a sugar-soft coating of radium dust as the young women pointed their brushes again and again.

Still, the unearthly glow could be disconcerting. Undressing in darkened bedrooms, they'd be startled by their own reflections glowing in the dark. The clothes they wore to work shined in their closets like limp apparitions. Even blowing their noses yielded glowing handkerchiefs.

Demand for radium dials increased when the United States entered World War I, so more and more women came to work at the plant. After the war, many of them were encouraged to return to domestic life, and a number of dial painters left the factory to get married and have babies. That's when the trouble had started for the women who worked at the West Orange factory in New Jersey. Miscarriages, severe joint problems, and toothaches were only harbingers of the misery to come.

The first documented case of radium jaw was noted the same year that

Marie visited the United States. A dial painter named Mollie Maggia went to the dentist in 1921 to have a painful tooth removed, and then, over the next several months, she lost the rest of her teeth and her jawbone disintegrated. She died at the age of twenty-four. Her official cause of death was listed as syphilis, but later tests on her glowing, exhumed corpse revealed that she was entirely free of sexually transmitted infection and had died, like a growing number of her coworkers, of radium poisoning.

As time went on, more and more of the radium painters developed painful, infected teeth and jawbones so rotten that chunks of them would break off during dental procedures. A well-known dentist and doctor from New York had become suspicious about the mysterious ailment, which was similar to "Phossy jaw," an affliction that resulted from phosphorus poisoning.

Each of the girls who had the condition had worked as a dial painter, and some of them were still lip pointing with radium paint. Besides rotting jaws, the girls suffered from severe bone maladies, with arthritic symptoms, leg fractures, and crumbling vertebrae. One young woman who hadn't worked with radium for years screamed and fainted when she looked in a mirror and saw the bones of her skull glowing underneath her skin on a dark night.

By 1925, Von Sochocky was no longer an owner of the US Radium Corporation. Ousted by his own company in 1921, he helped a physician working on the girls' behalf come up with a way to use an electroscope to test living humans for internal radioactivity. Because radium decays into radon, they reasoned, anyone with radium in their jaw should have higher than normal radioactivity readings on an electroscope. Von Sochocky and the physician carried the device to the hospital where a dying woman breathed into it and confirmed that she was, in fact, radioactive. She died soon after, and her autopsy established their findings. Frighteningly, her bones, and the remains of several other girls who had died, emitted enough radioactivity to fog X-ray films.

On February 5, 1925, Marguerite Carlough became the first of the dial painters to file suit against the US Radium Corporation, for $75,000, and later that year, two official reports linking radium to the dial workers' illnesses were finally published. The US Radium Corporation and other companies who made radium products continued to deny any fault on their part. Fortunately, the families of the sick and deceased young women, along with a few advocates, kept pushing to get the truth out.

Doctors and lawyers working for the dial painters were initially confused, because they couldn't track down any obvious victims at the other dial-painting plants outside West Orange. They didn't yet understand that it took months or years for the radium sitting inside the girls' bodies to eat away their bones and make tumor-inducing changes in their cells. The West Orange factory had been the first to open, so that's where the first cases began popping up.

Scores more would follow. At the newest factory in Ottawa, Illinois, none of the girls had heard about radium sickness and were happily continuing to lip point. Dentists in their town were warned by the Radium Corporation to keep silent about any problems.

Marie was right to be disgusted. Since 1914, scientists and physicians studying the biological effect of radium had understood that the element, which is chemically similar to calcium, could deposit itself in human bones. Short-term studies showed that exposure to radioactivity affected the blood by making it produce more red blood cells, which was considered a health benefit. However, constant overstimulation of bone marrow caused anemia, a shortage of red blood cells.

Marie wondered whether perhaps she should be doing more than simply having her Radium Institute employees tested for changes in their blood. Irène worked with radioactivity every day after all, and Marie greatly valued the health of her employees. She still believed that fresh air and rest could reverse the effects of radiation-induced anemia, but what if she was wrong?

No one understood that ingesting even the smallest amount of radium was more destructive than anyone could have imagined. As radium trapped inside the human body encounters tissue and is incorporated into bone, high-energy alpha particles produced by the decaying element severely damage frail biological systems, rotting bone and causing cancers. Although the radium girls hadn't suffered burns or cracked fingertips, it was as though they'd swallowed millions of tiny bombs. The alpha particles emitted from the radium they'd ingested were wreaking havoc on their bones and tissue, killing them from the inside out.

Missy's letter to Marie about the dial painters had arrived on the heels of news of the deaths of two of Marie's former students in January. After being sick for a few months, they'd died within days of each other, from severe anemia and leukemia. The men, Maurice Demenitroux and Marcel Demalander, had been preparing radium and thorium X for medical use in a poorly ventilated laboratory outside Paris. Marie had been told that they weren't using proper screens to protect themselves from radioactivity, and in her opinion, they hadn't taken enough fresh air. She'd always kept in the back of her mind Pierre's experiment, which showed that trapping animals in a chamber with large quantities of radon gas was fatal.

Marie had replied to Missy that she had had no radium fatalities in her own lab but reported the deaths of Demalander and Demenitroux and suggested that faulty ventilation equipment probably played a role. As she'd never visited the dial-painting facilities, she told Missy that she could make no comment on the risk to their workers. Sadly, she knew of no treatment for radiation sickness. Marie did, however, promise to look into radiation-related illnesses in France and keep Missy updated.

She knew that radiologists and nurses had died of X-ray-related illnesses following the war. She was less certain about death from exposure to radium. Secluding herself in the laboratory and surrounding herself with academics had shielded her from the long-term implications of her discovery as it made its way around the world.

Now, doubt had crept in, with worry close behind. Ghostly girls haunted her dreams, and she sometimes woke in the middle of the night convinced that all of her teeth had fallen out. One particular detail revealed by Missy gnawed at Marie's heart. Several of the dial painters, it seemed, had experienced extreme pain and stiffness in their legs, along with arthritic hips and backs.

Could Pierre have been sick with radium poisoning before he died? Had radium hollowed out his bones like it rotted the jaws of the dial painters? The two of them had always been willing to make sacrifices for science, but it had never before occurred to her that their work might have been killing him. Was it possible the wagon wheels that crushed his head had simply beaten radium to the finishing line?

She worried about Irène too. Much like her father, she had a slow, serious brilliance and had continued to follow in Marie's footsteps, working with radioactivity every day. In March, Irène had defended her doctoral thesis, describing her work studying the alpha particles given off by polonium to a thousand people in the Sorbonne's amphitheater, and for the past year she'd been working very closely with a bright young protégé of Paul Langevin named Frédéric Joliot. Marie suspected that their companionship extended beyond the lab, but at the moment she was more preoccupied with Irène's safety. Since receiving the letter from Missy, she'd been watching her daughter like a hawk, constantly reminding her to wash her hands before going outside for tea and reprimanding her when she didn't think she was being cautious enough with her samples.

Still, there was nothing she could do now. If she had opened Pandora's box, all that was left was to pray that her discovery did more good than harm in the long run. Marie looked down to discover that she'd been rubbing a shiny green leaf between the scarred ridges of her thumb and finger. She exhaled, unaware that she'd been holding her breath, and turned back to her white-tiled temple to resume her experiment.

Scene IV

The Steps of the Palace

1925

The largest glass roof in Europe hung suspended over their heads, a web of pale green threads and sky.

"We should stage an American rodeo in here," Loïe said. "There's plenty of room."

Gab shook her head, looking up. "I don't like horses."

Loïe laughed, remembering that long-ago day they'd gone riding together. Almost thirty years had passed since that lovely afternoon in Nice.

"You won't believe what they've built," she said, leading Gab across the expansive floor of le Grand Palais. "It's hardly recognizable."

For the International Exhibition of Modern Decorative and Industrial Arts, twin wrought-iron staircases had been temporarily covered to create a single "monumental staircase," which spanned the entire width of the Nave and ascended to the luxurious Salle des Fêtes on the second floor in a series of large recessed landings. Each of the landings was large enough to act as a stage, and the largest one had been specifically dedicated to theatrical productions. It was a temple to the latest style of art and fashion, which would later be called Art Deco, and the overall effect was that of an ancient Egyptian tomb or a Mesopotamian temple.

Loïe's dancers were currently up in the Salle des Fêtes, which was serving as a dressing room and staging area for the Fête de Nuit. Organized by several theater directors and the couturier Paul Poiret, the event was the most sought-after invitation in town. Loïe had a front-row seat at the foot of the Grand Staircase, but Gab was planning to sit somewhere closer to the back of the Nave. The cavernous foyer could hold 2,500 spectators, and rows of chairs stretched from the first stair of the Grand Staircase all the way back to the main entrance.

There would be other performers at the gala that night, but Loïe liked to think that, even after all these years, she was still the most original performance artist in Paris. Seduction and illusion were central themes of the extravaganza. The Paris Opéra, the Moulin Rouge, the Comédie Française, and the Folies Bergère would all put on short performances, interspersed with fashion shows featuring haute couture models.

Gab paged through the program.

"Eva Le Gallienne is performing a monologue written by Mercedes de Acosta tonight," she pointed out.

Loïe sighed. "Can't we forget about Isadora for one night?"

Mercedes de Acosta, an American playwright with a colorful reputation, had been dating Gallienne, a well-known actress, for several years. Mercedes, Loïe knew, was also rumored to have been Isadora Duncan's lover back in 1917. Which made it especially maddening that Isadora was currently writing a scandalous autobiography that threatened to expose the true nature of Loïe's relationship with Gab.

"Did you cable Mr. Cromwell?" Gab asked.

"Yes," Loïe said. "I told him to notify the publisher that we'd hold them responsible if they print what she's written about me." She hoped that would be sufficient to stomp out this fire.

Consequences be damned, Isadora still lived as freely as she danced. She slept with man after man, preaching a gospel of personal freedom, and mostly got away with it because she was so beautiful and talented. But the public was fickle, and they were growing weary of her. The scandalous dancer had been all over the newspapers recently. Her dance school in Russia had failed. Divorced, broke, and probably alcoholic, she was desperate for money. In December, her ex-husband had committed suicide, and in February, angry with countless men who had professed their undying love and now refused to give her a dime, she'd threatened to publish their love letters.

At the last minute, she'd changed her mind about the letters, but later she told the press that she was going to write her memoir to salvage her finances instead. Several American newspapers mocked her, publishing the same blurb: "Isadora Duncan, peeved dancer says she will tell all she knows. We wonder how long it will take."

Isadora had moved to France and, flying in the face of her detractors, had, it seemed, gotten right to work on writing. Luckily for Loïe, a few friends of Isadora's who had read through a scurrilous chapter on Loïe reported back to Gab. It was clear that, despite all Loïe had done for her, Isadora didn't care one bit whether she destroyed Loïe's reputation.

After they'd parted ways back in the winter of 1902, Duncan claimed she didn't even know Loïe. Now, she'd written an entire chapter on her, which began by recalling that they'd been introduced by a singer who said to her, "Sarah Bernhardt is such a great artist, what a pity, my dear, she is not a good woman! Now there is Loïe Fuller. She is not only a great artist but she is such a pure woman," winkingly adding, "Her name has never been smirched by any scandal with a man." In a single statement, Loïe's former protégé built her up and put in place the framework to tear her back down.

Isadora had written about arriving in Berlin to find Loïe "surrounded by her entourage. A dozen or so beautiful girls were grouped around her, alternately stroking her hands and kissing her…Here," Isadora wrote, "was an atmosphere of such warmth and sensuousness as I had never met before."

After praising Loïe's dancing, she'd gone on to write an entire paragraph about Gab.

In the midst of these nereids, nymphs, iridescent apparitions, there was a strange figure in a black tailor-made. She was shy, reticent, with finely moulded yet strong face, black hair brushed straight back from her forehead, with sad, intelligent eyes. She invariably held her hands in the pockets of her suit. She was interested in art, and, especially, spoke eloquently of the art of Loie Fuller. She circulated around the bevy of brightly coloured butterflies like some scarab of ancient Egypt. I was at once attracted by this personality, but felt that her enthusiasm for Loie Fuller possessed her entire emotional force, and she had nothing left for me.

After another glowing description of Loïe's genius and her "marvelous ephemeral art," she'd written about the red-haired dancer who had kissed her and then tried to strangle her, saying that she'd begun to ask herself what she was doing in the presence of "this troupe of beautiful but demented ladies."

Despite the fact that there was an entire subculture of wealthy, famous women who loved other women in Paris, Isadora's words were kindling for a fire that could burn Loïe to the ground. She'd seen what happened to Marie. Once the public envisioned you in a particular way, to swerve from that path exposed you to attack from all sides.

Loïe took a deep breath. "Can we please stop worrying?" she pleaded. "And enjoy this?"

Gab looked at her with dark, serious eyes and didn't say a word. For the thousandth time, Loïe wondered whether this dear woman, who had spent her entire life protecting her, would have been happier with someone else. She wasn't ashamed of Gab. She loved her. But only their close friends understood how tightly they were connected.

Always putting work first, Loïe had been determined to live a life where nothing held her back. She opened her wings toward whatever light attracted her at any moment, while Gab stayed behind, putting out fires.

She'd always been aware that living so selfishly hurt Gab, who had only wanted to settle down with Loïe and live a quiet life. Isadora had been right on that front at least. Loïe possessed every ounce of Gab's emotional force, and she was eternally grateful for that.

She reached over and squeezed Gab's hand.

"We will be fine," she whispered. "Even if the truth about us comes out. I wouldn't be here now without you."

Together they looked out at what they'd made. That afternoon, they'd draped the Grand Staircase and its platforms with four thousand square meters of silk taffeta. Light and supple enough to respond to the tiniest air current, it was shot through with purple, red, periwinkle, magenta, orange, green, gray, and brown. It had shimmered in the sunlight like the water in a Monet. Now it glowed softly in the lights of the palace.

The fabric, which she'd ordered from Bombay, absorbed and reflected the "vibrations" of all colors of light so beautifully. Tears had sprung to Loïe's eyes during the first rehearsal as she watched her creation come to life in the Grand Palais. She'd been working on smaller-scale versions of the dance for months, calling it the "Dance of Sirens," but now she had the means to put on a full-scale performance and she'd retitled it "La Mer Immense."

It was hard to believe that twenty-five years had passed since the exposition of 1900, when she'd danced in her little theater, just down the riverbank. Art and design had changed dramatically since then. Blocky geometry and columnar figures had replaced the sinuous Art Nouveau style that Loïe had personified. American jazz and its culture were all the rage, and new ideas about art, including surrealism, offered endless opportunity for inspiration.

Surrealism, which aimed to bridge the gap between dreams and reality, had taken hold in Paris around 1917, but Loïe had anticipated the movement long before then and continued to play with the idea of unconscious expression. Unlike most of her peers, who had faded from the public consciousness, Loïe was still burning bright after over thirty years in show business. It helped that she was brilliant at convincing people that everything she did was new and exciting.

"The public always makes me think of a man in whose hand we've placed a vial of radium salts, without telling him the nature of what we've given him," she'd recently told a reporter. "There is a very good chance that his first gesture would be to throw it away, thinking that it's of no value. But say to him abruptly that it's radium and he'll immediately close his hand and rave about the thing he despised only the moment before. So, you always have to come to him and say immediately that it's radium and repeat to him that it's radium."

She and Gab were continuing to explore filmmaking, and besides making moving pictures, Loïe wanted to merge film with live performance by choreographing a production that would feature a shadow wandering among icebergs. She imagined using the moving-picture screen as an imperceptible canvas, so that the dancer would come and go, leave the scene and move away to unreal distances on-screen before returning to the stage. Dance and projection, flesh, fabric, and light would merge, leaving the action whole and uninterrupted. She'd already worked out the details in her mind.

As usual, though, she had more ideas than time. Despite being so busy, she'd still seen friends and had run into old acquaintances. In 1924, when she designed the lighting for a new ballet called *Mercure*, Loïe had once again encountered Pablo Picasso, who created the sets and costumes. Although he'd never done a painting of her, Picasso had been influenced by her dances at the exposition, and in the summer of 1907, he'd alluded to her swirling veils in his groundbreaking masterpiece *Les Demoiselles d'Avignon*, which sparked the Cubist movement.

Several months after that, Marie Curie had joined Loïe in a box at the Champs Élysées theater to watch Loïe's dancers perform the *Ballets Fantastiques*. The presence of her friend brought grateful tears to her eyes. Loïe knew how much Marie disliked attention, especially from the French press. Still, the scientist seemed content now, with Irène at the Radium Institute and her gram of American radium.

When they'd parted, Loïe took her dear friend's hands in hers and kissed Marie's pale cheeks, saying that she hoped to see her again very soon. The scientist looked so old. It worried her immensely.

Now, being here with Gab at what might be the most important performance of her career, Loïe felt a sense of peace. Nothing Isadora or anyone else could write about her would take away her accomplishments. Newspapers might tear her reputation apart, but stages across the world would still be lit by her ideas, and every time dancers spun across a stage with wings of swirling silk, she would be there.

"Monsieur Astruc has saved me a chair in the front row," she said to Gab. "Are you sure you won't sit with me?"

"In front of all those people?" she asked, and Loïe imagined her again as the young girl spinning before the mirror in one of her robes, having a "look in ze glass."

"I'll see you afterwards then." Loïe smiled, leaning forward to kiss her cheeks and then watching her disappear into the crowd.

The celebration of modern design had populated the Grand Palais with the best-dressed celebrities and world elites. International royalty, along with the most sought-after designers in Paris and their wealthy clients, paraded and preened. Corsets had all but disappeared, and the gleaming new tunic-style dresses with their boyish shape and dropped waists bared arms and legs. Loïe moved to take her seat before the expanse of silk on the Grand Staircase, and as the upper crust of Parisian society moved to find their positions in the sea of chairs, she motioned to her dancers to take their places under the fabric.

When everyone but a few stragglers had been seated, M. Gabriel Autrec, the producer of the festival, nodded to Loïe. She stood and confidently signaled the orchestra's conductor before nodding, one by one, to her electricians and settling back into her chair. A hush fell over the crowd as the low, dark rumble of the tympani thrummed through the air. Soft light appeared and glimmered on the silk, overlaid by the percussive tones of a plucked harp. Bright columns of sound emerged from the woodwinds and brass, and Loïe closed her eyes for a moment when the bright yellow violin notes skittered across the deep blue tones of the string bass. She could almost feel the wind moving across water.

As Debussy's tone poem *La Mer* filled the Grand Palais with sound, the sea came to life, propelled by the veiled bodies of Loïe's dancers. They expertly manipulated the fabric, using their frames and air currents to create rolling waves. Blue and green light from rotating projectors danced across the silk, adding depth and reflection to the rhythm of the silken water.

The sea as a theme, and in particular *The Great Wave*, a Japanese wood-block print by Hokusai, had inspired countless French artists. As a nod to Hokusai, Debussy had gone so far as to have *The Great Wave* printed on the cover of his score for *La Mer*. In 1897, Camille Claudel, Rodin's former lover and a friend of Loïe's, had sculpted a stunning wave from green onyx marble, depicting an enormous wave curling over three dancing women, and Loïe's friend Pierre Roche had also created a strikingly realistic print of a foaming wave. Now she had brought their work to life.

In concert with the sound, the waves grew in intensity. One of Loïe's muses emerged from under the fabric to walk gracefully between the luminous swells, a siren clothed in white with long, flowing hair. The music grew agitated and enormous waves broke, the liquid silk almost close enough to brush Loïe's face. Other sirens appeared and vanished again beneath the waves, which bathed the spellbound spectators with soft breezes.

Later, the critic Gustave Fréjaville wrote that on that evening in the palace, she'd recreated the ocean, "with its waves and foam, with its immense mystery, its poetry and its legends, until the appearance, under moon rays, of brilliant people with dangerous charms."

Loïe's dancers were instruments in the great orchestra of light, and watching the figures beneath the thin fabric move reminded her of the first time she'd seen the luminous X-ray image of her flesh-veiled fingers in Thomas Edison's lab. That day, a thousand dances ago, a thousand adventures ago, had led her to Marie.

As silken waves washed over the steps of the palace, Loïe turned back to try to catch a glimpse of Gab. As usual, she couldn't spot her dear girl among the crowd, but as always, she knew Gab was there. Leaning back, Loïe thrilled in the surreal vision she'd conjured on the steps of the palace and contemplated what her next act would be.

Scene V

Spotlight

1929

The air in the ballroom was thick with conversation. Marie sat quietly, thinking about the Radium Institute. She missed her garden and hoped that things were running smoothly without her.

The high-pitched humming in her ears was barely noticeable over the background noise. Her work, she was now convinced, had damaged more than her fingertips. Marie was constantly tired. Her cataracts kept getting worse and there was a maddening ringing in her ears. At sixty-one, she couldn't help thinking that she'd aged more quickly than her friends. When she looked in the mirror, Marie barely recognized the white-haired, spectacled woman staring back at her through clouded eyes. She'd never been particularly vain, but she hated to think that her workers and colleagues at the Radium Institute might view her as elderly or weak.

Although Irène and Ève both worried about her health, she never complained to anyone except Bronya, and she had sworn her sister to secrecy. Marie knew it would probably be best to retire before radiation completely destroyed her, but she couldn't do it. She'd written to Bronya a few years before, "Sometimes my courage fails me and I think I ought to stop working, live in the country and devote myself to gardening. But I am held by a thousand bonds...Nor do I know whether, even by writing scientific books, I could live without the laboratory."

Life without research, to Marie, was life without reason.

She had more than her own health to worry about, though. Radium was now a documented killer, and it was impossible to deny the dual nature of her discovery. As her beautiful element became an unregulated commodity around the world, it had transformed from a panacea into a public health nightmare.

Soon after her ship docked in New York Harbor the week before, Missy Maloney had given her more horrifying news about the radium dial painters. At least fifteen of the factory workers were now known to have died, and countless more girls and young women were sick with cancer from licking brushes dipped in radium paint. Marie was devastated at the news.

For years, she'd been telling herself that with proper precautions, radium could be handled safely, but she couldn't regulate what people did with it. Even her own carefully controlled world of research had been touched by tragedy as Marie's lab, which had always followed the best safety practices, suffered its first casualties. Back in November of 1925, a Japanese researcher named Nobuo Yamada, who had been working with Irène to prepare highly radioactive polonium sources, had written that he was very ill with radiation poisoning. Yamada suspected that he was sick from exposure to "emanations." Less than two years after returning home to Japan, he fell down senseless, took to his bed, and died.

While on vacation in August of 1927, not long after hearing that Nobuo had died, Marie received bad news from closer to home. Irène had written that their kind, bubbly colleague Sonia Cotelle had become very ill. A Polish scientist who had come to the lab just after the war ended, Sonia was one of Marie's most trusted employees at the institute and was a specialist in working with the most dangerous products: complicated preparations of polonium, radiothorium, and mesothorium. Irène's letter recalled that "Fred went to Paris on Tuesday and found Madame Cotelle in very poor health. He strongly dissuaded her from [working with more polonium] because she has stomach problems, extremely rapid hair loss, etc." Her letter had gone on to note that when they tested her for radioactivity, Sonia's lips and urine had been "very active."

The practice of measuring liquid by sucking it up into glass pipettes was discouraged in the lab, but everyone knew that it still went on. Marie suspected that her friend had probably swallowed some polonium. Somehow, Sonia survived the incident. She returned to the lab after spending a few weeks taking fresh air in the mountains, at Marie's insistence, but the experience frightened everyone. Sonia's blood count hadn't returned to normal, yet she refused to abandon her work at the Radium Institute.

When her own daughter's blood count came back with abnormal results, Marie sent Irène off on a two-week trip, hoping that fresh air would cure her. She was relieved when Irène returned from the vacation with normal blood, renewed energy, and enthusiasm. All seemed to be well, but Marie worried constantly, especially since Irène had contracted tuberculosis during the war.

Her employees at the Radium Institute seemed healthy for the most part, but the exceptions now gave her pause. Like Marie, many individuals who worked with radioactivity had damaged skin on their hands. A few had lost fingers and one man lost his vision, but these had seemed like heroic sacrifices in the name of scientific progress.

What worried her more, in hindsight, were cases like that of the thirty-one-year-old researcher who had suddenly died of bronchitis. Such deaths weren't unheard of, but they were unusual. Two other lab workers, only thirty-three and forty-three years old, passed away from "tuberculosis," but their blood tests had shown abnormalities that might have been considered suspicious. Tuberculosis, as Marie knew all too well, preyed on weak immune systems that allowed the disease to reactivate and become deadly. Had radium indirectly killed them? Would working with radioactivity make Irène sick?

A blur of motion caught Marie's eye, and she looked up to see Missy waving from a table just in front of her. She was back in the States again thanks to the journalist, who had managed to raise enough money to buy another gram of radium for Marie. Although they weren't advertising the fact, Marie planned to donate the gift to the Radium Institute she'd established in Poland, so they could begin medical treatments for cancer.

For the past few days, Missy and Marie had been staying at the home of Henry Ford, the automobile magnate who had gotten his start working for Thomas Edison. Ford adored Edison and had organized "Light's Golden Jubilee" to celebrate the fiftieth anniversary of the invention of incandescent light and to dedicate the Edison Institute of Technology at Ford's village and museum complex in Dearborn, Michigan, where Edison's old research complex Menlo Park had been painstakingly reconstructed.

The sit-down, candlelit banquet was supplemented by electric light. Marie sat at the head table as a guest of honor and one of a handful of attendees asked to give a short speech, along with Thomas Edison, President Herbert Hoover, Henry Ford, and her friend Albert Einstein, who would speak over shortwave radio from Berlin. Even though she didn't normally enjoy giving such speeches, Marie was happy to have been included. She understood that the invitation was not just a speaking engagement but public recognition of the importance of her work. The speeches would be broadcast over NBC radio, and her words would be heard all over America, alongside those of Edison and Einstein.

As Marie, the banquet attendees, and America listened via NBC radio, Thomas Edison and the only other living man who had been present on the day Edison "brought light down from the heavens" reenacted the invention of the incandescent lightbulb. The reenactment, along with the simultaneous radio broadcast, was the brainchild of image-maker and public relations genius Edward Bernays. By asking the listening audience to dim their lights until Edison's bulb flared to life, he allowed millions to participate in the celebration while simultaneously creating a work of conceptual art. Sitting in the dark, Americans followed the dramatic radio show as they listened to the step-by-step narration. When Edison and his former assistant Francis Jehl finally connected the bulb to the battery and the filament burned bright, the radio announcer proclaimed that the bulb was lit and electric lights all over America flared back to life.

In the room where Marie sat, when the bulb was illuminated in the old Menlo Park building, President Hoover pushed a button and all of the ballroom's electric chandeliers blazed in dramatic fashion, turning the dangling crystal teardrops into sparkling diamonds. One observer remarked that it was like "an eclipse running backward."

Naturally, Marie thought of Loïe. She should have been there that night. Not only did she know Edison, Loïe was the one who had manipulated electric light into a transformational tool for theater, dance, and design. But when she looked around at the legendary men seated near her—Henry Ford, Orville Wright, J. P. Morgan, George Eastman, Will Rogers—it occurred to her that they probably wouldn't have invited Loïe anyway.

It was no wonder that Loïe had always claimed to be born in America but made in France. Despite their reputation as freethinkers and innovators, most Americans had never fully appreciated Loïe as an inventor or an artist. While at times they'd been dazzled by her special effects, they'd been too narrow-minded to see her as anything more than a short woman spinning onstage under colorful lights.

Paris had been Loïe's savior, and Marie's too, for that matter. Despite its shortcomings, the City of Light had welcomed them both and let them shine, on and off through the years, as they persevered through illness, death, scandal, and war. They were both part of the city now, visible in its art and architecture, its culture and its memory. Paris had adored Loïe until the day she died.

In those last years, Ève was the conduit between Loïe and Marie. Days and months ticked past as Marie kept up with the Radium Institute and Loïe and Gab managed their dance troupe and made films. At some point, Loïe had written to Marie that she was sad they didn't see much of each other anymore. Through her connections, Loïe had arranged lessons for

Ève with the composer and pianist Gabriel Pierné, but after performing successfully around Paris, Ève had suffered a crisis of confidence and at the last minute sent a tearful letter backing out of the American tour that Loïe and Gab had planned for her.

"Dear, dear Miss Fuller," she'd written, "I am awfully ashamed and anxious in writing these words to you because I know and I felt every day how much you worked on that business, and how much time you and Gab lost on that, and what love you showed for me in the whole thing."

Loïe had been very nice about the situation, although Marie was fairly certain the cancellation had caused problems for her. Now she wished they had scheduled one last lunch together. The dancer had died at two o'clock in the morning on New Year's Day of 1928.

Loïe had spent the last three months of her life in a room at the Plaza-Athénée hotel in Paris, looking out the window at the sky as she tried to overcome what the doctor thought was a bad case of bronchitis. During that time, her muses visited and danced for her, and friends stopped by, but she took a turn for the worse just after Christmas. Gab held Loïe's hand as the dancer took her last breath, and gently closed her dear companion's eyes for the last time.

It seemed appropriate to Marie that Loïe had breathed her last as celebrations waned, stage curtains were drawn, and lights were extinguished all around Paris. Ève had been the one to break the news to Marie, reading Loïe's obituary in *Le Journal*, but Marie didn't really believe her friend was gone until that evening, when snow arrived in the form of small, imperfect flakes that reflected every color of the rainbow and robed Paris in white.

Ève had written to Gab immediately:

Dear friend Gab,

I'm just hearing the sad news from the newspapers…I thought that Loïe was doing much better and can hardly believe this blow so sudden, so horrible for all those who love Loïe deeply. I don't know if we can see you, if it's not intrusive. If you would rather be alone? I'll be there on Wednesday in any case. I kiss you tenderly and sadly, dear Gab, and think of you and your Loïe.

Ève Curie

Later, on January 3, 1928, an obituary appeared in the European edition of the *Chicago Tribune and the Daily News*. It was headlined, "Loie Fuller Is Dead; Paris Mourns the Star Who Brought Light to Dance," and Loïe's cause of death was listed as bronchial pneumonia, following two months of "wasting illness." The article compared her fame to that of Isadora Duncan, which Loïe would have hated, but Isadora had died tragically nine months earlier when a long scarf wrapped around her neck got caught up in the wheels of an open-top automobile, breaking her neck. Comparing the two American modern dancers was irresistible to the press.

"La Belle Loie," the article said, "as every Frenchman of middle age knew her, was fifty-eight years old." Loïe had actually been almost sixty-six when she died, but continued to lie about her age from the grave. After detailing her most famous dances and her triumphant production of *La Mer* at the Grand Palais, the obituary continued, "Critics today are saying Loie Fuller's ideas were responsible for all modern stage lighting. Colored ribbons and fans, giving fire-effects and half the stunts which are now the common property of music halls were her invention."

When the interviewer from the *Chicago Tribune* had appeared in Loïe's hotel room following her death, Gab was still by her side. "In tears by the lilac-strewn bed where the dancer lay, Mlle. Bloch told the *Tribune* that she would see to it that the Fuller dancers continue the tradition of their founder." The obituary had gone on to quote one of France's leading writers: "'You are a great scientist, as well as a great artist,' Anatole France, one of the legions of her admirers once told [Loïe], for light was her greatest preoccupation." Loïe, Marie thought, might not have been a scientist in the traditional sense, but she had most certainly been an enthusiastic learner, a great observer, an innovative thinker, and a lover of science, which was precisely why Marie had liked her from the beginning.

One line in particular haunted Marie. "In recent years," it said, "Loïe's closest friends have whispered that she had become a victim of her great idea. 'Lumiere! Lumiere!' 'Light! Light!' was the cry of her last hours of delirium."

Less than a year before she died, Loïe had written:

> Oh! I am so tired—so tired! All inside me is so tired—just tired out. Have you ever been so tired that you could not even undress to go to bed? Well, I am just that way all-the-time except when some activity spurs me on. Then when the moment is over of mental activity, it all comes back again—and the tired feeling hurts me so that tears come in spite of me. Isn't it dreadful?
>
> There is so much to do— so much that has got to be done and I put off—put off because I am too tired! As I am writing this, there is a sensation of vibration throughout my system, but not evident. My eyes close with almost each word I write, and little "hurts" come in my head, first here and then there. My face is uncomfortable from, I suppose, the nerves. I am sleepy—I wonder if it is because I slept only very late last night. But I always go to sleep late—from twelve to two is my "wakest" time. I was born at 2 a.m.

Loïe's death had been the last straw for Marie, finally convincing her that she should speak out on radium's dangers. Her friend's unexpected demise brought back youthful visions of radium-lit butterflies, but the dreamy insects were now transformed into the specters of young dial painters lying in coffins, glowing with deadly dust.

Was Loïe a canary in a coal mine? Had her charming, vivacious friend really died of pneumonia, or had her death been hastened by the luminescent salts she'd applied to costumes and textiles day after day? It now appeared that radium's damage could be unpredictable and invisible. Perhaps even as Loïe scolded Marie about taking care of herself, radioactive salts had been killing the dancer from the inside, like a silkworm cocoon dissolved by the moth within?

Loïe hadn't needed radium therapy following her surgery for breast cancer, but after the surgery, she told Marie that the experience had made her come to think of radium as a savior. Had it been a savior, or had it been her killer? Marie would never know, but she didn't want any more bodies piling up on her doorstep.

In her suitcase at the Ford mansion was a speech she planned to give the following week at the Plaza Hotel in New York. Her words, written for the third annual dinner of the American Society of the Control of Cancer, would be broadcast across the country by radio. After praising the work being done by physicians to fight cancer with radiotherapy, she would warn of the dangers of radium in untrained hands. Besides encouraging safer laboratory practices, she planned to emphasize that radium should only be used in therapeutic fields by experts with several years of specialized training, and highlight the dangers of allowing unqualified corporations and individuals to dispense radium as a medicine. She hoped that people would listen.

As the Light's Golden Jubilee celebrations rolled on, Thomas Edison didn't seem to be feeling well, so the introductions were brief. One orator quoted Mr. Edison, saying, "All things come to him who hustles while he waits," which Marie found particularly amusing. Finally, President Hoover stood up to introduce the guest of honor, saying, "And now, Ladies and Gentlemen, no words of mine can satisfy your hearts. Mr. Thomas A. Edison."

To thunderous applause, the man who had invented the phonograph stepped up to the microphone. He had suffered from hearing loss his entire life and liked to say that he hadn't heard a bird sing since he was twelve years old. Now, he was almost completely deaf. Old and gray, he began his speech with a nod to technology: "I am told that my voice will reach out to the four corners of the world." He continued with a few emotional words of gratitude, pausing at times to collect himself.

In the speech that followed, President Hoover spoke affectionately of Edison, although the guest of honor had left to lie down in another room and wasn't there to hear Hoover's speech. Marie smiled when her friend Albert Einstein's voice came through the radio, even though there was so much crackling that she could barely understand his German. She smiled again when he managed to say the last few words, "Good night, my American friend," in English. Albert was a brilliant physicist, but he was constantly apologizing for his poor language skills.

When President Hoover stood to introduce Marie, she heard a door creak in the rear of the ballroom. Cool air brushed her cheek and the murmur of voices died down. The men around her offered to help, but she waved them away, rose from her chair, and moved forward to the microphone. Her thumb itched to rub the radium scars on her fingers, but she squeezed her hands into fists to keep them still.

Standing there, bathed in light, she looked out at the crowd before her. As always, she felt like an object of curiosity, but this was different. She wasn't simply being paraded about. Marie had been asked to speak because she was one of them, a giant of the new century. Her voice, with that of Edison and Einstein, was being carried across oceans and recorded for posterity. Like them, she had changed the course of science and society. Marie belonged.

Through her cataracts, the crowd looked hazy in the chandeliers' glare. She could feel the audience waiting. Marie finally understood that the fame she had fled for so many years was the very thing that would ensure that her work shined on long after she was gone. When she spoke about the dangers of radium in a few days, people would listen, and her words would help protect future generations from the missteps of the past.

A smile flitted across Marie's face and sparked a youthful glint in her gray eyes. The certainty that had guided her for so long may have faltered, but her mind was clear. She would give her speeches, collect her gram of radium, and go back home to France. There was more work to be done.

Curtain

The dancer and the scientist were approximately the same age when they swirled skyward in plumes of carbon, leaving piles of ash and minerals behind. Today, Marie's remains lie with Pierre's in a tomb beneath the Panthéon, while Loïe's ashes are just across the Seine in Père Lachaise Cemetery. One is famous and the other now almost forgotten. But like smoke and ashes, the spirit of their accomplishments flowed up and out, spreading through the atmosphere to inspire generations of dancers, artists, inventors, and scientists.

Marie Curie died at the age of sixty-six, in July of 1934. Her cause of death was recorded as aplastic pernicious anemia, which was almost certainly caused by exposure to radioactivity. Ève Curie went on to become an accomplished musician, journalist, and author, writing a prizewinning biography of her mother. Irène married Frédéric Joliot and each of them went on to win a Nobel Prize in chemistry for their discovery of artificial radioactivity.

Marie's legacy lives on in the Curie Institute in Paris, one of the leading medical biology and biophysics research centers in the world, which operates both a research facility and a hospital specializing in cancer treatment. The original Radium Institute now houses a lovely museum, called Musée Curie, where one can peer into Marie's laboratory, see equipment used to make revolutionary discoveries, and sit in her garden.

After Loïe's death, Gab kept her work alive. Loïe's troupe of dancers continued to perform for another ten years, with Gab at the helm. According to biographers Current and Current, the Loïe Fuller Dancers "remained a familiar sight [in Paris] as they traveled about in their white robes, white slippers and red cloaks." Under the name Gab Sorere, Gab kept making films, including some that featured Loïe's dances. She continued to cultivate Loïe's work with fluorescence as well, using Loïe's lab to produce chemicals for films and performances featuring fluorescent paint and black light, a type of ultraviolet light.

Loïe Fuller's patented fluorescent salts were later used to light the doorways of bomb shelters during World War II, and many of her inventions, including darkened theaters and colorful lighting gels, are still used in theaters today. In addition to modern dance, stage lighting and special effects, her name has been associated with the Rolls-Royce hood ornament, plastic wrap, modern lingerie, and even the invention of camouflage.

Like radium, the legends of Marie Curie and Loïe Fuller will keep shining on with a faint but steady light, inspiring us to dream bigger, work harder, and reach higher, dispelling the darkness that veils the path ahead.

Acknowledgments

In her notebooks, Loïe Fuller writes about studying the hues of tapestry threads, observing, "Under the microscope, in polarized light, the colors are countless. They shift, changing till the brain grows dizzy looking at them." Writing about Loïe and Marie was a similar experience—beautiful and dizzying at times. I couldn't have done it without the help of a number of people.

To begin with, I'm extraordinarily grateful for the biographers whose books introduced me to Loïe Fuller and Marie Curie and built a foundation for my research, especially Anne Cooper Albright, Rhonda K. Garelick, Richard Nelson Current, Marcia Ewing Current, Giovanni Lista, Ève Curie, Susan Quinn, and Barbara Goldsmith.

The guidance and expertise of two phenomenal women brought *Radiant* to life. My literary agent Rhea Lyons is a fountain of enthusiasm and positive energy who believed in my story idea from the start and helped to shape it into a book. I'm also eternally grateful to my editor Maddie Caldwell, who fell in love with Loïe and Marie, patiently read through my first drafts, and pulled me out of a hundred rabbit holes to keep me focused on the remarkable women at the center of this story. Thank you, Rhea and Maddie.

Thank you to my copy editor Rick Ball, who, in addition to rescuing me from mistakes and grammar faux pas, appears to be fluent in French, art history, and literature and gave me fantastic notes along with his corrections. Thank you to Jacqui Young at Grand Central Publishing as well, who organized images for the book, answered my questions, and did a hundred other things behind the scenes. Thank you, design and editing teams at Grand Central Publishing, for polishing the story and making it shine.

Peter Knapp and Blair Wilson first encouraged me to write a biography of a scientist, for which I'm grateful, and as I searched for an idea, my son, Charlie, pointed out that all the women represented on the periodic table are associated with radioactive elements, which led me to Marie Curie. Thanks, Charlie.

Several people patiently helped me locate and view documents at libraries and museums. I would especially like to thank Phil Karg and the staff at the New York Public Library's Jerome Robbins Dance Division collection; Anna R. Goodwin at the Maryhill Museum of Art; Michael Lange at the Bancroft Library (University of California, Berkeley); Maria Brandt, Sarah Gates, and Sue Grinols at the De Young and Legion of Honor Fine Arts Museums of San Francisco; and Paul Israel, director and general editor of the Thomas A. Edison Papers, at Rutgers University. While in Paris, I was fortunate to spend a few days doing research in the lovely Opera Library, for which I'm grateful to the Bibliothèque de Nationale France. A special thank-you to Michelle Montmorency, granddaughter of Sarah Paget Montmorency who donated the Joseph Paget Fredericks collection to the Bancroft Library, for giving me permission to use images from the collection.

I want to thank the Musèe Curie in Paris. Visiting Marie's lab, sitting in her garden, and exploring the exhibits in the old Radium Institute was a highlight of my visit to France. Some laboratory techniques are almost impossible to visualize by reading about them, and I was thrilled when Claude Charvy demonstrated the piezoelectric quartz electrometer on display, giving me a glimpse of the complicated technique perfected by Marie Curie for measuring radioactivity. I want to thank archivist Aurélie Lemoine as well, for helping me acquire photographs from the museum's collection, and Natalie Pigeard-Micault and Renaud Huynh for answering my questions.

Writing this book led me to two women as interested in Loïe Fuller as I am. I was thrilled to get insight into Loïe's dances from dancer-choreographer Jody Sperling, who is an expert on Loïe Fuller and the founder and artistic director of Time Lapse Dance. It was immensely helpful having conversations with Zeva Oelbaum, who is currently making a Loïe Fuller documentary titled *Obsessed with Light*.

Thank you to Natalie Godin, who translated several handwritten documents from French to English, and to rock star photographer Amber Procaccini for taking my headshot. Thank you to Robert Kruh, chemist, dean emeritus of the graduate school at Kansas State University, for giving my dad a 1903 Crookes Spinthariscope, which he then passed along to me, entrusting me with a piece of Marie and Loïe's history.

This book was written amid the whirlwind of life, and I don't know how I could have done it without the support of my friends and family. Thank you to my dad, Ron Lee, physicist, Kansas State University, Lawrence Livermore National Laboratory, for being my science advisor. Special thanks to Jean Lee, Ron Lee, Patti Wade, Bill Wade, Chuck Heinecke, Tim Alevios, Jennifer Wilson, Laurie Lindeen, and Mary Warner for reading through various drafts of my work and giving me input and encouragement. Thank you, Mom and Dad, and Jan and Chuck, for staying with the kids when we went to France.

Special thanks to my patient husband, Ken, who fell asleep on a bench at the Paris Opéra while I spent an hour searching for a hidden library—and to my kids Charlie, May, and Sarah, who love to tease me about my horrible French accent and are my biggest cheerleaders.

Finally, thank you, Loïe Fuller and Marie Curie, for inspiring me to tell your stories.

Bibliography

"1915 Panama-Pacific International Exposition in SAN FRANCISCO Rare 16mm Footage." Accessed n.d. https://www.youtube.com/watch?v=RY75exH6Rck.

"$20,000 Dollars Damages Wanted by Singer." *The Philadelphia Inquirer*, November 17, 1907. https://www.newspapers.com/image/168372733/.

Adler, Kathleen. "The Suburban, the Modern and 'Une Dame De Passy.'" *Oxford Art Journal* 12, no. 1 (1989): 3–13. www.jstor.org/stable/1360262.

"The Adolph B. Spreckels Residence." The Adolph B. Spreckels Residence. Accessed May 18, 2020. http://www.beyondthegildedage.com/2013/08/the-adolph-b -spreckels-residence.html.

Albright, Ann Cooper. *Traces of Light: Absence and Presence in the Work of Loïe Fuller*. Middletown, CT: Wesleyan University Press, 2007.

Anderson, Joseph L. *Enter a Samurai: Kawakami Otojirō and Japanese Theatre in the West*. Tucson, AZ: Wheatmark, 2011.

Aquarium at 1900 Paris Exposition. March 20, 2013. Photograph. https://www .worldfairs.info/forum/viewtopic.php?t=2343.

"The Aquarium at the Paris Exposition," n.d. https://books.google.com/books?id =PWrnAAAAMAAJ&pg=PA345&lpg.

"Archive Footage of Light's Golden Jubilee—Henry Ford." YouTube. The Henry Ford, n.d. https://www.youtube.com/watch?v=eTMoaeax--Y.

"At the Stage Door." *The Los Angeles Times*, July 16, 1915. https://www.newspapers.com /image/380487015/.

Augustin, Marion, Hélène Langevin-Joliot, and Natalie Pigeard-Micault. *Marie Curie: Une Femme Dans Son siècle*. Paris: Gründ, 2017.

"BIGAMY, SAYS LOIE FULLER: The Nautch Dancer Has Lawyer W. B. Hayes Arrested, and Produces a Marriage Agreement Which the Lawyer Says Is a Forgery—His Wife Stands by Him—Hayes Says the Girl Got a Good Deal of Money Out of Him—Photographs as Collateral." *New York Sun*, January 20, 1892.

Bru, Richard. n.d. http://www.bcn.cat/museupicasso/en/exhibitions/temporals /imatges-secretes/japonismo_ENG.pdf.

Chandler, Arthur. "The Paris Exposition Universelle of 1900, Chandler Expanded and Revised from World's Fair Magazine, Volume VII, Number 3, 1987," n.d. http://www.arthurchandler.com/paris-1900-exposition.

"A City Built on Air." Parisian Fields, September 13, 2015. https://parisianfields.com /2015/09/13/a-city-built-on-air/.

Clarètie, Jules. "Les Femmes Au Théâtre Et Dans Les Lettres. Un Théâtre De L'avenir. Le Théâtre Féministe. Une Répétition De La Tragédie De Salomé." *Le Temps*, November 8, 1907. https://gallica.bnf.fr/ark:/12148/bpt6k2391722 /f2.item.r=loie fuller laboratoire.texteImage.

Clark, William L. "New Conceptions Relative to the Treatment of Malignant Disease with Special Reference to Radium Needles." *Pennsylvania Medical Journal*, January 1921: 223. https://books.google.com/books?id=f9MyAQAAMAAJ&pg=PA223&lpg#v.

Colette. "The Vagabond by Sidonie-Gabrielle." *The Vagabond*. Farrar, Straus, and Giroux, Inc., 1955.

"Color Scheme for Ball Is Perfect: Loie Fuller's Spectacular Ballet to Hold Closing Rehearsal Thursday." *Oakland Tribune*, April 27, 1915. https://www .newspapers.com/image/80758080/.

Constance Paget-Fredericks. University of California; California Digital Library, n.d. https://oac.cdlib.org/ark:/13030/tf429007kj/?layout=metadata&brand=oac4.

"Courrier Des Théâtres." *Numéro Le Petit Parisien: Journal Quotidien Du Soir*, February 3, 1904. https://gallica.bnf.fr/ark:/12148/bpt6k5613223/f4.image.r=loie fuller radium dance?rk=21459;2.

Curie, Mme. Sklodowska. "Radium and Radioactivity." *Century Magazine*, January 1904. https://history.aip.org/history/exhibits/curie/article.htm.

Curie, Eve. *Madame Curie*. New York: Doubleday, Doran & Co., 1939.

Curie, Marie. *Autobiographical Notes: The Story of My Life, 1923*. Paris: Musée Curie, 2013.

———. Letter from Marie Curie to Henry Ford regarding Light's Golden Jubilee. Thehenryford.org, November 3, 1929. https://www.thehenryford.org/collections -and-research/digital-collections/artifact/487474/#slide=gs-486108.

———. *Pierre Curie*. United States: Dover Publications, 2013.

———. *Radioactive Substances*. Mineola, NY: Dover Publications, 2002.

Curie, Marie, and Pierre Curie. "Les Nouvelles Substances Radioactives Et Les Rayons Qu'elles Émettent [Radioactive Substances and the Rays They Emit]." *Sociète française de physique*, 1900. https://doi.org/10.5479/sil.322777.39088000898254.

Current, Richard Nelson, and Marcia Ewing. *Loie Fuller: Goddess of Light*. Boston: Northeastern University Press, 1997.

"Dancer and Wizard." *The Los Angeles Times*, November 1, 1896. https://www.newspapers .com/image/380186746/.

"Dances by Loie Fuller." *The San Francisco Examiner*, July 3, 1915. https://www.newspapers .com/image/457916615/.

"Dancing Feast for Charities." *The San Francisco Examiner*, May 8, 1915: 12. https://www.newspapers.com/image/457642348/.

"Dancing Lacks in Art Values: Fuller Depends Too Much on Mechanical Effects, Weaves a Colorful Fantasy with Their Aid." *The Los Angeles Times*, July 22, 1915. https://www.newspapers.com/image/380489076/.

"The Deadly Legacy of Dr. Von Sochocky's Radium Lives On." *The Record*, December 7, 1983: 23. https://www.newspapers.com/image/494433865/.

"Diagram Identifying People Shown in Irving R. Bacon's Light's Golden Jubilee and Edison Institute Dedication Mural." The Henry Ford. Accessed n.d. https://www.thehenryford.org/collections-and-research/digital-collections /artifact/44967/#slide=gs-192107.

"Discover the Grand Palais." RMN—Grand Palais. Accessed n.d. https://www .grandpalais.fr/en/discover-grand-palais-0.

"Doings of Actors, Authors and Musicians." *The Los Angeles Times*, December 12, 1909. https://www.newspapers.com/image/380142806/.

Doucet, Jérôme, and F. G. Dumas. "MISS LOÏE FULLER." *Numéro Revue Illustrée*, November 1, 1903. https://gallica.bnf.fr/ark:/12148/bpt6k6242667n/f22.item.r=loie fuller.texteImage.zoom.

Downer, Lesley. *Madame Sadayakko: The Geisha Who Bewitched the West*. New York: Gotham Books, 2003.

"Dr. Von Sochosky's Obituary." *Sand Springs Leader*, December 20, 1928: 12. https://www.newspapers.com/image/603744915/.

"Dramatic Matters." *Morning News*. April 5, 1904. https://www.newspapers.com /image/160036822.

"Dramatis Personae." *The Observer*. January 15, 1911. https://www.newspapers.com /image/258936829/.

Dumas, F. G., ed. "L' Ame De La Dance." *Revue Illustrée / F.-G. Dumas, Directeur*, November 1, 1903. https://gallica.bnf.fr/ark:/12148/bpt6k6242667n /f28.image.r=loie fuller.

Dumont, A., ed. "La Fête De Soleil." *Gil Blas*, June 23, 1914. https://gallica.bnf.fr /ark:/12148/bpt6k7537410c/f2.item.r=1914.

"The Eiffel Tower and Science—Official Eiffel Tower Website." La Tour Eiffel, November 21, 2018. https://www.toureiffel.paris/en/the-monument/eiffel -tower-and-science.

"El Tovar Hotel." Historic Hotels of America. Accessed n.d. https://www.historichotels .org/hotels-resorts/el-tovar-hotel/.

Ellis, Harry. "Loie Fuller's Troupe in Pri[n]ce Troubitzky's Garden (c. 1905): [Photographie] / Harry Ellis—Photographer." Gallica, January 1, 1970. https://gallica.bnf.fr/ark:/12148/btv1b525081243/f1.item.r=loie fuller 1925.zoom.

Emling, Shelley. *Marie Curie and Her Daughters: The Private Lives of Science's First Family*. New York: Palgrave Macmillan, 2013.

"Exposition Universelle." *Wikimedia*. n.d. https://upload.wikimedia.org/wikipedia /commons/b/be/P._Bineteau,_Exposition_universelle_de_1900_-_plan_général .jpg.

"Exposition Universelle 1900: Les Projects D'Initiative Privee." *La Pantheon De L'Industrie*. n.d., 1037 edition. https://gallica.bnf.fr/ark:/12148/bpt6k9641748x /f1.image.r=francois deloncle telescope.

Faidit, Jean-Michel. "The Centenary of the Sun Festival at the Eiffel Tower." European Southern Observatory Website, n.d. https://www.eso.org/public/outreach /eduoff/vt-2004/FinalEvent/fe-reports/fe-rec-faidit.pdf.

"The Fate of the House Built on Sin: Pathetic Tragedies in American Social Life That Have Followed Defiance of the Moral Law." *Star Tribune*, October 4, 1914. https://www.newspapers.com/image/180868646/.

Flammarion, Camille. *Mysterious Psychic Forces An Account of the Author's Investigations in Psychical Research, Together with Those of Other European Savants*. S.l.: Project Gutenberg, 1907.

"Frenchman Raves O'Er Loie Fuller: Claretie Wants to See Her in Salome." *Hartford Daily Courant*, February 18, 1907. https://www.newspapers.com/image /369187444/.

Fröman, Nanny. "Marie and Pierre Curie and the Discovery of Polonium and Radium." NobelPrize.org. Accessed June 7, 2020. https://www.nobelprize.org/prizes /themes/marie-and-pierre-curie-and-the-discovery-of-polonium-and-radium.

Fuller, Loie, Gabrielle Bloch, and undefined Plieux de Diusse. "Patent ApplicationFR534881DA·1921-03-19Application of Negative Films to Cinematic Projections March 19, 1921." Espacenet. European Patent Office. Accessed n.d. https://worldwide.espacenet.com/patent/search/family/008925804 /publication/FR534881A?q=FR534881A.

Fuller, Loie. *Fifteen Years of a Dancer's Life, with Some Account of Her Distinguished Friends*. London: H. Jenkins limited, 1913.

———. "How I Became Interested in Radioactive Matter." *How I Became Interested in Radioactive Matter*. New York Public Library for the Performing Arts, n.d. from Loie Fuller's notebooks.

"Gailhard to Resume Chisel: Veteran Retiring Director of Paris Opera to Be a Sculptor Again." *New York Times*, December 20, 1907. https://timesmachine.nytimes.com/timesmachine/1907/12/20/101732060.html?auth=login-email&pageNumber=3.

Garafola, Lynn. *Diaghilev's Ballets Russes*. New York: Da Capo Press, 2010.

Garelick, Rhonda K. *Electric Salome: Loie Fuller's Performance of Modernism*. Princeton, NJ: Princeton University Press, 2009.

Gbur, Greg. "Paris: City of Lights and Cosmic Rays." Scientific American Blog

Network. *Scientific American*, July 4, 2011. https://blogs.scientificamerican.com /guest-blog/paris-city-of-lights-and-cosmic-rays/.

———. "The Spinthariscope—See Atoms Decay Before Your Eyes!" Skulls in the Stars, April 26, 2011. https://skullsinthestars.com/2011/04/25/the-spinthariscope -see-atoms-decay-before-your-eyes/.

Goldsmith, Barbara. *Obsessive Genius: the Inner World of Marie Curie*. New York: W. W. Norton, 2005.

Griffith, M. "Loie Fuller: The Inventor of the Serpentine Dance." *Strand Magazine*, 1894.

Griffith, M. Dinorben, and Camille Flammarion. "A Wedding Tour in a Balloon." *Strand Magazine*, January 1899. https://archive.org/details/StrandMagazine_097 /mode/2up.

Harmon, Ada Douglas. *The Story of an Old Town*. Glen News Printing Company, 1928.

Heilbron, J. L. "Fin De Siecle Physics at the Turn of the Century: Science, Technology, and Society in the Time of Alfred Nobel." Accessed n.d. https://web .stanford.edu/dept/HPS/Fin-de-siecle physics.pdf.

Herrera, Aurora. *Body Stages: The Metamorphosis of Loïe Fuller*. Madrid: La Casa Encendida, 2015.

"Historic American Buildings Survey/Historic American Engineering Record/Historic American Landscapes Survey—About This Collection." Library of Congress Prints & Photographs Online Catalog, January 1, 1970. http://www.loc.gov /pictures/search/?q=Old Tavern fullersburg&co=hh.

"Homage Paid M. Curie for Benefits of Radium: Little Gray Woman Still Weary from Recent Illness Acknowledges Plaudits at Cancer Center Dinner and Warns Against Use of Element by Untrained Hands." *The Brooklyn Daily Eagle*, November 1, 1929. https://www.newspapers.com/image/59880449/.

"How Lights Are Worked for La Loie, The Curious Mechanism Which Produces the Marvelous Stage Effects." *The Journal*, March 15, 1896. https://www .loc.gov/resource/sn84031792/1896-03-15/ed-1/?sp=20&r=-0.12,-0.01,1.337 ,0.574,0.

Huffington, Arianna Stassinopoulos. *Picasso: Creator and Destroyer*. New York: Simon & Schuster, 1988.

Huysmans, J. K. *Parisian Sketches*. UK: Dedalus Ltd, 2004. First published in France, 1880.

"The Image Makers." BillMoyers.com, April 14, 1983. https://billmoyers.com /content/image-makers/.

"Index Du Forum." L'Aquarium de Paris—Paris 1900—Photos, illustrations, vidéos. Accessed May 14, 2020. https://www.worldfairs.info/forum/viewtopic .php?t=2343.

"Is a Princess of Pearl Tints." *Los Angeles Herald* 34 edition (March 3, 1907): sec. 153. https://cdnc.ucr.edu/?a=d&d=LAHI19070303.2.95&e.

Jardins, Julie Des. "American Memories of Madame Curie." *Celebrating the 100th Anniversary of Madame Marie Sklodowska Curie's Nobel Prize in Chemistry*, 2011: 59–85. https://doi.org/10.1007/978-94-6091-719-6_4.

Jiminez, Jill Berk. *Dictionary of Artists' Models*. London: Fitzroy Dearborn Publishers, 2001.

"Jollier." *The Tribune* (Coshochton, Ohio), February 8, 1925. https://www.newspapers.com/image/321891286/.

Khrapak, Vyacheslav. "Reflections on the American Lyceum: The Legacy of Josiah Holbrook and the Transcendental Sessions." *University of Oklahoma Journal of Philosophy & History of Education* 64 (2014): 47–62.

"La Fête Du Soleil à La Tour Eiffel En 1904." Société astronomique de France. Accessed n.d. https://saf-astronomie.fr/fete-du-soleil-tour-eiffel-1904/.

"La Fete Du Soleil En 1914." *L'Astronomie* 28 (1914): 322–24. http://articles.adsabs.harvard.edu//full/1914LAstr..28..322./0000356.000.html.

"La Loie Fuller and Many White Robed Maidens Will Present Gorgeous Pageant of Elaine." *The San Francisco Examiner*, October 3, 1915. https://www.newspapers.com/image/457799602/.

"La Loie Is Not Insane." *The Journal*. June 4, 1896. https://www.loc.gov/resource/sn84031792/1896-06-04/ed-1/?sp=2&q=loie fuller june 4 1896&r=0.122,0.842,0.756,0.324,0.

"'La Loie' Talks of Her Art: Why She Does Not Think Much of Muslin-Twirling and Toe-Kicking Imitators," March 1, 1896. https://timesmachine.nytimes.com/timesmachine/1896/03/01/issue.html.

"Lady Scientist of Distinction." *Butte Miner*, November 26, 1906. https://www.newspapers.com/image/348390622.

Ļaviņa, Dace. "Symbiosis of Modernisation and National Identity in the Legacy of the 'Baltars' (Baltic Art) Porcelain Painting Workshop, 1924–1930." *Art History & Criticism* 15, no. 1 (January 2019): 37–55. https://doi.org/10.2478/mik-2019-0003.

Le Petit Journal Parti Social Français. February 2, 1904. https://gallica.bnf.fr/ark:/12148/bpt6k616696b/f3.item.r=loie fuller radium.zoom.

Lemaire, Philippe. "Exposition Universelle Et Internationale De Paris 1900." Pavillons—Exposition Paris 1900, n.d. https://www.worldfairs.info/expolistepavillons.php?expo_id=8#2425.

Lista, Giovanni. *Loïe Fuller, Danseuse De La Belle Époque*. Paris: Hermann, 2006.

"Loie Fuller." *Ambassades Et Consulats: Revue De La Diplomatie International*, January 1928. https://gallica.bnf.fr/ark:/12148/bpt6k65056231/f54.item.r=loie fuller.texteImage.

"Loie Fuller As a Moral Agent." *San Francisco Call*, May 14, 1893. https://www.newspapers.com/image/92948655/.

"Loie Fuller Dances Done in Color Riot: Marvelous Effects Obtained by Light as Company Weaves to Classical Music." *San Francisco Examiner*, June 2, 1915. https://www.newspapers.com/image/457361334/.

"Loie Fuller Girls in Goodbye Dance." *San Francisco Examiner*, December 17, 1915. https://www.newspapers.com/image/457577572/.

"Loie Fuller Invents a New Dress That Lights Up a Theatre." *New York Times*, February 5, 1911.

"Loie Fuller Is Dead: Paris Mourns Star Who Brought Light to Dance." *Chicago Tribune and the Daily News*, January 3, 1928. https://gallica.bnf.fr/ark:/12148/bpt6k4775867w.r=loie fuller?rk=21459;2.

"Loie Fuller Knows Light: Famous Dancer Is an Authority in This Line on Stage." *Sioux City Journal*, November 22, 1925. https://www.newspapers.com/image/509210726/.

"Loïe Fuller, La Fée Lumière Est Morte." *Le Journal*, January 3, 1928. https://gallica.bnf.fr/ark:/12148/bpt6k7624847t/.

Loie Fuller Papers. New York Public Library, Jerome Robbins Dance Division. Folders 1–77 ed. *ZBD–113 vols. Micro Film Reels 1–4.

"Loie Fuller's Radium Dance." *The Maud Mercury*, August 5, 1904. https://www.newspapers.com/image/581148726/.

"Loie Fuller's 'Salome': Drama Without Words Is Drawing All Paris." *Indianapolis News*, November 27, 1907.

"Loie Fuller Teaches Dance in Happy Way." *San Francisco Examiner*, May 23, 1915. https://www.newspapers.com/image/457711154/.

"Loie Fuller, The Eiffel Tower." *Cincinnati Enquirer*, July 15, 1914. https://www.newspapers.com/image/33523394/.

"Loie Fuller: The Serpentine Inventor's Influence on Fashion." *The Standard Union*, March 25, 1893.

"Loie Is Determined: She Will Push Her Suit Against Lawyer Hayes; Not Afraid of His Threats." *Courier News*, January 5, 1892.

"London Managers Loaf Two Week: Whole Fortnight Passes Without a New Production Being Brought Out." *Philadelphia Inquirer*, January 29, 1911. https://www.newspapers.com/image/168647724/.

Lubenau, Joel O., and Edward R. Landa. "Radium City: A History of America's First Nuclear Industry." heinzhistorycenter.org. Senator John Heinz History Center, 2019. https://www.heinzhistorycenter.org/magazine/Radium-City.pdf.

"Madame Curie Now Professor Sorbonne: Her Chair the Most Important Ever Held by a Woman." *Vancouver Daily World*, August 1, 1906. https://www.newspapers.com/image/68365081/.

"Madame Curie Pays Visit to Canonsburgh Radium Plant: Quizzes Manager

After Inspection of Processes." *Pittsburgh Daily Post* 5AD: sec. 1921. https://www.newspapers.com/image/87224581/.

Makaryk, Irene Rima. *April in Paris: Theatricality, Modernism, and Politics at the 1925 Art Deco Expo*. Toronto: University of Toronto Press, 2018.

"Many Face Ruin As Dancer Plans to Bare Love Notes." *Buffalo Times*, February 15, 1925. https://www.newspapers.com/image/494224751.

Marian, Maid. "One Day with the New Dancer from Paris: From Breakfast to Midnight with Loie Fuller." *The Journal*, March 1, 1896. https://www.loc.gov/resource/sn84031792/1896-03-01/ed-1/?sp=33&q.

"Marie Curie Heads List of Notables." *Clarion-Ledger*, May 4, 1928. https://www.newspapers.com/image/202705429/.

"The Married Columnist." *Miami Tribune*, March 30, 1925. https://www.newspapers.com/image/616514133/.

McAuliffe, Mary. *Twilight of the Belle Epoque: The Paris of Picasso, Stravinsky, Proust, Renault, Marie Curie, Gertrude Stein, and Their Friends through the Great War*. Lanham, MD: Rowman & Littlefield, 2017.

McClure, J. B. *Edison and His Inventions*. Chicago: Rhodes & McClure, 1894.

Mesch, Rachel. *The Hysterics Revenge: French Women Writers at the Fin De Siecle*. Nashville, TN: Vanderbilt University Press, 2006.

"Minneapolis Will Join Nation in Celebrating Light's Golden Jubilee." *Star Tribune*, October 20, 1929. https://www.newspapers.com/image/180325903/.

"Miss Loie Fuller Dances in Paris as Salome." *New-York Tribune*, December 1, 1907. https://www.newspapers.com/image/78349289/.

"Miss Loie Fuller: A Gossip Over the Breakfast Table about Skirt Dancing." *Westminster Budget*, November 29, 1895. https://www.newspapers.com/image/34433084/.

Moore, Kate. *The Radium Girls: The Dark Story of America's Shining Women*. Turtleback Books, 2018.

Morinni, Clare de. "Loie Fuller: The Fairy of Light." *Dance Index* I, no. 3 (March 1942).

Morisot, Berthe. *A Horse and Carriage on a Woodland Road*. Accessed May 15, 2020. http://www.arthistory.upenn.edu/ashmolean/Morisot/Morisot_entry.html.

Morris, Edmund. *Edison*. New York: Random House, 2019.

"Most Important Professorship Ever Held by a Woman: Madame Curie Given Charge of Sorbonne Laboratory." *Oakland Tribune*, July 15, 1906. https://www.newspapers.com/image/76997007/.

"The Most Wonderful Dance in the World." *The Journal*, March 1, 1896. https://www.loc.gov/resource/sn84031792/1896-03-01/ed-1/?sp=33&q=loie fuller 1896 the journal.

"Mysterious Deaths Caused by Radioactivity Is Belief." *Bridgeport Telegram*, June 22, 1925. https://www.newspapers.com/image/6984969.

"National Recording Registry Includes Four National Archives Sound Recordings."

National Archives and Records Administration. Accessed n.d. https://www.archives.gov/press/press-releases/2006/nr06-87.html.

"New Illusion Shown By La Loie Fuller: Makes Stage Dancers Seem Diminutive." *San Francisco Examiner*, June 15, 1915. https://www.newspapers.com/image/457414772/.

"Nineteen Hundred and Nineteen by William Butler Yeats." William Butler Yeats—Famous poems, famous poets.—All Poetry. Accessed n.d. https://allpoetry.com/Nineteen-Hundred-And-Nineteen.

Noguchi, Yone. "Sada Yacco." *New York Dramatic Mirror*, February 17, 1906. http://www.botchanmedia.com/YN/articles/Sadayacco.htm.

Nones, Phillip. "Paul Paray: The Conductor Who Popularized Florent Schmitt's Ballet La Tragédie De Salomé (1907/10) for Half a Century." Florent Schmitt, April 4, 2020. https://florentschmitt.com/2018/05/18/paul-paray-the-conductor-who-popularized-florent-schmitts-ballet-la-tragedie-de-salome-1907-10-for-half-a-century/.

"Noteable Book Exhibit to Be Shown at Fair." *San Francisco Examiner*, March 24, 1915. https://www.newspapers.com/image/457557132/.

"Notes and Correspondence: Madame Curie Receives Gram of Radium and Many Honors." *Journal of Industrial & Engineering Chemistry* 13, no. 6 (1921): 573. https://doi.org/10.1021/ie50138a039.

Novy, Yvon de. "En Causant avec Miss Loïe Fuller [Chatting with Miss Loie Fuller]." Edited by Gaston de Pawlowski. *Comoedia*, April 23, 1925. https://gallica.bnf.fr/ark:/12148/bpt6k76528100/f4.

O'Dell, Cary. "'Light's Golden Jubilee' (October 21, 1929)." www.loc.gov, 2005. https://www.loc.gov/static/programs/national-recording-preservation-board/documents/LIGHT'S GOLDEN JUBILEE.pdf.

Offen, Karen. "Depopulation, Nationalism, and Feminism in Fin-De-Siecle France." *American Historical Review* 89, no. 3 (1984): 648. https://doi.org/10.2307/1856120.

"Oil Painting of the Banquet given to Thomas Alva Edison at America's Tribute to Him by the Leaders of Industry, Science, Literature, and Art, on the 50th Anniversary of His Invention of the Electric Incandescent Lamp." The Henry Ford. Flickr. Yahoo!, October 20, 2011. https://www.flickr.com/photos/thehenryford/6264288152.

"Old Tavern, Ogden Avenue, Fullersburg, Du Page County, IL." Library of Congress. Accessed n.d. https://www.loc.gov/item/il0298/.

"Overview of the Edison Motion Pictures by Genre: History of Edison Motion Pictures: Articles and Essays: Inventing Entertainment: The Early Motion Pictures and Sound Recordings of the Edison Companies: Digital Collections: Library of Congress." Library of Congress. Accessed May

14, 2020. https://www.loc.gov/collections/edison-company-motion-pictures
-and-sound-recordings/articles-and-essays/history-of-edison-motion-pictures
/overview-of-the-edison-motion-pictures-by-genre.

Panama Pacific Expo World's Fair in San Francisco 1915—Rare Narrated Nitrate Films. n.d.
https://www.youtube.com/watch?v=9t_PyZpbfFU.

"The Papers of Thomas A. Edison." National Archives and Records Administration. Accessed May 14, 2020. https://www.archives.gov/nhprc/projects/catalog
/thomas-edison.

"Paris 1900 Exposition: History, Images, Interpretation." Ideas, n.d. http://www
.arthurchandler.com/paris-1900-exposition.

"The Paris Exposition, First Impression of the New Great Show in France." *New York Sun,* June 3, 1900. https://www.newspapers.com/image/207637911/.

Picasso and Braque Go to the Movies. Madman Cinema, Contemporary Arts Media
(distributor), 2009.

Pigeard-Micault, Natalie. *Les Femmes Du Laboratoire De Marie Curie.* Paris: Éd. Glyphe, 2013.

"Propose De Coulisses [Behind the Scene]." *Gil Blas,* November 1894. https://
gallica.bnf.fr/ark:/12148/bpt6k7521549f/f3.item.r=loie fuller.zoom.

Quinn, Susan. *Marie Curie: A Life.* New York: De Capo Press, 1995.

"The Radium Dance." *El Paso Times,* April 1, 1904. https://www.newspapers.com
/image/429194369/.

"Radium Dances: Weird and Fantastic Spectacle Performance Invented by Loie
Fuller." *Buffalo Commercial,* March 14, 1904. https://www.newspapers.com/image
/279112665/.

"Radium Kills Dial Painters." *Pittsburgh Post Gazette,* May 30, 1925.

"Radium Makes Dial Painters Seriously Ill." *Daily Oklahoman,* September 13, 1925.
https://www.newspapers.com/image/442017871/.

"Radium Necrosis, New Occupational Disease in Women; Developed by Women Painting Watch Dials in Factory." *The Gazette,* May 30, 1925. https://www.newspapers
.com/image/419822557/.

"Radium on the Stage." *St. Louis Post-Dispatch,* April 6, 1904. https://www.newspapers
.com/image/138865196/.

"Radium Poisoning Kills Inventor." *Times Union,* November 14, 1928. https://www
.newspapers.com/image/559953582/.

"Radium The Most Valuable of Metals and Its Wonderful Light Giving Properties."
St. Louis Post-Dispatch, September 8, 1901. https://www.newspapers.com/image
/138260816/.

Radvanyi, Pierre. "Physics and Radioactivity after the Discovery of Polonium and
Radium." *Chemistry International* 33, no. 1 (n.d.). https://old.iupac.org/publications
/ci/2011/3301/8_radvanyi.html.

Radvanyi, Pierre, and Jacques Villain. "The Discovery of Radioactivity." *Comptes*

Rendus Physique 18, no. 9–10 (2017): 544–50. https://doi.org/10.1016/j.crhy .2017.10.008.

"A Remarkable Woman." *Sydney Morning Herald*, December 26, 1906. https://www .newspapers.com/image/124069969/.

Rentetzi, Maria. "Marie Curie and the Perils in Radium." *Physics Today*. American Institute of Physics, April 27, 2017. https://physicstoday.scitation.org/do /10.1063/PT.6.4.20171107a/full/.

Sherard, R. H. "Flammarion the Astronomer: His Home, His Manner of Life, His Work." *McClure's Magazine*, 1894. https://todayinsci.com/F/Flammarion_Camille /FlammarionCamille-Bio.htm.

"Shines like the Sun: It Is Claimed That Radium, the New Mineral, Will Light the World." *Larned Eagle Optic*, February 22, 1901. https://www.newspapers.com /image/382891875/.

"Spreckles Pay Tribute to Art: Couple Entertains Notables in Worlds of Art and Literature at Brilliant Function." *San Francisco Examiner*, April 1, 1915. https:// www.newspapers.com/image/458054800/.

Staley, Richard. *Einstein's Generation: The Origins of the Relativity Revolution*. Chicago: University of Chicago Press, 2008.

"Stars and Stripes." *The Press* (Kansas City, Kansas), September 8, 1893. https:// www.newspapers.com/image/484660482/.

Stevenson, Ian. "'Like a Beast at Bay': Marie Curie's Secret Stay in Highcliffe." Dorset Life. Accessed June 8, 2020. https://www.dorsetlife.co.uk/2012/12 /like-a-beast-at-bay/.

"The Theatres." *The Times*, January 30, 1911. https://www.newspapers.com/image /33233484/.

The Thomas A. Edison Papers at Rutgers University. Accessed May 19, 2020. http://edison.rutgers.edu/NamesSearch/SingleDoc.php?DocId=X0980B.

"Thomas Edison National Historical Park (U.S. National Park Service)." National Parks Service. U.S. Department of the Interior. Accessed May 14, 2020. https://www.nps.gov/edis/index.htm.

"Thomas Edison's Golden Jubilee Speech." *Thomas Edison's Golden Jubilee Speech*. The Victrola Guy, n.d. https://www.youtube.com/watch?v=G4SbydoXWLg.

Tiggelen, René Van, and Luc De Broe. *Radiology in a Trench Coat: Military Radiology on the Western Front During the Great War*. Brussels: Verlag nicht ermittelbar, 2013.

"Tired, Tenacious, Triumphant: Marie Curie Visits the United States in 1921." *Journal of the British Society for the History of Radiology* 36 (December 2012): 19–36. http://www.bshr.org.uk/journals/IL36.pdf.

"Un Roman Dans un Laboratoire: L'aventure de Mme. Curie et de M. Langevin." *Le Petit Journal*, November 5, 1911. https://gallica.bnf.fr/ark:/12148/bpt6k619529k/.

Vaughan, Ernest, and Georges Clemenceau, eds. "Mme. Curie and Loie Fuller."

L'Aurore: Literary, Artistic, Social / Dir. Ernest Vaughan; Red. Georges Clemenceau, October 23, 1907.

Waleffe, Maurice de, ed. "Marie Curie and Loie Fuller at Champs Elysees Theater." *Numéro Paris-Midi*, May 1, 1925. https://gallica.bnf.fr/ark:/12148/bpt6k47353672/f3.item.r=loie fuller mme curie.zoom.

Warner, Deborah Jean. "The Spinthariscope and the Smithsonian." Smithsonian Institution Archives, January 9, 2018. https://siarchives.si.edu/blog/spinthariscope-and-smithsonian.

"Watch Dial Painter Asks $75,000, Avers Radium Poisoned Her." *Pittsburgh Post Gazette*, March 10, 1925. https://www.newspapers.com/image/86281026/.

Wirtén, Eva Hemmungs. *Making Marie Curie: Intellectual Property and Celebrity Culture in an Age of Information*. Chicago: University of Chicago Press, 2016.

"Woman Professor Gives Lecture: Madame Curie Given Rousing Reception by Large Crowd at Paris Sorbonne." *Buffalo Evening News*, November 26, 1906. https://www.newspapers.com/clip/48263875/.

"Women Are Forging to the Front in Science." *Albuquerque Citizen*, December 16, 1906. https://www.newspapers.com/image/77634140/

"World's Tribute to Edison Voiced by Hoover." *Detroit Free Press*, October 22, 1929. https://www.thehenryford.org/collections-and-research/digital-collections/artifact/167439/#slide=gs-255809.